The Freedom and Power of

FORGIVENESS

The Freedom and Power of

FORGIVENESS

JOHN F. MacARTHUR

CROSSWAY BOOKS • WHEATON, ILLINOIS
A DIVISION OF GOOD NEWS PUBLISHERS

First printing, 1998

Printed in the United States of America

ISBN 0-89107-979-3

Library of Congress Cataloging-in-Publication Data

MacArthur, John 1939-
   The freedom and power of forgiveness / John F. MacArthur.
     p.   cm.
   ISBN 0-89107-979-3 (alk. paper)
   1. Forgiveness—Religious aspects—Christianity.   I. Title.
BV4647.F55M33   1998
234'.5—dc21

                                        98-11274
                                          CIP

11	10	09	08	07	06	05	04	03	02	01	00	99	98
15	14	13	12	11	10	9	8	7	6	5	4	3	2	1

CONTENTS

INTRODUCTION

Vengeance is popular today; forgiveness is not. Retaliation is often portrayed as a virtue reflecting healthy self-esteem. It is heralded as an inalienable right of personal freedom. Vengeance is evidence of macho strength.

Dirty Harry takes aim at the perp and, challenging him to flee, intones, "Go ahead. Make my day." That is the existential moment in which his persona is defined. He will achieve personal fulfillment if he can kill the miscreant.

Our society is drunk on the grapes of human wrath. Road-rage, disgruntled employee rampages, drive-by shootings, and other crimes of vengeance are the hallmarks of this generation. No wonder so many people are wracked with guilt, anger, depression, and other destructive emotions.

Early in my pastoral ministry I noticed an interesting fact: nearly all the personal problems that drive people to seek pastoral counsel are related in some way to the issue of forgiveness. The typical counselee's most troublesome problems would be significantly diminished (and in some cases solved completely) by a right understanding of what Scripture says about forgiveness.

People who come for counseling generally fit into one or both of two categories. There are some who need to understand how God's forgiveness is extended to sinners; and there are others who need to learn to be forgiving. In other words, some people are struggling with their own guilt; others have a sinful propensity to blame others and withhold forgiveness for wrongs done. (And many people struggle with both guilt and blame.)

Both tendencies are spiritually and emotionally debilitating. Both are capable of making life wretched. Both can spawn a multitude of related problems. And both can be remedied only by a better understanding of and obedience to what Scripture teaches about forgiveness.

I have often defended the notion that doctrine is inherently practical. What we believe determines how we think, how we behave, and how we respond to life's trials. Abstract beliefs never remain abstract; they inevitably manifest themselves in behavior. A right belief system therefore lies at the foundation of all truly righteous conduct.

Yet I frequently hear people complain that biblical exposition and doctrinal instruction are too impractical. Here is a topic that utterly refutes that notion, for there is no way to deal with either guilt or blame unless we comprehend what Scripture teaches about forgiveness. In other words, the most important practical aspects of Christian living ultimately hinge on the soundness of our doctrine on issues such as guilt, forgiveness, reconciliation, and all related topics.

This book examines forgiveness from the perspective of what Scripture teaches about the subject. My concern, as always, is sound doctrine. But my ultimate aim is to show the practical ramifications of this vital doctrine and to help you, the reader, learn to respond biblically to your own guilt, as well as to forgive others who have wronged you.

In the process, we will address a number of important questions about forgiveness and how it affects our personal lives:

- Can we be sure of God's forgiveness?
- If Christians are forgiven already, why do they need to confess sin in their daily lives?
- How are we supposed to confess our sins? Do we confess to other people, or to God alone?

• Does God ever withdraw His forgiveness from someone who has received it?

• Should the forgiveness we extend to others be *unconditional*?

• How do we reconcile Jesus' teaching on forgiveness with His instructions for carrying out discipline against people who willfully live in sin?

• If we are to forgive seventy times seven, as Jesus taught Peter, do we ever have cause for questioning the legitimacy of a repeat offender's repentance?

• Isn't God concerned about justice too? If I simply forgive those who have wronged me, where's the justice in that?

Forgiveness is not an easy subject, especially in a complex age such as ours. It has become fashionable these days to speak of "forgiving" oneself (often a dodge for those who refuse to deal rightly with guilt), while laying blame for *our* shortcomings at the feet of parents, government, or society as a whole. Can these modern ways of handling guilt and blame be reconciled with Jesus' teaching on forgiveness? I believe they cannot, and in this book we will explore together what Scripture has to say about the subject and see why God's principles of forgiveness are infinitely superior to all human ways of reckoning with guilt, blame, mercy, and justice.

Almost no concept is more important to the Christian faith than forgiveness. The Gospel itself is a message about God's forgiveness, and Christ's teaching was full of exhortations to His people to be forgiving to one another. He set an incredibly high standard, teaching us to forgive even the most stubborn offenders.

In fact, let's be honest: the standard at times seems impossibly high. How can we overcome our natural human inclinations and learn to forgive the way God demands of us? That is part of what we will explore in this book.

But, first of all, though, we must come to grips with what Scripture teaches about sin, guilt, and *God's* forgiveness. And when we do, we will actually be thankful that the standard Jesus set is so high—because it's based on the forgiveness God Himself extends to us. Our need of divine forgiveness is infinitely greater than any forgiveness we might ever be called upon to extend to our fellow sinners. The person who keeps this truth in view will never have a serious problem forgiving others.

God is the consummate forgiver. And we depend every day on His ongoing forgiveness for our sins. The least we can do is emulate His forgiveness in our dealings with one another.

Yet there is a natural, sinful tendency for all of us to minimize our own sins and magnify our blame of others—to treat ourselves with mercy and demand retribution against others. If we would only learn to be more repulsed by our own sin than we are at the wrongs others commit against us, we would be well on the road to spiritual health. On the one hand, we urgently need forgiveness. On the other, we desperately need to forgive.

These things were constant themes in the teaching of Christ during His earthly ministry. His parables, His preaching, and even the Lord's Prayer all emphasized the truth that those who are forgiven must also be forgiving. Some of His harshest sayings were spoken to people who were unwilling to forgive.

Already you might detect that forgiveness is not an altogether comfortable study to pursue. In fact, I soon realized while preparing the material for this book that there are fewer topics *more* convicting.

Yet in the big picture the message is positive and hopeful. Without God's forgiveness we would have no hope whatsoever. And when we learn to forgive others, a host of life's difficulties suddenly are settled. Forgiveness, we discover, is the starting point for resolving life's most troubling problems.

So I offer this book with the hope that it will be a remedy for many caught in the grip of modern humanity's spiritual and emotional malaise. If you are struggling to forgive, or are searching for forgiveness, this book is for you. If you are grappling with guilt, or angrily blaming others, this book is for you too. As we study the freedom and power of God's ultimate gift, my prayer is that your heart will be drawn closer to our God, who is always eager to forgive—and that you too will learn to be an eager forgiver.

ONE

> ➔➤➤➤

THE GROUND OF ALL FORGIVENESS

He made Him who knew no sin to be sin on our behalf,
so that we might become the righteousness of God in Him.

—2 CORINTHIANS 5:21

Forgiveness. Nothing is more foreign to sinful human nature. And nothing is more characteristic of divine grace.

Fallen humanity finds God's forgiveness terribly hard to understand. As individual sinners, we all know firsthand what a struggle it can be to forgive others who have wronged us. Some people therefore find it impossible to envision Almighty God as anything other than stern and unforgiving. Others, knowing that Scripture teaches us God is merciful, imagine that He is so completely indulgent that no sinner really has anything to fear. Both misconceptions are fatally wrong concerning divine forgiveness.

Compounding that problem, our attitude toward forgiveness tends to vary, depending on which side of the equation we look at. When we are on the receiving end of mercy, we naturally esteem forgiveness as one of the highest of all virtues. But when we are the aggrieved party, forgiveness often seems a gross violation of justice!

And yet, all would no doubt recognize *both* justice and mercy as great virtues. Who among us does not desire to be forgiven when we know we have done wrong? And who does not despise injustice, particularly when we are the ones against whom a wrong has been committed?

So how do we reconcile these two great virtues, justice and mercy? More important, how can *God* reconcile them? If He hates injustice, how can He countenance the forgiveness of a transgressor? How can a perfectly holy God pardon sinners?

That's easy for God, you may be thinking. *After all, He can simply choose to forgive us and declare all our offenses null and void. He can just excuse the sinner and let sin go unpunished.*

But that is a deficient view of God and an unbiblical way of looking at forgiveness. God cannot and will not simply acquit transgressors by ignoring the evil they have done. To do so would be unjust, and God is a God of perfect justice.

Here we must be extremely careful to keep our thinking biblical. Some people tend to take the grace and forgiveness of God for granted, while ignoring His absolute righteousness. Others thunder a lot about the justice of God, while saying little about His grace. Both truths must be kept in balance if we are to understand what Scripture teaches about forgiveness.

FIRST, THE BAD NEWS

God does not forgive by simply looking the other way when we sin. The Bible repeatedly stresses that God will punish every sin. Galatians 6:7, for example, gives us this solemn warning: "Do not be deceived, God is not mocked; for whatever a man sows, this he will also reap." In Exodus 23:7 God says, "I will not acquit the guilty." Nahum 1:3 is unequivocal: "The LORD will by no means leave the guilty unpunished." In the gospel message itself, "God's wrath is revealed . . . against all ungodliness and unrighteousness" (Rom. 1:18).

Scripture describes the relationship between God and the sinner as enmity (Rom. 5:10; 8:7). God hates sin, and therefore all who sin have made themselves God's enemies. "God is angry with the

wicked every day" (Psalm 7:11, KJV). He hates those who do iniquity (Psalm 5:5).

All sinners are in the same boat. Those who violate some minor
point of God's law are as guilty as if they had broken every commandment (Jas. 2:10). And the real truth is that no one's sins are
trivial (Rom. 3:10-18). All people are born with an insatiable pen-
chant for sin (Ps. 58:3). They are spiritually dead (Eph. 2:1), revel-
ing in their own sin, objects of God's holy anger (v. 3), and utterly
without hope (v. 12). From the human perspective, this is a truly
desperate state of absolute futility.

God, on the other hand, is perfect, infinitely holy, absolutely
flawless, and thoroughly righteous. His justice must be satisfied by
the punishment of every violation of His law. And the due penalty
of our iniquity is infinitely severe: eternal damnation. Nothing we
can offer God could possibly atone for our sin, because the price of
sin is too high.

Fallen humanity's predicament is as bleak as it can be. Every
person is a sinner, caught under the looming sword of God's
judgment. By nature we are "children of wrath" (Eph. 2:3),
utterly enslaved to our own sin (John 8:34). We have no innate
ability to love God, to obey God, or to please Him by any means
(Rom. 8:7-8).

The situation seems irreversible: we are accountable to a holy
God whose justice must be satisfied, and yet we are guilty sinners,
incapable of doing anything whatsoever to satisfy God's justice. Left
to ourselves, we would all be doomed.

Any hope of the sinner's ever being justified by any means
would seem to be out of the question. God Himself says it is an
abomination to justify a sinner, equal to the sin of declaring an innocent person guilty: "He who justifies the wicked and he who condemns the righteous, both of them alike are an abomination to the
LORD" (Prov. 17:15). "He who says to the wicked, 'You are righteous,' peoples will curse him, nations will abhor him" (Prov. 24:24).

Again and again, God Himself expressly forbids anyone to
declare a sinful person righteous.

NOW, THE GOOD NEWS

But Scripture tells us that God *does* justify the ungodly (Rom. 4:5). He covers their transgressions (v. 7). He refuses to take their misdeeds into account (v. 8). He declares them righteous, completely forgiving their sins. Do you see why the Gospel is such good news?

How can God grant such forgiveness without compromising His own standard of justice? How can He justify sinners without rendering Himself unjust? How can He forgive sinners without breaking His own Word, having already sworn that He will punish every transgression?

The answer is: *God Himself has made His Son, Jesus Christ, the atonement for our sins.*

Multitudes of Christians would nod their heads knowingly at the sound of that statement. But comparatively few are actually well-equipped to articulate the doctrine of the Atonement clearly, or to defend it against the many attacks that the enemies of truth constantly lob its way.

So while it may seem like we're about to cover ground that is familiar to many readers, I would urge you not to skim this section or assume you have heard it all before. I hope, in the remainder of this chapter, to unfold the truth about Christ's substitutionary work in such a way that you will gain a fresh, new appreciation of the depth and significance of this most vital of all Christian doctrines.

This truth lies at the very heart of the gospel message. It is the most glorious truth in all of Scripture. It explains how God can remain just while justifying sinners (Romans 3:25-26). And it is the only hope for any sinner seeking forgiveness.

THE MINISTRY OF RECONCILIATION

Perhaps the most important single passage in all of Scripture about Christ's substitution on sinners' behalf is found in 2 Corinthians 5. Notice how the idea of forgiveness permeates the context. In fact, *reconciliation* is Paul's whole theme in this passage:

God . . . reconciled us to Himself through Christ, and gave us the ministry of reconciliation, namely, that God was in Christ reconciling the world to Himself, not counting their trespasses against them, and He has committed to us the word of reconciliation. Therefore, we are ambassadors for Christ, as though God were entreating through us; we beg you on behalf of Christ, be reconciled to God.
                                                    — 2 COR. 5:18-20

Variations on the word *reconcile* are used five times in those few verses. Paul mentions, for example, "the ministry of reconciliation" (v. 18). That is his description of the evangelistic task. "The word of reconciliation" (v. 19) refers to the gospel message. This is how he characterizes the Gospel: it is a message of reconciliation. The duty of every minister of the Gospel is to tell sinners how they can be reconciled to God.

Reconciliation to God presupposes complete forgiveness. So our theme of forgiveness is very much at the heart of this passage.

The truth is glorious: God has a plan by which He can accomplish the very thing that seemed so completely impossible. There *is* a way to satisfy His justice without damning the sinner. He can both fulfill His promise of vengeance against sin and reconcile sinners. He can remain just while justifying the ungodly (Rom. 3:26). "Lovingkindness and truth have met together; righteousness and peace have kissed each other" (Ps. 85:10).

THE AUTHOR OF RECONCILIATION

Notice that the sinner's reconciliation is both initiated and obtained on the sinner's behalf wholly by God. The redeemed person contributes nothing of any merit whatsoever to the process. Paul says this clearly: "Now all these things are from God, who reconciled us to Himself through Christ" (2 Cor. 5:18).

The relationship between God and the sinner is *never* restored because the sinner decides to change his ways and make amends with God. In the first place, no sinner ever would or could take such a step toward God. Remember that the sinner is in total bondage to sin, morally unable to love or obey God; he is willfully at enmity with Him (Rom. 8:7-8).

Furthermore, as we have seen, no sinner could possibly do enough to satisfy the demands of God's perfect righteousness. Sinners who think they deserve God's favor only compound their sin with self-righteousness. Their baseless hope of earning divine merit is actually a further insult to the infinite holiness of God, whose only standard is an absolute perfection unattainable by fallen humanity.

Sinners have no way to quench God's righteous anger, no capacity to satisfy His holy justice, and no ability to meet His standard of absolute perfection. In other words, no sinner could ever atone for sin. Sinners have broken the law of God and are therefore banished eternally from His presence.

Self-reformation is out of the question. Even if sinners *could* reform themselves, they could never pay the price to atone for wrongs already done. "Turning over a new leaf" cannot nullify sin already on the record.

To make matters worse, a sinner's best efforts at good works are always tainted with sin and therefore cannot merit God's holy favor. "But we are all as an unclean thing, and all our righteousnesses are as filthy rags" (Isa. 64:6, KJV). John Bunyan, who saw this truth clearly, once said that the best prayer he ever prayed had enough sin in it to damn the whole world.

So it is ridiculous to think that a sinner might simply decide to be reconciled to God and therefore effect a reconciliation.

Why does this truth deserve so much stress? Because many people have the misguided notion that reconciliation is something the sinner is supposed to accomplish by deciding to stop rejecting God. Often you'll hear some well-meaning Christian attempt to evangelize non-Christians by suggesting that by a sheer act of the will, any sinner can end his or her rebellion against God and in doing so, effect a reconciliation. That is a deficient understanding of the Gospel, based on a deficient understanding of the seriousness of human depravity. To suppose that any sinner could or would choose to restore a right relationship with God is to grossly underestimate the bondage of sin and its power over the sinner's will.

Besides, the greatest impediment to our salvation is not even our hostility against God. It is *His* wrath against us. The reconciliation Paul describes in 2 Corinthians 5 is not accomplished because we decide to accept God, but because He decides to accept us.

Therefore, if any reconciliation is going to be accomplished, God Himself must be the author and finisher of it. Reconciliation with God can never be accomplished by a sinner's self-efforts, because all such efforts are themselves inherently sinful. That leaves the sinner with only one hope: if reconciliation is to be achieved, God Himself must be the initiator and author of it.

God is not at all a reluctant Savior. It was He who came seeking Adam and Eve after they fell (Gen. 3:9). It was He who sought His wayward people and pleaded with them to repent and receive His salvation. It was God weeping through the tears of Jeremiah for His sinful people (Jer. 13:15-17). It was God who was depicted in the story of Hosea going into the slave prostitute market and bringing His unfaithful, sin-stained wife back and treating her with love as if she were a chaste, virgin bride (Hos. 3:1-3).

By contract, the gods of the pagans were either hostile and demanded appeasement to withhold their murderous intent—or they were indifferent and needed to be awakened to the cries of their worshipers. God is neither hostile nor indifferent. He is by nature a Savior.

This is the good news about forgiveness—"namely, that God was in Christ reconciling the world to Himself, not counting their trespasses against them" (2 Cor. 5:19). There *is* a way for sinners to be reconciled to God. Through the atoning work of Christ, God Himself has accomplished what seemed impossible. The enmity can be removed, the sin forgiven, and the fellowship restored—by God Himself, not by the sinner. That is what the gospel message proclaims.

Romans 5:10-11 says, "While we were enemies, we were reconciled to God. . . . [We] exult in God through our Lord Jesus Christ, through whom we have now received the reconciliation." God provides that reconciliation. He accomplishes it. And we dare not think we can contribute one ounce of merit to the process.

Paul echoes the same theme in Colossians 1:21-22: "Although you were formerly alienated and hostile in mind, engaged in evil deeds, yet He has now reconciled you."

Wherever the language of reconciliation is found in the New Testament, the stress lies on *God's* working to bring it about. Nowhere is the sinner ever portrayed as the one who can accomplish reconciliation. Nowhere are sinners ever led to think that they can work their way back into God's favor. The opposite is true.

On the other hand, however, nowhere in Scripture is God ever depicted as reluctant to reconcile sinners to Himself. On the contrary, it is God Himself who lovingly initiates and effects reconciliation on behalf of the sinner—and He offers reconciliation to all who will believe.

When the apostle Paul pleaded with sinners, "We beg you on behalf of Christ, be reconciled to God" (2 Cor. 5:20), he was not suggesting they should seek to make amends with God, but was simply urging them to receive what *God* was offering *them*.

This is the distinctive of Christian forgiveness. Every manmade religion ever concocted teaches that there is something the sinner must do in order to appease God. Biblical Christianity alone teaches that God has supplied on the sinner's behalf all the merit that is necessary to please Him.

THE MEANS OF RECONCILIATION

Here, then, are the basic truths underlying the Christian doctrine of forgiveness: God is the one who must accomplish forgiveness of sins; it is not possible for the sinner to earn his way back into God's favor. And if God is going to show mercy to sinners, He cannot do so in a way that violates His perfect justice. He has sworn to punish the guilty, and that oath must be fulfilled; otherwise, justice is not satisfied. So, until God's wrath against the guilty is fully meted out, forgiveness remains an impossible violation of divine righteousness, and no one can be reconciled to God.

The wrath of God against sin therefore poses the biggest obstacle of all to any sinner's forgiveness.

Do you find that truth shocking? Many modern readers will. Too many people think of divine grace as a sort of benign forbearance, by which God simply excuses sin and looks the other way— as if grace involved a lowering of the divine standard in order to accommodate what is unholy. Scripture teaches no such thing. Again, God Himself has sworn that every transgression and disobedience will receive a just penalty (cf. Heb. 2:2), and He cannot relinquish His perfection in order to indulge the wicked. To do so would compromise His own righteousness.

So how does God reconcile sinners to Himself? On what grounds can He extend forgiveness to sinners? Here we are brought face to face with the need for atonement. If God's wrath is to be satisfied, if God is going to be *propitiated* to the sinner, a suitable atonement is required. God must fulfill the demands of justice by pouring out His wrath on a substitute. Someone must bear the sinner's punishment vicariously.

And that is precisely what happened at the cross.

The apostle Paul distills the whole Gospel in one simple statement in 2 Corinthians 5:21: "He made Him who knew no sin to be sin on our behalf, so that we might become the righteousness of God in Him."

You may read that and think, *What does that have to do with forgiveness?*

The answer is, everything. While on the face of it this may seem a hard verse to understand, it sets forth the ground of all forgiveness. The truth the apostle Paul means to convey here is the whole basis for how God redeems sinners. I doubt there is a more important verse anywhere in Scripture for understanding the Gospel.

This profound truth is the key to understanding divine forgiveness: God made the sinless Christ to be sin on our behalf, so that we might become in Him the very righteousness of God. Let's carefully dissect this crucial verse of Scripture.

Substitution

First, it speaks of substitution. It means that Christ died *our* death. He bore the punishment for *our* sin. He Himself suffered the wrath of God that we deserved. God "made Him who knew no sin to be sin on our behalf, so that we might become the righteousness of God in Him."

In simple language, the apostle Paul's point is this: God treated Christ like a sinner and punished Him for all the sins of all who would believe, so that He could treat them as righteous and give them credit for Christ's perfect obedience.

Think about the profound implications of this truth: Christ's death was a payment for the sins of those who would believe. He substituted for them before the bar of judgment. He bore their guilt and suffered punishment in their place. And the true nature of the suffering He sustained was infinitely more than the humiliation and nails and flogging that accompanied His crucifixion. He received the full weight of God's wrath against sin.

In other words, as Christ hung on the cross bearing others' sins, God the Father poured out on His own sinless Son every ounce of divine fury against sin. That explains Christ's cry at the ninth hour, "'Eloi, Eloi, lama sabachthani?' which is translated, 'My God, My God, why hast Thou forsaken Me?'" (Mark 15:34). There's a very real sense in which God the Father *did* forsake the Son—judicially. As Christ hung there, God was discharging against His own Son the unrestrained fullness of His fierce wrath and displeasure against our sin!

When we think about this, it is a shocking doctrine. God the Father heaped punishment on His own Son for guilt that rightfully belonged to others! Yet, astonishing as it is, this is the clear teaching of Scripture. The apostle Peter wrote, "He Himself bore our sins in His body on the cross, that we might die to sin and live to righteousness" (1 Pet. 2:24). Isaiah 53, picturing the sufferings of Christ in prophetic language, says:

> *Surely our griefs He Himself bore, and our sorrows He carried; yet we ourselves esteemed Him stricken, smitten of God, and afflicted. But He was pierced through* for our transgressions, *He was crushed for* our *iniquities; the chastening for* our *well-being fell upon Him, and* by His scourging we are healed . . . the Lord has caused the iniquity of us all to fall on Him.*
> — ISA. 53:4-6, *emphasis added*

Isaiah goes on to add this staggering statement: "The Lord was pleased to crush Him, putting Him to grief. . . . He would render Himself as a guilt offering" (v. 10).

The death of Christ *"pleased"* God? That is exactly what Scripture teaches. Repeatedly the Bible says Christ died as a "propitiation" for our sins (Rom. 3:25; Heb. 2:17; 1 John 2:2; 4:10). The word *propitiation* speaks of an appeasement, a total satisfaction of the divine demands on behalf of the sinner. This is a marvelous truth. It means Christ paid the full price—the ransom—for sin on behalf of those He redeemed.

People often misunderstand what this ransom involved. "The Son of man came . . . to give His life a ransom for many" (Mark 10:45; cf. 1 Tim. 2:6). But contrary to what many think, the "ransom" spoken of in such passages is not a payoff to Satan. Satan is in no position to demand a payment for the redemption of souls. (See Appendix 1 for further discussion of this.)

Instead, the "ransom" paid is an atonement rendered to satisfy the justice of God. Christ ransomed His people by paying on their behalf the penalty for their sin that was demanded by divine righteousness. The price of redemption was the full wrath of God against an innocent, perfectly righteous victim! That, and that alone, could atone for the guilt of sinners.

Many find this doctrine distasteful. Liberal theologians often protest that this notion of atonement makes God seem harsh and unsophisticated. They deny that God demands any payment—particularly a blood sacrifice—in order to be propitiated toward sinners. God, they protest, has no need to "get even" with the sinner for sin or to demand a payment of any kind. They claim divine goodwill is a sufficient basis for the forgiveness of sinners. If God wants to forgive sin, they say, He can do so freely.

But to hold such a view is to relinquish God's justice for the sake of His benevolence. It makes God's forgiveness cheap, and perfect righteousness expendable. Far from exalting God, the liberal view demeans Him by compromising His righteousness.

Scripture plainly teaches that only a blood sacrifice can atone for sin and appease the wrath of God against the sinner. God told Old Testament Israel, "The life of the flesh is in the blood: and I have given it to you upon the altar to make an atonement for your souls: for it is the blood that maketh an atonement for the soul" (Lev. 17:11, KJV). Hebrews 9:22 states it succinctly: "Without shedding of blood there is no forgiveness."

So atonement by shedding of blood is absolutely essential to the forgiveness of sins. Forgiveness is impossible without a satisfactory, substitutionary sacrifice. Scripture teaches this plainly. The wrath and justice of God must not be downplayed in our understanding of His forgiveness.

Another grave misunderstanding about Christ's sacrifice on the cross is fast gaining new popularity these days. Known as the "governmental theory of the Atonement" (or sometimes "moral government theology"), this teaching suggests that Christ's death was proof of God's wrath against evil, a graphic demonstration of God's displeasure over sin—but not a literal payment for sins. Those who advocate this view deny that our guilt was actually transferred to Christ, and they also deny that His righteousness can be imputed to sinners.

Moral government theologians often sound evangelical. They speak and write a lot about "revival." (In fact, a site on the World Wide Web touting this kind of theology is called "Revival Theology Resources.") They quote writers whose names are familiar to evangelicals, such as Charles Finney and Albert Barnes. Occasionally they will insist that they believe in a *kind* of substitutionary atonement. But the distinctive of their theology is their insistence that neither guilt nor righteousness can be transferred from one person to another. So they have ruled out the only kind of substitution that ultimately matters for the biblical doctrine of justification.

That is why the "governmental" view of the Atonement is actually a serious compromise of the central truth of the Gospel. It amounts to a denial that Christ's death on the cross was payment for *anyone's* sins. In effect, it leaves sinners with no atonement at all and suggests that in order to gain justification they must amend their own lives, rid themselves of their own sin, and cleanse themselves from further defilement by sustaining a life of obedience. Since Scripture clearly teaches that such self-reformation is impossible (Jer. 13:23), this view of the Atonement in effect nullifies the biblical promise of salvation. (See Appendix 1: "How Are We to Understand the Atonement?")

But as noted earlier, all the self-reformation in the world cannot atone for past sins, nor can it provide the perfect righteousness necessary to please God. The whole error of apostate Israel consisted in thinking they could establish a righteousness of their own, apart from the righteousness God provides on believers' behalf: "Not knowing about God's righteousness, and seeking to establish their own, they did not subject themselves to the righteousness of God" (Rom. 10:3).

The clear teaching of the Bible, from beginning to end, is that sinners cannot atone for their own sins in any way. A perfect sacrifice was therefore needed to atone for sin on their behalf. This involved shedding the blood of an innocent substitute (this means death, not merely bloodletting). And the substitute must bear on the sinner's behalf the full punishment for guilt, not merely a token penalty (cf. Isa. 53:5). Only such a perfect sacrifice could satisfy the demands of God's justice and thus propitiate Him toward sinners. That is exactly what Scripture says Christ's sacrifice provided:

God set [Christ] forth as a propitiation by His blood, through faith,
to demonstrate His righteousness, because in His forbearance God
had passed over the sins that were previously committed, to demon-
strate at the present time His righteousness, that He might be just and
the justifier of the one who has faith in Jesus.

— ROM. 3:25-26, NKJV

We unequivocally reject the liberal notion that this doctrine of vicarious atonement places God in the same category as ancient heathen gods who supposedly demanded blood sacrifices in order to be mollified. The atoning work of Christ has nothing whatsoever in common with pagan notions about propitiation and offended deities. The God of Scripture is not at all like the gods of ancient Canaan, or even the more sophisticated gods of Greek mythology. He is not temperamental and irritable, requiring some sacrificial inducement in order to placate a fiery temper. We're not to think of God's wrath as equivalent to a bad mood. His righteous hatred of sin is a fixed and holy disposition, not a volatile temperament. His demand that sin be atoned for is an essential matter of divine righteousness, not a fatuous need for vengeance.

Nor should anyone imagine that Christ's sacrifice was necessary to overcome some reluctance on the Father's part to save sinners. God is inherently loving and eager to save, taking no pleasure in the death of any sinner (Ezek. 33:11).

Still, it is the clear teaching of Scripture that, as a simple matter of divine justice, the only acceptable atonement for sin was a blood sacrifice, a suffering substitute who would bear the full wrath of God on the sinner's behalf. Since it had to be one who "knew no sin," Christ is the *only* worthy substitute, and His dying on the cross rendered the atonement that was necessary to provide forgiveness for sinners.

This doctrine of substitutionary atonement is therefore the whole ground of God's forgiveness. Apart from Christ's atoning work, no sinner would ever have any hope of salvation.

The entire foundation of the sinner's reconciliation to God is the reality that Christ died bearing the guilt of our sin. He died in our place and as our substitute. He took our punishment and freed God to impute righteousness to us.

Imputation

The notion of imputation is important in explaining 2 Corinthians 5:21. *Imputation* speaks of a legal reckoning. To impute guilt to someone is to assign guilt to that person's account. Likewise, to impute righteousness is to reckon the person righteous. The guilt or righteousness thus imputed is a wholly objective reality; it exists totally apart from the person to whom it is imputed. In other words, a person to whom guilt is imputed is not thereby actually made guilty in the real sense. But he is accounted as guilty in a legal sense. It is a reckoning, not an actual remaking of the person's character.

The guilt of sinners was imputed to Christ. He was not in any sense actually tainted with guilt. He was merely reckoned as guilty before the court of heaven, and the penalty of all that guilt was executed against Him. Sin was imputed, not imparted, to Him.

This is a remarkable statement: "[God] made Him who knew no sin *to be sin* on our behalf." It cannot mean that Christ *became* a sinner. It cannot mean that He committed any sin, that His character was defiled, or that He bore our sin in any sense other than by legal imputation.

Christ had no capacity to sin. He was impeccable. This same verse even says, "[He] knew no sin." He was spotless. He had to be spotless in order to serve as the perfect substitute. He was holy, harmless, undefiled—separate from sinners (Heb. 7:26). He was without sin (Heb.4:15). If sin had besmirched His character in any sense—if He had become an actual sinner—He would have then been worthy of sin's penalty Himself and thus unqualified to render payment for the sins of others. The perfect Lamb of God could not be other than spotless. So the phrase "[God] made Him . . to be sin" *cannot* mean that Christ was tainted with actual sin.

What it means is simply that the guilt from *our* sins was imputed to Him, reckoned to His account. Many Scriptures teach this concept: "He was pierced through for our transgressions, He was crushed for our iniquities" (Isa. 53:5). "He Himself bore our sins in His body on the cross" (1 Pet. 2:24). He bore "the sins of many" (Heb. 9:28).

So in 2 Corinthians 5:21, Paul's simple meaning is that God treated Christ as if He were a sinner. He imputed our guilt to Him and exacted from Him the full penalty for sin—even though Christ Himself knew no sin.

The guilt He bore was not His guilt, but He bore it as if it were His own. God put *our* guilt to Christ's account and made Him pay the penalty for it. All the guilt of all the sins of all who would ever be saved was imputed to Jesus Christ—reckoned to His account as if He were guilty of all of it. Then God poured out the full fury of all His wrath against all of that sin, and Jesus experienced it all. That's what this verse means when it says God made Christ to be sin for us.

Justification

This verse also contains the answer to that troubling question of how sinners can be justified. In the same way that the guilt of sinners was imputed to Christ, His righteousness is imputed to all who believe.

Scripture repeatedly teaches that the righteousness by which sinners are redeemed—the whole ground on which they are made acceptable to God—is a righteousness that is *imputed* to them. As early as Genesis 15:6 we read that Abraham "believed in the LORD; and He reckoned it to him as righteousness." Romans 4 uses Abraham's justification as the model for how all believers are justified.

So the notion of imputation is crucial to understanding how sinners can be reconciled to God. Christ was "made . . . to be sin" because our guilt was imputed to Him. We become righteous by the imputation of His righteousness to us. It is that simple.

Note the important implications of this: Christ, dying on the cross, did not actually *become evil* in order to bear our guilt. By the same token, we do not actually have to *become perfect* in order to be credited with His perfect righteousness. How is the righteousness of justification obtained? Only by imputation. Just as God put our sin to Christ's credit, He puts Christ's righteousness to our credit.

That means our forgiveness is not dependent on some prior moral reform on our part. Every believer is forgiven immediately, just like the thief on the cross. No works of penance are necessary, no meritorious rituals. Forgiveness costs us nothing, because it already cost Christ everything.

The union with Christ that accompanies every sinner's true conversion will inevitably result in a changed life (2 Cor. 5:17). Every true Christian is being conformed to the image of Christ (Rom. 8:29-30). But that life-change in no sense merits divine forgiveness. Forgiveness is fully ours before the first evidences of Christlikeness are even visible, because Christ's atoning work has already paid the price of our sin in full, and at the same time provided us with a garment of perfect righteousness that is the birthright of every believer.

When God looks at the Christian—even the most godly, most consistent Christian you can imagine—He does not accept that person on the virtue of the Christian's own good life. He considers that person as righteous solely by virtue of the imputed righteousness of Christ. That is the whole point of 2 Corinthians 5:21. That is what Scripture means when it says God "justifies the ungodly" (Rom. 4:5). And that is the very heart of the gospel message.

Christ's perfect righteousness is infinitely superior to any righteousness that we might devise on our own. That's why the apostle Paul, discarding years of fastidious pharisaical obedience to the law, said it was now his great hope to "be found in Him, not having a righteousness of my own derived from the Law, but that which is through faith in Christ, the righteousness which comes from God on the basis of faith" (Phil. 3:9). Paul said that the highest kind of righteousness it is possible to obtain for oneself is like "dung" (v. 7) compared to the righteousness of Christ that is imputed to believers.

The believer is clothed with the righteousness of Jesus Christ. The perfection of that righteousness is what defines every believer's standing before God. It is why all Christians are given such a high position of privilege (seated with Christ in the heavenlies, according to Ephesians 2:6). It is why Scripture says that "there is therefore now no condemnation for those who are in Christ Jesus" (Rom. 8:1). Their sins are already eternally forgiven, and as believers they are covered with the perfect righteousness of Christ.

How does one obtain this forgiveness? By believing. In Romans 4 Paul's whole point is that sinners are justified only through an imputed righteousness, and that imputation occurs only through faith:

> What then shall we say that Abraham, our forefather according to the flesh, has found? For if Abraham was justified by works, he has something to boast about, but not before God. For what does the Scripture say? "And Abraham believed God, and it was credited to him as righteousness." Now to the one who works, his wage is not credited as a favor but as what is due. But to the one who does not work, but believes in Him who justifies the ungodly, his faith is credited as righteousness.
>
> — vv. 1-5

Faith is the *only* prerequisite to this justification. No work can earn it. No ritual can be the instrument by which it is obtained. In fact, Paul goes on to point out in verse 10 that Abraham was justified *before* he was circumcised (cf. Gen. 15:6 with Gen. 17:10). So circumcision, as important as it was in the covenant God made with Abraham, *cannot* be a requirement for justification or a means to it.

If God justifies the ungodly solely through faith (Rom. 4:5), of what does this faith consist?

It is a refusal to trust anything *but* Christ for salvation. It means the abandonment of self-righteousness and a single-minded reliance on Christ alone for salvation. It therefore involves a sincere love for Christ and hatred for all that displeases Him.

He offers forgiveness and eternal life freely to all who will come to Him. "The Spirit and the bride say, 'Come.' And let the one who hears say, 'Come.' And let the one who is thirsty come; let the one who wishes take the water of life without cost" (Rev. 22:17).

Dear reader, if you understand that you are a sinner and long for freedom and forgiveness from your sin, turn to Christ even now. He will not cast out any who come to Him (John 6:37). He is eager to forgive and reconcile sinners to Himself. All else that we have to say about forgiveness is moot if you do not know the forgiveness of God for your sins. You need read no further if this issue remains unsettled between you and God. "As though God were entreating through us; we beg you on behalf of Christ, be reconciled to God" (2 Cor. 5:20).

JUSTICE AND FORGIVENESS RECONCILED

In Christ, God's justice and His mercy are reconciled. "Lovingkindness and truth have met together; righteousness and peace have kissed each other" (Ps. 85:10). These two seemingly irreconcilable attributes of God have been reconciled.

God has reconciled sinners to Himself. I hope you can begin to appreciate the wonder of this reality. All Christians are forgiven an unpayable debt, not because we deserve it, not as a reward for doing penance by which we somehow pay for our own sins, but solely on the basis of what God Himself has done for us.

That inestimable gift of free forgiveness becomes the ground on which all other kinds of forgiveness are based, and also the pattern for how we are to forgive others. As we probe more deeply into this subject of forgiveness, please keep in mind all that God has done in order to provide forgiveness for us. If we keep in perspective how much God forgave, and how much it cost Him to forgive, we will soon realize that no transgression against us can ever justify an unforgiving spirit. Christians who hold grudges or refuse to forgive others have lost sight of what their own forgiveness involved.

God's forgiveness is the pattern by which we are to forgive, and the best model of that is Christ Himself. In the chapter that follows, we will examine what may be the most graphic example of divine forgiveness anywhere in Scripture.

TWO

➤➤➤

CHRIST'S
DYING PRAYER

They crucified Him. . . . But Jesus was saying,
"Father, forgive them; for they do not know what they are doing."

−LUKE 23:33-34

If anyone ever had good reason not to forgive, it was the Lord Jesus. He was the ultimate and only true victim—totally innocent of any wrongdoing. He never wronged another individual, never spoke a lie, never committed an unkind or unloving act, never broke the law of God, never had an impure thought. He never yielded to any evil temptation whatsoever.

Scripture says, "[He] committed no sin, nor was any deceit found in his mouth" (1 Pet. 2:22). He "has been tempted in all things as we are, yet without sin" (Heb. 4:15). He is "holy, innocent, undefiled, separated from sinners" (Heb. 7:26).

No one was *less* worthy of death than He. Even the evil Roman governor Pontius Pilate testified repeatedly, "I find no guilt in this man" (Luke 23:4; cf. Mark 15:14; John 19:4, 6).

And yet Pilate, conspiring with other evil men, using false and trumped-up charges, condemned Christ to death and killed Him in the most brutal manner imaginable. Throngs of people were whipped into a frenzy of hatred, demanding His death unjustly (Mark 15:11-14).

Through it all, Christ was led as a lamb to the slaughter (Isa. 53:7). Submitting to the indignity and injustice, He surrendered His life without resistance, without threat, and without retaliation. In fact, all that suffering and injustice was for the express purpose of making Him an atoning sacrifice for the sins of the very ones who put Him to death!

Forgiveness was what filled his heart, not condemnation or revenge. He had said, "The Son of Man did not come to destroy men's lives, but to save them" (Luke 9:56, margin). "For God sent not his Son into the world to condemn the world; but that the world through him might be saved" (John 3:17, KJV).

You might think, *It was one thing for Christ to be so forgiving. He knew it was in God's plan for Him to die. He had a mission to fulfill, and it involved His death. He understood all that from the beginning. Surely God does not expect me to suffer such wrongs so easily!*

But the manner of Christ's dying is explicitly set forth as an example for every Christian to follow:

> *Christ also suffered for you, leaving you an example for you to fol-*
> *low in His steps, who committed no sin, nor was any deceit found*
> *in His mouth; and while being reviled, He did not revile in return;*
> *while suffering, He uttered no threats, but kept entrusting Himself*
> *to Him who judges righteously.*
>
> — 1 PET. 2:21-23

TURN THE OTHER CHEEK

The principle of forgiveness was a feature of Christ's teaching from the beginning. The Sermon on the Mount includes a whole section instructing the disciples to suffer patiently when wronged: "You have heard that it was said, 'An eye for an eye, and a tooth for a tooth.' But I say to you, do not resist him who is evil; but whoever slaps you on your right cheek, turn to him the other also" (Matt. 5:38-39). Many people misunderstand the intent of that passage, so it is worth a closer look.

First, it is important to understand that Christ was not teaching universal pacifism. Some have suggested that this section of the Sermon on the Mount rules out the use of force or violence in every situation. However, that cannot be, because Romans 13:4 expressly assigns civil authorities the right and duty to "bear the sword"— meaning to use force, including deadly force when necessary—in the capacity of "an avenger who brings wrath upon the one who prac- tices evil." So a policeman who kills a criminal in order to stop the commission of a crime, or an executioner who kills someone judged guilty of a capital offense, is acting with an explicit mandate from God.

Second, the passage does not rule out self-defense in wantonly criminal attacks. Jesus is teaching how we should respond to insults and affronts against our personal dignity (vv. 39-42), not criminal threats to life and limb. Furthermore, this passage certainly does not suggest that a husband should refuse to defend his wife, or that a father should decline to protect his children. Those who see in this passage that kind of radical pacifism have twisted Jesus' intent.

Third, Christ was not nullifying any principle of Old Testament law. He was correcting an *abuse* of the law found in rabbinical tradi- tion. The eye-for-an-eye principle was given by divine inspiration to Moses, and therefore it could not have been an evil principle: "If a man injures his neighbor, just as he has done, so it shall be done to him: fracture for fracture, eye for eye, tooth for tooth; just as he has injured a man, so it shall be inflicted on him" (Lev. 24:19-20; cf. Exod. 21:24; Deut. 19:21).

We know that Christ was not declaring this law null and void, because He himself stated in Matthew 5:17-18, "Do not think that I came to abolish the Law or the Prophets; I did not come to abolish, but to fulfill. For truly I say to you, until heaven and earth pass away, not the smallest letter or stroke shall pass away from the Law, until all is accomplished." So there is no possibility that Christ meant to alter or amend the moral standard of the Old Testament law.

What did He mean then? If verse 39 doesn't actually rescind the eye-for-an-eye law and replace it with a kinder, gentler principle, what is the point of this passage?

Here's the issue: the eye-for-an-eye principle was given to govern matters of civil justice. It was a guideline for judges meting out punishment for civil infractions, to insure that the punishment fit the crime. It was a merciful principle, limiting the punishment according to the gravity of the offense. And in all cases where the eye-for-an-eye principle applied, *judges* were to find the offender guilty and assess the penalty, not the injured individual (Exod. 21:22-24; cf. Deut. 19:18-21). Nowhere did the Old Testament ever permit an individual to take the law into his own hands and apply it against those who had wronged him personally.

Unfortunately, rabbinical tradition obscured the necessary distinction between matters of civil justice and petty personal wrongs. The rabbis had misapplied the eye-for-an-eye principle, employing it to argue that individuals are justified in seeking personal revenge for all wrongs done against them.

Jesus was simply correcting that misconception. He was also making some necessary distinctions between public and personal offenses, between profound and petty ones. A slap on the cheek is no real injury. Let the one who wishes to follow Christ simply turn the other cheek. But if the victim deems the assault a criminal offense, let him go through the proper procedures of civil law and allow *others* to determine guilt and assess penalties. No one has a right of personal retaliation. To do so is to make oneself judge, jury, and executioner. That violates the spirit of everything the law teaches about civil and personal justice.

So Jesus' instructions about turning the other cheek establish two categories of offense: one petty and personal, the other profound or public. In the latter case, someone besides the victim must determine guilt and assess the penalty. In the former case, the injured party wishing to glorify God should simply suffer the wrong patiently.

DO NOT RESIST HIM WHO IS EVIL

Jesus' words in Matthew 5:39 sum up the principle that applies to petty personal offenses: "Do not resist him who is evil; but whoever slaps you on your right cheek, turn to him the other also."

That verse has been badly misapplied over the years. One cult in the 1970s was famous for applying the *King James* translation of that verse ("resist not evil") in the most extreme fashion, going so far as to worship Satan alongside Christ!

Obviously, Christ was not teaching that evil agents should simply be allowed to have their way in all circumstances. Jesus Himself opposed evildoers constantly, through both His teaching and His actions. On two occasions He even made a whip of cords and drove out those who were profaning His Father's house (Matt. 21:12; John 2:15).

Elsewhere, Scripture instructs us to resist the devil (Jas. 4:7; 1 Pet. 5:9). We are to oppose false teachers by refuting their lies (Titus 1:9). We are to resist evil in the church by excommunicating evildoers (1 Cor. 5:13; see chapter 7 for a fuller discussion of church discipline). Paul even taught that church leaders who continue in sin should be rebuked "in the presence of all, so that the rest also may be fearful of sinning" (1 Tim. 5:20).

It is equally clear, for reasons already mentioned, that the principle of nonresistance and the turn-the-other-cheek rule cannot be meant to keep civil government from punishing evildoers. To apply these principles in the civil arena would be to surrender society to chaos. Civil government is ordained by God precisely "for the punishment of evildoers and the praise of those who do right" (1 Pet. 2:13-14; cf. Rom. 13:4). Justice obligates us both to uphold the law and to insist that others do so as well. Reporting crime is both a civic responsibility and an act of compassion. To excuse or help cover up the wrongdoing of others is an act of wicked complicity with evil. To fail to protect the innocent is itself a serious evil (Jer. 5:28-29).

So there's absolutely no room in Scripture for the notion that our response to evil should always be passive nonresistance. That cannot be what Jesus is teaching in Matthew 5:39.

But what did Jesus mean when He said, "Do not resist him who is evil"?

Again, He was forbidding personal retaliation, revenge, spite,

resentment, or a combative response in the face of a personal or
petty injury. The word translated "resist" speaks of a militant
reprisal. The idea involves personal vengeance. Christ is simply
teaching exactly the same principle the apostle Paul set forth in
Romans 12:17-19:

> *Never pay back evil for evil to anyone. Respect what is right in the*
> *sight of all men. If possible, so far as it depends on you, be at peace*
> *with all men. Never take your own revenge, beloved, but leave room*
> *for the wrath of God, for it is written, "Vengeance is Mine, I will*
> *repay," says the Lord.*

In this manner we can often overcome evil by doing good (v. 21).

A LAMB TO THE SLAUGHTER

Someone will point out that Christ's crucifixion was neither petty
nor private. So it doesn't really fit in the category of those minor personal offenses we ought to overlook, does it?

No, but it *does* clearly fit in a third category of offenses Jesus also
mentions in His Sermon on the Mount: persecution for righteousness' sake. Our Lord taught that we are to suffer gladly when our
suffering is for the sake of righteousness:

> *"Blessed are those who have been persecuted for the sake of righteous-*
> *ness, for theirs is the kingdom of heaven. Blessed are you when men*
> *revile you, and persecute you, and say all kinds of evil against you falsely,*
> *on account of Me. Rejoice, and be glad, for your reward in heaven is*
> *great, for so they persecuted the prophets who were before you."*
> *— MATT. 5:10-12*

Notice the response Christ calls for when this type of wrong is suffered: "Rejoice, and be glad." That is not describing a giddy, capri-
cious joy. It isn't talking about a masochistic delight over suffering.
It is a calm, settled peace—exactly the kind of spirit shown by Christ
Himself in the midst of His trials.

Scripture repeatedly portrays Christ as a lamb led to the slaughter: "He was oppressed and He was afflicted, yet He did not open His mouth; like a lamb that is led to slaughter, and like a sheep that is silent before its shearers, so He did not open His mouth" (Isa. 53:7). The emphasis is on His silence and His passivity. He was suffering for righteousness' sake, and it would have been wrong of Him to fight back. Why?

In the first place, He had no legal recourse. Both official Rome and the Jewish Sanhedrin conspired together to kill Him. In this case, although the offense against Him was both profound and public, He had no means to seek legal redress. There was no higher earthly court of appeal to which He could go. His only option was insurrection. He put a stop to that idea in the Garden of Gethsemane when He rebuked Peter and told Him to put His sword away (John 18:11). Violent resistance was not justified in such an instance, no matter how wrong His persecutors were, and regardless of how totally innocent He was.

Jesus reminded Peter that if He were inclined to resist, He could simply pray to the Father and immediately have heavenly armies dispatched to His aid: "He will at once put at My disposal more than twelve legions of angels" (Matt. 26:53). So Christ *could* have stopped His crucifixion if he had chosen to.

But had He done that, His earthly work would have been incomplete, and sin would have remained unatoned for. The Father had given Him this cup to drink, and He would submit to the Father's will, no matter what the cost. He would overcome evil with good.

One of the significant factors about the crucifixion narratives in all four Gospels is the silence of Christ before His accusers. When legitimate questions were put to Him, He answered honestly but briefly. For the most part, however, He remained silent. The high priest was frantic to find some reason to accuse Him, but Matthew 26:63 records, "Jesus kept silent" (cf. Mark 14:61). Brought to Pilate, he stood in utter silence while the chief priests and scribes listed false accusations against Him (Matt. 27:12). Mark 15:4-5 records the following: "And Pilate was questioning Him again, saying, 'Do You make no answer? See how many charges they bring against You!' But Jesus made no further answer; so that Pilate was astonished." When Pilate pressed Jesus about where He was from, John 19:9 records, "Jesus gave Him no answer." Luke says Herod also "questioned Him at some length; but He answered him nothing" (Luke 23:9).

That is why Peter, an eyewitness to much of the drama, wrote, "While being reviled, He did not revile in return; while suffering, He uttered no threats, but kept entrusting Himself to Him who judges righteously" (1 Pet. 2:23).

"FATHER, FORGIVE THEM"

When Christ *did* speak in those final hours before He gave up His life, it was clear that His mind was not on revenge—not even on self-defense. *Forgiveness* was the predominant theme of His thoughts throughout the whole ordeal of His crucifixion.

For example, at the height of His agony, at the very moment when most victims of crucifixion might scream out in fury with a curse, He prayed for forgiveness for His tormentors: "Father, forgive them; for they do not know what they are doing" (Luke 23:34).

Bishop J. C. Ryle wrote, "These words were probably spoken while our Lord was being nailed to the cross, or as soon as the cross was reared up on end. It is worthy of remark that as soon as the blood of the Great Sacrifice began to flow, the Great High Priest began to intercede."

Do you see the glory of that? Although Christ is the sovereign, eternal, omnipotent God, He did not threaten, He did not condemn, He did not pronounce doom on His crucifiers. Instead of lashing out against them, He prayed for them.

Jesus had earlier taught, "Love your enemies, and pray for those who persecute you" (Matthew 5:44). But who would have thought that teaching would be carried to such an extreme?

Like so many aspects of our Lord's death, this manifestation of divine mercy was a fulfillment of Old Testament prophecy. Isaiah

53:12 foretold it: "He poured out Himself to death, and was numbered with the transgressors; yet He Himself bore the sin of many, *and interceded for the transgressors.*"

This was the hour for which Jesus had come (John 13:1). Many times His enemies had sought to kill Him before His time (cf. John 7:30; 8:20). "I lay down My life," He said. "No one has taken it away from Me, but I lay it down on My own initiative. I have authority to lay it down, and I have authority to take it up again. This commandment I received from My Father" (John 10:17-18). Everything that was happening in those dreadful hours was according to "the predetermined plan and foreknowledge of God" (Acts 2:23). It was all coming to pass *"in order that the Scripture might be fulfilled"* (John 19:28; cf. vv. 24, 36; Mark 15:28).

This was the reason for which He had come (John 3:17). The whole point of the Incarnation was forgiveness. It was the very thing Jesus was dying for. It was what He was praying for. And it is what He exemplified in His death. Again, He gave us an example we are solemnly charged to follow. If you don't feel somewhat inadequate to answer that calling, perhaps you have not understood the full significance of it.

The scene at the cross includes a remarkable contrast. Here is Jesus, humbly submitting Himself to His Father's will, "obedient to the point of death, even death on a cross" (Phil. 2:8). And there is the mob, jeering, taunting, egging the murderers on, determined at all costs to fulfill their evil deed. They came together in that awful, sacred moment—the solitary, spotless Lamb and the murderous, contemptible crowd: "And when they came to the place called The Skull, there they crucified Him" (Luke 23:33). Again, it was all coming to pass according to "the predetermined plan and foreknowledge of God" (Acts 2:23), *"in order that the Scripture might be fulfilled"* (John 19:28). But at that moment, surely only the Lamb Himself understood that God's will was being done.

Inevitably someone will ask whom Christ was praying for. Was it the Jews who had conspired to sentence Him to death? The

Roman soldiers who actually nailed Him to the cross, then gambled for His clothing? The mocking crowd who taunted Him?

The answer must be all of the above, and more. In one sense the scope of that prayer surely extends beyond the people who were there that day, to every person who has ever trusted Christ and so received His forgiveness. After all, our sins put Him there. We are every bit as culpable as the men who actually drove those nails through His sinless hands and feet.

Now, "Father, forgive them" was not a prayer for immediate, unconditional, indiscriminate forgiveness of everyone who participated in Christ's crucifixion. Rather, it was a plea on behalf of those who would repent and trust Him as their Lord and Savior. Jesus was praying that when they came to grips with the enormity of what they had done and sought God's forgiveness for it, He would not hold it against them. Forgiveness does not belong to those who stubbornly persist in unbroken unbelief and sin and rebellion. Those who carried their steely hatred of Him to the grave were not absolved from their crime by this prayer.

Forgiveness is offered to all, freely (Rev. 22:17). God is as eager to forgive as the prodigal's father was. He pleads for every sinner to turn to Him in humble repentance (Ezek. 18:3-32; Acts 17:30). Those who do, He promises to receive with open arms and unrestrained forgiveness. But those who remain in infidelity and defiance will never know God's forgiveness.

So Christ was praying for those who would repent of their evil deed. The sin they were guilty of was so unbelievably horrific that if these people had not actually heard Him pray for their forgiveness, they might have assumed their sin was unforgivable. (See Appendix 2, "What Is the Unforgivable Sin?")

Why did He pray, "*Father*, forgive them," when in the past He had simply forgiven sinners Himself (cf. Luke 7:48)? After all, hadn't He already shown that "the Son of Man has authority on earth to forgive sins" (Matt. 9:6)?

Yes, but now as our sin-bearer, He was taking our place, dying in our stead, having surrendered every divine prerogative, including His own life, on our behalf. He hung there before God as a representative of sinful humanity. And so He appealed to *the Father* to forgive the transgressors. He was at that moment identifying Himself with the very ones whose irrational hatred of Him had brought Him all these sorrows. Such is the wonder of divine mercy!

Jesus' words, "For they do not know what they are doing" (Luke 23:34) obviously do not mean that those who killed Him were wholly ignorant of the awful *reality* of their crime. The Jewish leaders knew that they had falsely accused Him (Matt. 26:59). Pilate knew that Jesus was an innocent man (Luke 23:4). Anyone even slightly aware of what was going on would have seen that a great injustice was being done (Mark 14:56).

Yet these were blind people led by blind rulers (Acts 3:17). They were all utterly ignorant of the magnitude of their atrocity. They were completely blind to the spiritual light of divine truth.

Their ignorance, however, did not excuse them. Ample evidence testified to the truth of who Jesus was. The people had heard Him teach, and they "were amazed at His teaching; for He was teaching them as one having authority, and not as their scribes" (Matt. 7:28-29). They had witnessed His mighty works (John 10:32-33). In all probability, some of those now clamoring for His death were the same people who earlier had followed Him just for His miracles' sake. Some of them may have even been among the multitudes He fed (John 6:26). Perhaps many of them had been part of the throng who just a week earlier had hailed Him as He entered the city (Matt. 21:8-11)! Surely these people could not have been ignorant of the many things Jesus had said and done in their presence. Two things are certain: their ignorance itself was not excusable, and ignorance certainly did not excuse their crime of murder.

Yet our Lord in His great mercy prayed for their forgiveness. Spiritually, they were blind, utterly insensitive to the awful reality of what they had done. It was not as if they consciously and deliberately were trying to snuff out the Light of the world. Their own minds were utterly blind to that true Light, and therefore they could not have understood the full enormity of their crime. "If they had understood it, they would not have crucified the Lord of glory" (1 Cor. 2:8).

Was Jesus' prayer for their forgiveness answered? It certainly was.

THE PARDONED THIEF

The first answer to that prayer came in a most dramatic way, even before Jesus died.

Both Matthew and Mark record that Christ was crucified between two thieves. These men were probably insurrectionists as well as robbers. Roman law rarely crucified men for mere thievery, so the two criminals were probably guilty of crimes against the government as well. They may have been in league with Barabbas, who was both a robber (John 18:40) and a murderer and was also guilty of sedition against Rome (Luke 23:18-19).

In any case, these were men who lived their lives outside the law. The crimes of which they were guilty had been deemed capital offenses, and one of the thieves ultimately confessed that unlike Christ, they were both indeed worthy to suffer death (Luke 23:41).

So these were grossly immoral men, and the hardness of their hearts is evident in the fact that even while they were being crucified, in the midst of their own excruciating agonies, they both poured scorn on Christ. When the chief priests and scribes taunted Him by saying, "He saved others; He cannot save Himself. He is the King of Israel; let Him now come down from the cross, and we shall believe in Him" (Matt. 27:42), "the robbers also who had been crucified with Him were casting the same insult at Him" (v. 44; cf. Mark 15:32).

Imagine how deeply ingrained someone's rancor would have to be to jeer at an innocent victim while the mocker himself was deservedly in the same predicament! These men were unspeakably evil malefactors. Surely they were the very worst of a bad lot surrounding Christ while He was dying. How amazing to think that Christ sought God's forgiveness for people as evil as this!

Luke, who recorded Jesus' prayer for His adversaries' forgiveness, also adds a remarkable postscript to the account of the two thieves. There came a point in the taunting where one of the two thieves experienced a dramatic change of heart. Watching Jesus suffer such abuse silently, without returning threat or insult to His taunters, that thief was smitten in conscience and repented. As both hung there dying, that man pleaded with the Savior, "Jesus, remember me when You come into Your kingdom!" (Luke 23:42).

His simple statement was actually a profound confession of faith. The man had clearly come to see the depth of his own guilt. He confessed that his own punishment was just and that Christ was guiltless (v. 41). His behavior immediately changed from wicked taunting to humble praise. He implicitly acknowledged Jesus' rightful claim to be Lord of the kingdom of heaven (v. 42). It is unlikely that the condemned criminal appreciated the full significance of Christ's death, but at that very moment, while that thief was receiving the due penalty for his crimes against Rome, Christ was atoning for the man's sins against God.

How did the man's scorn give way so quickly to worship? Flesh and blood had not revealed the truth to Him, but his eyes had been opened by a sovereign act of God. In the final moments of his earthly life, God graciously gave him a new heart. He had done nothing to merit divine grace. On the contrary, right up to the very end he was cursing, taunting, and mocking Christ, even though he himself faced certain death and after that, divine judgment.

But the sight of Christ's suffering in silence, the Lamb of God being led to the slaughter, awakened in that thief's heart a holy fear of God, and he finally rebuked his cohort: "Do you not even fear God, since you are under the same sentence of condemnation?" (Luke 23:40)—and with that statement rebuked himself as well. "We indeed [are suffering] justly," he confessed (v. 41), "but this man has done nothing wrong."

Knowing that he was utterly without hope on his own, the thief asked Christ for the smallest of favors: "Remember me." The request is reminiscent of the desperate plea of the publican who "was even unwilling to lift up his eyes to heaven, but was beating his breast, saying, 'God, be merciful to me, the sinner!'" (Luke 18:13). It was a cry of despair, a last-gasp appeal for the smallest token of mercy, admittedly undeserved.

Jesus, eager to forgive even the most hateful scorner, granted the man's request, and far more: "Truly I say to you, today you shall be with Me in Paradise" (v. 43).

Wrapped up in that promise was the full forgiveness of every evil deed the man had ever done. Nothing was required from the sinner himself to atone for his own evildoing. No works of penance were assigned him, no threat of Purgatory was made; he did not even receive a rebuke for having waited so long to come to Christ. He was immediately granted full entrance into the heavenly kingdom: "*Today* you shall be with Me in Paradise." Christ's atonement was sufficient to obtain full and free forgiveness for this most vile of sinners.

Scripture records no other words between Jesus and the dying thief. Both were suffering unspeakable agony. Soon both would enter Paradise, Christ having paid the price of the thief's sins, and the thief having been clothed in the perfect righteousness of the sinless Savior. A miracle of forgiveness had occurred!

SUPERNATURAL PHENOMENA

All of this occurred under a somber veil of darkness. Matthew says, "From the sixth hour darkness fell upon all the land until the ninth hour" (27:45). The darkness that fell upon the land was no mere eclipse. It could not have been. Passover always fell on the full moon, making a solar eclipse on this particular day out of the question. This was a supernatural darkness signifying divine judgment. God had judged humanity's sins, and as a result, the Light of the world was about to die. It was the most solemn moment in the history of the universe, and only darkness was appropriate for such a moment.

Matthew also records a remarkable series of incidents that happened at the moment of Jesus' death.

And Jesus cried out again with a loud voice, and yielded up His spirit. And, behold, the veil of the temple was torn in two from top to bottom, and the earth shook; and the rocks were split, and the tombs were opened; and many bodies of the saints who had fallen asleep were raised; and coming out of the tombs after His resurrection they entered the holy city and appeared to many.

– 27:50-53

Christ's death was no chance mishap, though it must have appeared to everyone present that chaos now ruled. The Shepherd was stricken and the sheep scattered. To the little band of observers who remained in the flock, all of this surely seemed a great victory for the forces of evil. Nature itself seemed in chaos. Darkness, an earthquake, and overwhelming gloom prevailed. It appeared to the human eye that the universe had been plunged into utter hopelessness.

Nothing could be further from the truth. Christ Himself remained in complete control. He had told the Pharisees, "I lay down My life so that I may take it again. No one has taken it away from Me, but I lay it down on My own initiative. I have authority to lay it down, and I have authority to take it up again" (John 10:17-18). Chaotic as the events may have seemed, at no time did God relinquish His sovereign control to the evildoers. On the contrary, numerous times in the crucifixion accounts we are told, "that the Scripture might be fulfilled" (John 19:24, 28, 36). All things were proceeding in accord with the divine plan.

When Christ died, He simply bowed His head and yielded up His Spirit. No one could have taken His life from Him against His will. At no time did He lose his deity or His sovereignty. All that occurred was part of His plan—a plan designed to make possible the forgiveness of sins.

What seemed like chaos in nature at the moment of Christ's death was actually a meaningful series of supernatural events, orchestrated by God, signifying that forgiveness was complete.

The Veil Rent

Notice that the veil of the Temple was torn "from top to bottom" (Matt. 27:51). That speaks of the veil that separated the Holy of Holies from the rest of the Temple. That veil marked a line no one was to cross, except for the high priest, who entered once a year with the blood of a sacrifice on the Day of Atonement.

Much of the book of Hebrews, especially chapters 9 and 10, discuss the significance of this veil, which signified "that the way into the holy place [had] not yet been disclosed" (Heb. 9:8). The annual sacrifices only symbolized a perfect sacrifice, yet to come, which, when offered, would put an end to all sacrifices forever (Heb. 10:11-12). The New Covenant, based on the shedding of Christ's blood, was then initiated.

Inherent in the New Covenant promises is the guarantee that sins are forgiven forever (vv. 16-17). "Now where there is forgiveness of these things, there is no longer any offering for sin" (v. 18). Therefore, according to the book of Hebrews, every believer can boldly approach the Most Holy Place—the true, heavenly mercy-seat—by the blood of Jesus (v. 19).

The tearing of the high-hanging veil from top to bottom signified that it was God Himself who tore the veil. Forgiveness was both complete and permanent. From that day on, the ceremonies and priestly functions in the Temple had no more significance. Within a generation, the Temple itself was destroyed, and with that, the Mosaic sacrificial system was sovereignly terminated.

The Earth Shaken

Matthew 27:51 continues, "The earth shook; and the rocks were split." Earthquakes in the Old Testament were always a graphic object lesson about divine wrath. When God delivered the law to Moses at Sinai, "the whole mountain quaked violently" (Exod. 19:18). Even in the Psalms, the shaking of the earth always signified the terror and wrath of the Lord (18:7; cf. 68:8; 77:18; 97:4). The

final judgment will commence with a global earthquake like none
ever seen before (Heb. 12:26-27; Rev. 6:14-15).

The earthquake of Matthew 27:51 accompanied the wrath of
God against sin, poured out on His own Son. This moment marked
the culmination of God's judgment against our sin, as the Son of
God yielded up His spirit, and the earth shook in horror.

The Dead Raised

At that same moment, another miracle occurred: "The tombs were
opened, and many bodies of the saints who had fallen asleep were
raised" (Matt. 27:52). The other Gospels do not mention this incident.
"Many," not all, of the saints in and around Jerusalem were raised. The
term is relative and could refer to as few as a dozen or so. The low-key
way in which Scripture describes this miracle seems to rule out a wide-
scale resurrection. These people rose from the dead, no doubt in glo-
rified bodies, and "after His resurrection they entered the holy city and
appeared to many" (v. 53). There were enough of them to establish that
this miracle had indeed occurred. No more is said about these people.
Having borne witness of the Resurrection, they no doubt ascended to
glory—forerunners of the event described in 1 Thessalonians 4:16.

All of these phenomena occurred instantaneously, and thus at the
darkest hour earth has ever known these miracles of triumph signaled
that something truly wonderful was occurring. Christ had purchased
forgiveness. The Great Shepherd had given His life for the sheep.

And even at that moment God was redeeming sinners.
Matthew 27:54 records: "Now the centurion, and those who were
with him keeping guard over Jesus, when they saw the earthquake
and the things that were happening, became very frightened and
said, 'Truly this was the Son of God!'"

A CENTURION BELIEVES

A centurion was an army officer with command over a hundred
men. This particular officer was undoubtedly the one supervising

the crucifixion of Christ and the two thieves. He and some of his troops had probably kept guard over Jesus since the trial in the Praetorium, Pilate's Jerusalem residence. They may even have been among the soldiers who arrested Jesus in the Garden of Gethsemane the night before; so they may have witnessed the entire ordeal from the very beginning.

These same soldiers doubtless participated in Jesus' scourging. They would have been the very ones who dressed Him in a mock robe, placed a crown of thorns on His head, blindfolded Him, beat Him, spat on Him, and taunted Him (Matt. 27:27-30; Luke 22:63-64). They were the same men who had nailed His hands and feet to the cross, then cast lots for His garments and brazenly taunted Him in the midst of His agonies.

They had heard Pilate declare Jesus' innocence, so they knew He was no insurrectionist. Nothing about His actions or behavior made Him any real threat to Rome or the nation of Israel. To these soldiers He must have seemed a stark contrast to the many criminals they had helped crucify. Their taunting suggests they initially wrote Him off as a lunatic or a deranged religious fanatic.

But the supernatural darkness, the earthquake, and the way Christ endured His sufferings all began to have an effect on these soldiers. Mark says that the manner of Jesus' death finally opened their eyes to who He really was: "And when the centurion, which stood over against him, saw that he so cried out, and gave up the ghost, he said, Truly this man was the Son of God" (Mark 15:39, KJV). These soldiers had undoubtedly watched countless victims of crucifixion die, but none had ever died like Jesus. The strength required to cry out as Jesus did was unheard of at this stage of crucifixion.

Matthew says that not only the centurion but also the soldiers with him "became very frightened" (Matt. 27:54, KJV). The Greek expression refers to extreme fright—a kind of panic. This sort of fear often occurred when people realized who Jesus really was. In fact, the expression used here is the same one Matthew employed to describe the disciples' reaction when they saw Jesus walking on water (14:26) and the reaction of the three disciples on the Mount of Transfiguration when they saw Christ in His glory (17:6).

These soldiers at the foot of the cross suddenly realized whom they had crucified, and the result was sheer terror. As fearful as the darkness and earthquake must have been, they were nothing compared to the realization that the One whom they had killed was indeed the Son of God—the very One whom the Jewish rulers had wanted crucified for claiming to be the Son of God! And so in the centurion's statement of faith, he borrowed the very words used by the Jewish leaders who accused Jesus before Pilate ("He made Himself out to be the Son of God," John 19:7).

The testimony voiced by the centurion seems to be a genuine confession of faith on behalf of him and his men. "*Truly* this was the Son of God!" (Matt. 27:54). Luke records that the centurion's response was an act of genuine worship: "He began praising God" (23:47). Ancient tradition says the centurion's name was Longinus and that he was soundly converted and became one of the earliest members of the Christian Church.

That centurion and also any of the soldiers who shared his faith were an immediate answer to Jesus' prayer for His tormentors. God Himself saved those men in answer to His Son's dying plea for mercy on their behalf.

How do we know? Because salvation is *always* a work of divine grace. The faith of these men was proof of God's work in their hearts. "No one can say, 'Jesus is Lord,' except by the Holy Spirit" (1 Cor. 12:3). Jesus made it clear, even to Peter, that God is the source of all true faith (Matt. 16:16-17). Only God Himself could have changed the hardened hearts of that centurion and his men.

UNTOLD MULTITUDES

The centurion and his men were not the only ones struck with fear at the manner of Jesus' death. Luke records that Christ's crucifixion ended in sadness and terror for most of those who had clamored for His death: "And all the multitudes who came together for this spectacle, when they observed what had happened, began to return, beating their breasts" (Luke 23:48).

Hours before, this had been a bloodthirsty mob, shrieking with vicious delight for the death of Jesus. Now that they had what they wanted, it left them with nothing more than despair, grief, and horror. The triumph they had expected left them hollow and hopeless. The crowd dispersed, and everyone slunk back to their homes in fear. The beating of their breasts signified alarm and a measure of remorse. But unlike the centurion, who worshiped God, these people were lacking genuine repentance. Unlike the soldiers, they made no confession of sin and no confession of faith in Christ.

Still, that prayer from the cross was being answered by God. It seems apparent from the biblical accounts that many of these same people were among the 3,000 who were added to the Church in one day (Acts 2:41). Who knows how many of those people, and the thousands of others saved in Jerusalem in the weeks that followed, had been part of the bloodthirsty mob at the crucifixion.

Peter, addressing the multitudes at Pentecost, implied that many of them were the same ones who had actually participated in the crucifixion of Christ. Peter actually charged them with guilt for the deed: "Therefore let all the house of Israel know for certain that God has made Him both Lord and Christ—this Jesus *whom you crucified*" (Acts 2:36, emphasis added).

And they did not deny their guilt. It had evidently weighed heavily on them since they walked away from Calvary beating their breasts. When they heard Peter's words, "they were pierced to the heart, and said to Peter and the rest of the apostles, 'Brethren, what shall we do?'" (v. 37).

Peter then urged them to repent and trust Christ, and the result was dramatic: "Those who had received his word were baptized; and there were added that day about three thousand souls" (v. 41).

They, too, were God's answer to His Son's dying prayer. Jesus' prayer, in a sense, led to the miracle at Pentecost.

But the 3,000 converted at Pentecost were only the beginning. It could very well be that by the end of the apostolic era the majority of those who actually participated in putting Christ to death were brought into the Kingdom in answer to His prayer for forgiveness!

Furthermore, in a sense every pardoned sinner who ever lived is an answer to Christ's prayer. Since our guilt put Him on the cross in the first place, we bear responsibility for His death just as surely as those who actually drove the nails through His hands and feet. And the forgiveness He extended on the cross to those who put Him to death is the same forgiveness He extends to sinners today. We who have experienced such forgiveness have a solemn duty to extend a similar mercy to others as well (Eph. 4:32).

What a high standard He set for us! His refusal to retaliate, His silent acceptance of others' wrongs against Him, His prayer of forgiveness, His eagerness to forgive—all set an example we are expected to follow.

How quickly our flesh recoils from following that example! When we suffer wrongfully, it becomes very easy to rationalize a counterattack and painfully difficult to follow our Lord's steps. But like Him, we must keep entrusting ourselves to the One who "judges righteously" (1 Pet. 2:23).

Can we look at this scene on the cross and understand the depth of His passion, then justify our own unwillingness to forgive any offense our neighbor might have committed against us? The answer is obvious. Should we not have mercy even as we have received mercy (cf. Matt. 18:21-35)? As those who have been forgiven much, we owe much, both to our Lord and to our fellow servants (cf. Luke 7:47). May the Lord grant us grace to follow in His steps of mercy!

THREE

IF WE CONFESS OUR SINS . . .

*If we confess our sins, He is faithful and just
to forgive us our sins and to cleanse us from all unrighteousness.*

—1 JOHN 1:9

One of the first verses many new Christians memorize is 1 John 1:9, because the promise of forgiveness and cleansing is such a rich comfort to those who have struggled all their lives with guilt.

But that verse is the focus of some controversy these days. A handful of popular teachers are claiming that since Christians are *already* forgiven, they should never ask God for forgiveness, and to do so is an expression of unbelief. They insist that 1 John 1:9 has nothing to do with Christians.

One of the best-known proponents of this view is Bob George, popular author and radio speaker. George characterizes Christians who pray for forgiveness as people "who live in daily insecurity . . . [Christians] who doubt whether all their sins are forgiven."[1]

George and several others who share his views claim the *only* way to enjoy one's liberty in Christ is to forget about guilt forever and embrace God's forgiveness as a wholly accomplished fact because of Christ's work.

There's enough truth in that viewpoint to make it extremely confusing to many sincere believers. As we saw in chapter 1, believers' sins *are* forgiven, atoned for by Christ. Christians are freed from the guilt of their sins and are clothed in the perfect righteousness of Christ. Their justification before God is an accomplished fact. Scripture says, " There is therefore now no condemnation for those who are in Christ Jesus" (Rom. 8:1). "Who will bring a charge against God's elect? God is the one who justifies; who is the one who condemns?" (Rom. 8:33-34). "Christ redeemed us from the curse of the Law" (Gal. 3:13).

So from the perspective of God's judgment-throne, the sins of believers are forgiven even before they are committed. God as Judge has thoroughly punished Christ for our sins, and He refuses to hold those sins against us in judgment. "Blessed are those whose lawless deeds have been forgiven, and whose sins have been covered. Blessed is the man whose sin the Lord will not take into account" (Rom. 4:7-8). All Christians are in this blessed state, and those truths are the whole basis of our liberty in Christ. That much is undeniably true.

But it is not the *full* truth. Don't get the notion that because of justification God pays no mind whatsoever to our sin. Don't think for a moment that believers can simply wallow in sin without provoking God's displeasure. Don't view personal remorse over sin as some sort of hindrance to spiritual health. Don't conclude that praying for God's forgiveness is something a Christian should never do. Such thinking is patently unbiblical; heresy is not too strong a word for it. Christians who think they can sin without causing offense to God and without seeking their heavenly Father's forgiveness are badly deceived.

Let's take a closer look at these issues.

ARE BELIEVERS SUPPOSED TO PRAY FOR FORGIVENESS?

I recently received a newsletter from one of these ministries known for teaching that Christians should never seek God's forgiveness. In a cover article, the founder of the ministry writes:

You've probably heard people pray like this: *And Lord, we ask you to forgive us for all our sins.* But hold it. Why do forgiven Christians ask God's forgiveness? Do they not believe they are forgiven? If they believe they're forgiven, then why do they ask for it repeatedly? Their prayers reveal unbelief.

A few paragraphs later, he proposes what he thinks is a better way to pray:

How frequently do you hear someone pray, "And, Lord, I thank You that I stand before You a completely forgiven man. Thank You that I am as spotless as the driven snow"? Those words are rare, but they thrill the heart of God because they demonstrate faith that the man believes God who says we are forgiven in Christ (Eph. 4:32). There is no way you are going to cozy up to God if you feel He is increasingly upset with you. To feel secure, you must believe that He does not hold one single sin against you. Here is a bold statement: It is impossible for a Christian to ask God's forgiveness for a besetting sin the umpteenth time, then snuggle up to Him. He will feel like God's patience is being stretched to the limit.

There's one fatal problem with that whole approach to the subject of forgiveness: it's the very opposite of what the Scriptures teach.

Christ clearly taught His disciples to pray, "Forgive us our sins" (Luke 11:4). Those who argue against praying for forgiveness generally try to explain away that phrase in the Lord's Prayer by suggesting that it belongs to another dispensation—either the Old Covenant under Moses' law, or some yet—future legal dispensation. They believe Jesus was teaching law, not grace, when He gave the Lord's Prayer. Therefore, they insist, teaching people to petition God for forgiveness is tantamount to living under law, not grace. And to expect Christians to pray in the manner set forth in the Lord's Prayer, according to this view, is legalistic.

One man who advocates this view wrote me a letter in which he said:

The Lord's Prayer belongs to the Old Covenant era, when law, not grace, was the governing rule. Does any believer today really imagine that God's forgiveness is contingent on how we forgive, so that we earn His forgiveness by forgiving others? Is it true that if I do not forgive others God will not forgive me? And are Christians supposed to fear that God will withdraw His forgiveness from believers who refuse to forgive those who have wronged them? We must conclude that the provisions of the Lord's Prayer are law, not grace. *Conditional forgiveness does not apply to Christians.*

That reveals a basic misunderstanding. Forgiveness is not offered on different terms in the Old Testament and New Testament eras. Even under the Old Covenant, salvation was always by grace, not by law. Believers were justified through faith alone, not by works. Paul's whole argument in Romans 4 is that the saved of all time are redeemed in exactly the same manner as Abraham: on the ground of a righteousness that is imputed through faith alone (vv. 1-5). That includes Old Testament saints living under Moses' Law, such as David (vv. 6-8). Their sins were forgiven in the same way ours are, and they too were clothed with a perfect righteousness imputed to them by faith.

In other words, limiting the Lord's Prayer to the Old Covenant era—or any other dispensation—does not alter the plain fact that Jesus was teaching already-justified people that they should pray for God's forgiveness.

WHY ARE WE SUPPOSED TO SEEK GOD'S FORGIVENESS IF HE HAS ALREADY JUSTIFIED US?

If justification takes care of sin past, present, and future, so that there is no condemnation for those who are in Christ (Rom. 8:1), why do believers need to pray for forgiveness? Aren't we praying for something that is already ours?

Let's back up and look at the subject biblically. First of all, it is a simple matter of fact that Scripture plainly teaches redeemed people to pray regularly for forgiveness. That is clear in many of the penitential psalms (Ps. 6; 32; 38; 51; 102; 130; 143); it is clear in the Lord's Prayer; and it is also what 1 John 1:9 describes.

As long as we live in a sinful world, with our own sinful tendencies, there is a sense in which Christians, though eternally cleansed by the washing of regeneration (Titus 3:5), still need daily cleansing from the effects of their sins.

The perfect illustration of these two kinds of cleansing is found in the apostle John's account of the Last Supper, when Jesus wanted to wash Peter's feet. At first Peter was reluctant to have Christ serve him in such a humiliating fashion. He told the Lord, "Never shall You wash my feet!" (John 13:8).

Jesus replied, "If I do not wash you, you have no part with Me."

Peter, always brash, decided that a foot-washing would therefore not be sufficient for him: "Lord, not my feet only, but also my hands and my head" (v. 9).

Jesus' reply draws a clear distinction between two kinds of cleansing: "He who has bathed needs only to wash his feet, but is completely clean; and you are clean, but not all of you" (v. 10).

Bathing illustrates the forgiveness of justification. Those who are justified are forgiven the penalty of sin forever. They do not need to be justified again. The day-to-day effects of their sin still need to be dealt with, however. Sin needs to be confessed and forsaken regularly, and the pardon of a loving but displeased Father must be sought.

The verb tenses in 1 John 1 also demonstrate this. A literal rendering of verse 7 reads, "The blood of Jesus His Son keeps cleansing us from all sin." And the verb tense in verse 9 also denotes continuous action: "If we are continually confessing our sins."

So neither the confession nor the cleansing spoken of in 1 John 1 is a one-time, finished event. These verses simply do not support the idea that God pays no heed to the believer's daily transgressions, as if our justification once and for all made sin an utterly moot point for the Christian.

Yet the question nonetheless seems to trouble many Christians. Why must we seek God's forgiveness if He has *already* granted forgiveness in justification?

The answer is that divine forgiveness has two aspects. One is the *judicial* forgiveness God grants as Judge. This is the forgiveness that was purchased by the atonement Christ rendered on our behalf. This kind of forgiveness frees us from any threat of eternal condemnation. It is the forgiveness of justification. Such pardon is immediately complete and never needs to be sought again.

The other is a *parental* forgiveness God grants as our Father. He is grieved when His children sin. The forgiveness of justification takes care of *judicial* guilt, but it does not nullify His fatherly displeasure over our sin. He chastens those whom He loves, for their temporal good (Heb. 12:5-10).

So the forgiveness Christians are supposed to seek in their daily walk is not pardon from an angry Judge, but mercy from a grieved Father. This is the forgiveness Christ taught us to pray for in the Lord's Prayer. The opening words of the prayer, "Our Father," demonstrate that a parental rather than a judicial relationship is in view. (This is also true in 1 John 1, where "fellowship . . . with the Father, and with His Son Jesus Christ" is the subject matter, again suggesting that the forgiveness in verse 9 is a parental rather than a judicial forgiveness.)

Judicial forgiveness deals with the *penalty* of our sins. Parental forgiveness deals with sin's *consequences*. Judicial forgiveness frees us from the condemnation of an aggrieved, omnipotent Judge. Parental forgiveness sets things right with a grieving and displeased but loving Father. Judicial forgiveness gives us an unshakable *standing* before the throne of divine judgment. Parental forgiveness deals with the *state* of our sanctification at any given moment and is dispensed from a throne of divine grace (Heb. 4:16). As Judge, God is eager to forgive sinners; but as a Father He is equally eager to keep on forgiving and cleansing His children from the defilement of their sin.

IS GOD EVER ANGRY WITH HIS OWN CHILDREN?

The mere suggestion that God can be displeased with His own children is enough to raise the defenses of many who believe that never, under any circumstances, can the sins of a child of God provoke divine displeasure. One Christian who was confused about these issues sent an e-mail to our ministry:

> Are you saying God will become angry with His own children? If we're clothed with Christ's righteousness, how could God even see our sin? And if He can't even see our sin, how could He ever be displeased by it? I thought God was never displeased with any Christian, because He accepts us in Christ, as if we were as righteous as Christ. And He is *well-pleased* with His beloved Son.
>
> Besides, if we believe God gets angry with His own children when they sin, can we honestly say we believe He has forgiven us in the first place?

Unfortunately, more and more Christians seem confused by such questions. Bad Bible teaching has pushed the concept of radical grace to the point where some seem to believe that God is obligated by the terms of justification to blithely accept the believer's sin and disobedience. Some who have imbibed these doctrines evidently imagine that because Christ has atoned for our sin, God is no longer entitled to object when we disobey.

But to hold such a view, one must ignore or explain away several important doctrines of Scripture.

For example, as we have seen already, Scripture clearly teaches that God disciplines His children who disobey:

> *You have forgotten the exhortation which is addressed to you as sons, "My son, do not regard lightly the discipline of the Lord, nor faint when you are reproved by Him; for those whom the Lord loves He disciplines, and He scourges every son whom He receives." It is for discipline that you endure; God deals with you as with sons; for what*

*son is there whom his father does not discipline? But if you are with-
out discipline, of which all have become partakers, then you are illegitimate children and not sons. Furthermore, we had earthly fathers
to discipline us, and we respected them; shall we not much rather be
subject to the Father of spirits, and live? For they disciplined us for a
short time as seemed best to them, but He disciplines us for our good,
so that we may share His holiness. All discipline for the moment seems
not to be joyful, but sorrowful; yet to those who have been trained by
it, afterwards it yields the peaceful fruit of righteousness.*

– HEB. 12:5-11

What is the nature of the parental discipline God administers to His
children? This is crucial to understanding the nature of the forgiveness Jesus taught His disciples to seek.

Bob George draws a stark contrast between *punishment* and *discipline*. He writes:

> Though ["discipline" and "punishment"] are often thought to
> mean the same thing, they are very different. The confusion
> of the two concepts probably comes from our experiences
> with well-meaning but fallible human parents, who often dis-
> ciplined us in love, but also sometimes punished us in frus-
> tration and anger. We then project those characteristics upon
> God, and assume that he acts the same way. However, noth-
> ing could be farther from the truth. This error is one of the
> final strongholds of legalism that must be corrected in order
> to enable a person to rest in God's grace. Let's begin by get-
> ting a proper definition of the terms.
>
> *Punishment* is a penalty imposed on an offender for a
> crime or wrongdoing. It has retribution in view (paying some-
> one back what he deserves) rather than correction. . . .
>
> *Discipline*, on the other hand, is totally different. Discipline
> is training that develops self-control, character, and ability.[2]

There is some truth in what George is saying. Sheer punishment
often has no goal other than the administration of justice. The death

penalty, for example, has no remedial design. Its aim is not to reha-
bilitate the offender, but to mete out the due penalty of a capital
crime.

And it is also true that discipline sometimes carries none of the
punitive connotations of chastisement. George's example of discipline is a basketball coach who puts his team through a hard work-
out in order to get them ready for competition. The goal is not to
punish the players, but to get them in shape. George writes:

> Punishment and discipline sometimes *feel* the same to one on
> the receiving end! But the sharp difference can be seen in both
> the *attitude* and the *goal* of the one doing it. The attitude behind
> punishment is *anger* and *indignation*, and its goal is justice; the
> attitude behind discipline is love, and its goal is the benefit and
> development of the person.[3]

Is it true, however, that discipline *never* involves punishment? Is
it also true that punishment never serves a corrective purpose?

No, it is not. For example, George himself illustrates "punishment" with an anecdote about a policeman who cited him for
speeding. He writes:

> You see, the law officer isn't interested in why you were
> speeding; he doesn't care whether or not you did it on pur-
> pose; nor is he interested in hearing about all the other days
> that you did abide by the law. All he knows is that you broke
> the law, and here is your penalty. You will also notice that he
> did nothing to compliment the 50 other drivers he saw that
> were within the speed limit. He just sat there, unresponsive,
> until there was a violation, then he got into action. That's
> punishment.[4]

But if George means to imply that a traffic citation serves no corrective purpose, he is quite wrong. Speeding tickets are designed
partly to punish and partly to deter future offenses. If the fine is
costly enough, it helps remind the offender not to commit repeat

violations. That is part of the lawmakers' intent when they establish the fines—and it is also quite often the officer's stated intent when he writes the citation. ("I'm going to cite you to help you remember not to speed next time.")

So a traffic ticket is partly punitive and partly corrective. *Many* punishments involve a measure of corrective discipline. And discipline—particularly the parental discipline described in Hebrews 12—often includes a punitive aspect as well.

George wants to separate the two in a way that suggests they are mutually exclusive. He is expressly denying that God's discipline of believers involves any punitive aspect. George writes, *"God, under the New Covenant, never deals with His children on the basis of punishment....* He is not dealing with us in anger, nor with a demand for justice."[5]

But does that square with what Scripture actually says? No, it does not. The basketball coach comparison is not the imagery Hebrews 12 employs. Rather, that passage pictures a displeased Father. Scripture pictures God administering discipline to believers with a rod. Yes, He disciplines His children in love, and for their good, and with a goal that is more corrective than it is punitive. But there is nonetheless a punitive element in the discipline described by the writer of Hebrews. This is firm yet loving parental chastisement—a spanking, not merely a practice drill prescribed by a benign coach-figure.

Furthermore, correction itself always contains the recognition that something is being done wrongly. Any good coach benches the undisciplined player, or makes him pay (as well as learn) by special workouts. That may include a punitive purpose, and it should produce a sense of shame.

This is crucial, because God's hatred of our sin is a manifestation of His love for us. His love is like that of a parent, not the detached benevolence of a coach who merely hopes his team will win. And the punitive element of the Lord's discipline is as much a manifestation of His love as is the corrective element.

The words used in Hebrews 12 to describe this discipline are important. They are rendered, in various translations, as "scourging," "chastening," "rebuke," and "chastisement." Those are fitting terms to convey what the writer of Hebrews is describing. They imply a parental punishment, colored by disapproval, mixed with sternness and a degree of severity. *Anger* is not too strong a term, with the caveat that we are describing a fatherly variety of indignation, and not the wrath of an offended judge.

Scripture itself repeatedly employs the language of holy anger to describe God's disapproval of His children's sins. For example, Moses recounted the Lord's response to the rebellion of the Israelites at Kadesh-barnea:

> *Then the LORD heard the sound of your words, and* He was angry *and took an oath, saying, "Not one of these men, this evil generation, shall see the good land which I swore to give your fathers, except Caleb the son of Jephunneh; he shall see it, and to him and to his sons I will give the land on which he has set foot, because he has followed the LORD fully." The LORD* was angry *with me also on your account, saying, "Not even you shall enter there."*
> — DEUT. 1:34-37, *emphasis added;*
> *cf. 3:26; 4:21*

He described a similar incident at the foot of Sinai, when the Israelites worshiped a golden calf:

> *I fell down before the LORD, as at the first, forty days and nights; I neither ate bread nor drank water, because of all your sin which you had committed in doing what was evil in the sight of the LORD to provoke Him to anger. For* I was afraid of the anger and hot displeasure with which the LORD was wrathful against you in order to destroy you, *but the LORD listened to me that time also. The LORD* was angry enough with Aaron to destroy him; *so I also prayed for Aaron at the same time.*
> — DEUT. 9:18-20, *emphasis added*

When Solomon did what was evil in the sight of the Lord, 1

Kings 11:9 records, "Now the LORD was angry with Solomon because his heart was turned away from the LORD."

Moses, Aaron, and Solomon were all redeemed men, fully justified through faith. Their standing before God was in no sense dependent on their works. Their sins were fully forgiven in the judicial sense. Yet Scripture says they angered God because of their sin.

Similarly, Christ was "indignant" with the disciples for refusing to allow children to come to Him (Mark 10:14). He rebuked Peter on several occasions, at one point addressing him as "Satan" (Mark 8:33). He also harshly rebuked James and John (Luke 9:55-56, NASB margin).

So the notion that God is always benign, never displeased with His children, is quite foreign to Scripture. The idea that His discipline never includes any punitive component is also simply wrong. The promise of God to those whom He loves is that He will chasten them as a father chastens his children. That chastening, though done in love and always for our benefit, is nonetheless a true expression of divine anger over sin—even the sins of His own children.

Listen to this provision of the Davidic Covenant:

> *"So I will establish his descendants forever, and his throne as the days of heaven. If his sons forsake My law, and do not walk in My judgments, if they violate My statutes, and do not keep My commandments,* then I will punish their transgression with the rod, and their iniquity with stripes. *But I will not break off My lovingkindness from him, nor deal falsely in My faithfulness."*
>
> – PS. 89:29-33, *emphasis added*

Christians never need to fear facing God's wrath as their eternal Judge, but they will definitely face His fatherly disapproval and correction when they sin. According to Hebrews 12, such discipline is the strongest evidence of His love for us. So don't ever buy into the notion that God is never angry over His children's sin. The fact that He is vexed with our sin is the very proof of His fatherly love for us.

WHAT DOES CONFESSION ACCOMPLISH?

What happens when we, as already-justified believers, confess our sins and seek God's fatherly forgiveness? First of all, it is important to understand that we do not lose our salvation when we sin. Confessing sin is not a matter of regaining lost salvation or renewing our justification.[6] Scripture teaches that those whom God justifies, He also glorifies (Rom. 8:30). The elect don't fall out of the process before reaching the goal. "He who began a good work in you will perfect it until the day of Christ Jesus" (Phil. 1:6). Our sin might displease God, but it cannot separate us from His love (Rom. 8:38-39).

But what does Scripture say? "If we confess our sins, He is faithful and righteous to forgive us our sins and to cleanse us from all unrighteousness" (1 John 1:9). *Forgiveness* and *cleansing* are the two aspects of that promise. As we have seen, the forgiveness spoken of here refers to a parental forgiveness, not the forgiveness of justification. It speaks of a subjective, relational kind of forgiveness. It is simply a restoration to the place of blessing in the eyes of a displeased father.

Similarly, the cleansing spoken of in these verses is not the washing of regeneration. Regeneration imparts new life, often pictured in Scripture as the washing of the heart (Jer. 4:14; Titus 3:5); but the continual cleansing described in 1 John 1:7-9 is a spiritual washing to rid believers of the defilement caused by sin in their daily walk. This type of cleansing is the very thing Jesus was illustrating when He insisted on washing Peter's dusty feet.

Clearly it is believers who are being addressed in 2 Corinthians 7:1: "Therefore, having these promises, beloved, let us cleanse ourselves from all defilement of flesh and spirit, perfecting holiness in the fear of God." There Paul indicates that we, by means of obedience and true repentance, participate in an ongoing cleansing from sin.

So 1 John 1:9 likewise is speaking of an ongoing pardon and purification from sin, not the cleansing and forgiveness of salvation. We're not to think that the pardon of justification and the washing of regeneration eliminate any need for Christians to deal with the subjective reality of sin in their lives. In the words of Puritan commentator Matthew Henry:

> The Christian religion is the religion of sinners, of such as have sinned, and in whom sin in some measure still dwells. The Christian life is a life of continued repentance, humiliation for and mortification of sin, of continual faith in, thankfulness for, and love to the Redeemer, and hopeful, joyful expectation of a day of glorious redemption, in which the believer shall be fully and finally acquitted, and sin abolished for ever.[7]

That's why Scripture teaches us to be continually confessing our sins and seeking God's daily forgiveness and cleansing. He is both faithful and just to forgive-*faithful* because it is His promise to us in the covenant relationship, and *just* because He has already made atonement for our sins.

CAN WE AVERT GOD'S DISCIPLINE BY CONFESSING AND SEEKING HIS FORGIVENESS?

Does God's forgiveness utterly nullify the fact that we have sinned? When we confess our sin and seek God's forgiveness, will He immediately withdraw His discipline and free us from the consequences of our sin?

Some believe that forgiveness should nullify all sin's consequences. This issue inevitably arises, for example, when a Christian leader who has fallen into immorality professes repentance and then wants to return to a position of leadership in the church. Predictably, the fallen leader will plead his case by pointing out that God has forgiven him for his sin, so past sins should not be a factor in considering him for church leadership.

Yet, the basic biblical requirement for all elders and deacons in the church is that they must be "above *reproach*" (1 Tim. 3:2, 10; Titus

1:6-7). The expression speaks of the leader's public reputation. "Above reproach" means there is nothing of which he can be accused. It does not speak of sinlessness, or no one could qualify. But a man who is "above reproach" is someone whose life is not marred by any obvious sinful defect or scandal that hinders him from standing before the flock as an example of consistent godliness.

Some sins, particularly scandalous sexual sins, carry a reproach that cannot be blotted out even though the offense itself is forgiven (Prov. 6:32-33). Forgiveness restores the person to a right relationship with God, but the stigma and scandal of the sin sometimes remains. In such cases a man may be forgiven and yet disqualified from spiritual leadership, because his life has not been a model of godly virtue.

God promises to deal mercifully with those who confess and forsake their sins. Scripture says, "He who conceals his transgressions will not prosper, but he who confesses and forsakes them will find compassion" (Prov. 28:13).

However, there is no promise in Scripture that God's forgiveness will eradicate *all* the consequences of our sin. We have already observed that forgiveness does not necessarily erase the public reproach attached to scandalous sins. Forgiveness also does not necessarily avert divine discipline for sin.

When David sinned with Bathsheba, for example, many months passed before David was humbled enough to confess his sin and seek forgiveness. Scripture records that Bathsheba went through her entire pregnancy and delivered a son before Nathan came to confront David about his transgression.

During those months of disobedience, David was evidently suffering severe emotional and spiritual distress because of his sin. He wrote of that time, "When I kept silent about my sin, my body wasted away through my groaning all day long. For day and night Your hand was heavy upon me; my vitality was drained away as with the fever-heat of summer" (Ps. 32:3-4).

This was all part of God's discipline against David. His peace was taken away, and the weight of his guilt even affected him physically.

In spiritual terms, his unconfessed sin ruined the sweetness of his fellowship with God. The relationship was hindered on David's end. The problem was not that God refused fellowship with David; rather, David's own sin kept him from seeking God as he had when his conscience was clear. In Psalm 51, a psalm about this specific episode of sin, David wrote, "My sin is ever before me" (v. 3). Sin obscured David's view of God and thereby became an impassable barrier to the rich joy of the fellowship David had always enjoyed with the Lord. Compare David's comment in Psalm 51 with the confession he made when he was pure before God: "I have set the LORD always before me; therefore my heart is glad and my glory rejoices" (Ps. 16:9). But while David's sin remained unconfessed, it was the sin that was always before him, obscuring his view of God.

For God's part, He was "displeased" (2 Sam. 11:27, KJV). But it was God who sought David's restoration.

The story is well-known. Nathan the prophet confronted David with his sin. He did so subtly, by telling the wayward king a parable whose moral lesson described precisely the kind of wrong David had committed (2 Sam. 12:1-4). Failing to recognize himself in the parable, David decreed a death sentence against whoever was guilty of such a crime.

"You are the man!" was Nathan's chilling reply (v. 7). Then, continuing, Nathan prophesied about God's discipline against David:

> "Thus says the Lord God of Israel, 'It is I who anointed you king over Israel and it is I who delivered you from the hand of Saul. I also gave you your master's house and your master's wives into your care, and I gave you the house of Israel and Judah; and if that had been too little, I would have added to you many more things like these! Why have you despised the word of the LORD by doing evil in His sight? You have struck down Uriah the Hittite with the sword, have taken his wife to be your wife, and have killed him with the sword

of the sons of Ammon. Now therefore, the sword shall never depart
from your house, because you have despised Me and have taken the
wife of Uriah the Hittite to be your wife.' Thus says the LORD,
'Behold, I will raise up evil against you from your own household;
I will even take your wives before your eyes, and give them to your
companion, and he shall lie with your wives in broad daylight.
Indeed you did it secretly, but I will do this thing before all Israel,
and under the sun.'"

– vv. 7-12

David's immediate response was confession, followed by sincere repentance. The record of his repentance is Psalm 51.

Yet the Lord did not withdraw His discipline in return for David's confession. God stayed the death sentence David himself had unwittingly decreed, but He did not rescind His chastisement altogether:

Nathan said to David, "The LORD also has taken away your sin;
you shall not die. However, because by this deed you have given occa-
sion to the enemies of the LORD to blaspheme, the child also that is
born to you shall surely die."

– vv. 13-14

Here is a perfect example of how justification erases sin's eternal condemnation, but not necessarily its temporal consequences. God forgave David's sins, but He did not erase the consequences—even though some of those consequences were divinely imposed as a means of punitive discipline.

In fact, David bore the consequences of that sin for the rest of his life. From this point on, his life became a chronicle of tragedy. As Nathan foretold, David's own wives were defiled in broad daylight by someone in his own household—his son Absalom (2 Sam. 16:22). Nathan's words to David make clear that God permitted this as a consequence of David's sin and as a way of chastening him. Could God have sovereignly stopped all the evil consequences of David's sin? Yes. Why did He not, especially after David repented?

Scripture does not provide a complete answer to that question, but we are given a hint in 2 Samuel 12:14, where God says to David that the discipline would occur "because by this deed you have given occasion to the enemies of the LORD to blaspheme." If God had allowed David to suffer no consequences for his act, the enemies of God would have had occasion to dishonor Him.

Furthermore, the chastening was part of God's covenant with David, and proof of God's love for him. In 2 Samuel 7:14 God promised, "I will be a father to him and he will be a son to Me; when he commits iniquity, I will correct him with the rod of men and the strokes of the sons of men, but My lovingkindness shall not depart from him, as I took it away from Saul, whom I removed from before you."

God had made an inviolable covenant with David and his house forever. And at the heart of that covenant was a vast promise of divine mercy for David. But along with the mercy came divine chastening when David sinned. The same principle applies to all the elect: "Whom the Lord loveth he chasteneth, and scourgeth every son whom he receiveth" (Heb. 12:6, KJV; cf. Prov. 3:12).

Far from being evidence that God has not *really* forgiven our sins, His loving discipline is proof that He has not cast us away. "For what son is there whom his father does not discipline? But if you are without discipline, of which all have become partakers, then you are illegitimate children and not sons" (Heb. 12:7-8).

WHAT DOES IT MEAN TO CONFESS OUR SINS?

The aim of genuine confession is not to avoid the earthly consequences of our sin. Read David's prayer of repentance in Psalm 51 and take note of this. David's confession focused entirely on sin's *guilt*, not its consequences. When he prayed the prayer recorded in that Psalm, David had already learned that he would suffer horrible consequences for his sin. His own children would dishonor him. His wives would be taken from him and made to commit adultery in broad daylight. The child he had conceived in his adultery with

Bathsheba would die, bringing him almost unbearable grief. God had already told him through the mouth of Nathan that all these things would certainly occur. David knew they were coming when he wrote Psalm 51.

Yet that great prayer of repentance includes no mention of sin's consequences. David made no complaint against the severity of God's discipline. His outrage in that Psalm was reserved for his own sin. That's because it was the *sin* that most disturbed David, not the *chastisement*. He wrote:

> *I know my transgressions, and my sin is ever before me. Against You,*
> *You only, I have sinned, and done what is evil in Your sight, so that*
> *You are justified when You speak and blameless when You judge.*
> — PS. 51:3-4

David was saying he regarded his discipline as totally just. Let no one question the righteousness of God for His treatment of David. David himself simply admitted that he was guilty as charged and deserved whatever consequences the Lord saw fit to bring against him.

That is precisely what it means to confess our sins. In 1 John 1:9, the word translated "confess" is the Greek verb *homologeo*, literally, "say the same." To confess our sins is to say the same thing as God says about them. Confessing our sins therefore means acknowledging that God's perspective of our transgressions is correct.

I once heard a Bible teacher claim that all God requires for forgiveness is that we simply name our sins—cite them—and He forgives. Another preacher I heard claimed all that is necessary is that we be aware of our sins. That is not what this verse teaches. Nor does confession merely mean *admitting* our sins. One can admit one's sin without truly agreeing with God's perspective. Acknowledging guilt is not the real sense conveyed by the word *homologeo*. Instead, to "confess" our sin in the truest sense involves despising the sin, being grieved by it, and judging it. That is what it means to say the same thing as God concerning our sin.

Must we keep a list of sins and confess every individual offense in order to get cleansing? That is not what this passage suggests. Agreeing with God concerning our sin is a constant attitude, not something done mechanically with a sin by sin checklist. Again, the verb tense in 1 John 1:9 speaks of continual confession. The apostle John is not calling for a one-to-one ratio of sins and confessions, but rather a constant, perpetual agreeing with God concerning our sin. And when we find ourselves, like David, enslaved to a particular sin, the only way to restore joy and harmony in our fellowship with God is repentance and confession.

TO WHOM DO WE CONFESS?

The confession spoken of in 1 John 1:9 is not confession to an earthly priest. Roman Catholicism is well-known for taking this verse, marrying it to James 5:16 ("Confess your sins to one another"), and employing those verses as justification for the priestly confessional booth.

Multitudes live in fear that if they do not regularly recite an inventory of their sins and seek the absolution of a priest, they might die with unconfessed sin and end up in hell. In effect, that makes confession of sin a meritorious work, as if the act of confession, combined with acts of penance, could somehow contribute to the atonement necessary to erase sins. All of that is foreign to Scripture, and certainly foreign to 1 John 1:9. This passage has nothing to do with confessional booths and rosary beads.

Here again, the verb tense is significant. Remember, "If we are confessing our sins" speaks of a continuous attitude, not a sacramental routine. This is in essence the apostle John's description of all true Christians—those who are continually saying the same thing as God about their sin. He is describing a characteristic of the true believer, not establishing a sacrament for doing penance.

In fact, there is nothing whatsoever in this context about confessing to other people. The confession the apostle has in mind is wholly Godward.

Is there ever a time when Christians ought to confess their sins to fellow Christians? We know that confession to God is *always* appropriate. Is person-to-person confession ever necessary? Yes. There are at least two situations that warrant this type of confession.

One is when we are seeking help from stronger, more mature Christians who can help us bear a burden, hold us accountable, pray for us, or otherwise be of help in overcoming bad habits and the difficult circumstances of sin (Gal. 6:2). That is the kind of confession in view in James 5:16: "Confess your sins to one another, and pray for one another so that you may be healed. The effective prayer of a righteous man can accomplish much."

The other time when person-to-person confession is appropriate is when we confess an offense to someone whom we have sinned against, in order to seek their forgiveness. This is part of the reconciliation necessary when we have directly wronged someone (Matt. 5:24). This is not to suggest that we are obligated to confess to someone every time we have an evil thought about them. But when our sins have caused another person real hurt, confession to the injured party is an appropriate, and even necessary, aspect of reconciliation.

However, what is in view in 1 John 1:9 is a Godward confession that ought to be characteristic of every Christian.

DO OUR SINS REMAIN UNFORGIVEN
IF WE FAIL TO CONFESS?

One author whose works I read several years ago was an advocate of the checklist view. He believed that Christians should inventory their specific sins and confess them one by one. According to him, God forgives only the sins we specifically confess. All sins committed in ignorance, and sins forgotten or otherwise unconfessed, remain utterly unforgiven until the judgment-seat of Christ. At the *bema*, he said, Christ will deal with those unconfessed sins and punish us for them (though he believed Christ's work on the cross would guarantee that our punishment for those unconfessed sins would not include hell).

This man was a Protestant, but his view is very similar to the Catholic notion of Purgatory. It is at least as serious an error as the teaching of those who say Christians should never confess their sins, because if Christ's atonement does not provide judicial forgiveness for *all* our sins, then Christians will have to atone (at least partially) for some of their own sins. Such a doctrine is an implicit denial of the sufficiency of Christ's atonement.

Again, believers *already* have the fullest kind of judicial forgiveness. The apostle John wrote later in this same epistle, "I am writing to you, little children, because your sins *have been forgiven* you for His name's sake" (1 John 2:12). He used the past tense there to underscore the fact that the eternal question of our forgiveness is forever settled. The threat of condemnation for our sins is gone (Rom. 8:1).

Again, 1 John 1:9 is simply speaking about an attitude that is characteristic of *all* true Christians: they are the ones who as a pattern are saying the same thing as God about their sin. When they cover their sin, as David did, they do not prosper. They forfeit their joy. They reap divine displeasure. They experience divine chastening.

But when they confess and forsake their sin, there is the guarantee of divine compassion (Prov. 28:13). God, who disciplines sinning saints because of His love for them, also delights to shower the brokenhearted and repentant with His mercy and compassion.

FOUR

PUT THAT ON MY ACCOUNT

*Accept him as you would me. But if he has wronged you in any
way, or owes you anything, charge that to my account.*

—PHILEM. 17-18

Scripture everywhere teaches that those who have been forgiven
much are obligated to forgive others (Matt. 18:23-35; Eph. 4:32;
Col. 3:13). Christians are therefore to be characterized by a forgiving spirit.

God's forgiveness of sinners is sometimes referred to as *vertical*
forgiveness. The sinner's forgiveness toward others is *horizontal* forgiveness. In the chapters that follow, we will look at several passages
of Scripture that deal with horizontal forgiveness and probe the
issue of how we are to forgive one another.

We begin with a look at one of the shortest books in all the
New Testament. The epistle to Philemon is also the briefest and
most personal of all of Paul's inspired works. Even though the
word *forgiveness* never appears in the book, that is the whole subject of the epistle. It is a superb case study on how forgiveness
should operate in the life of every believer. It also graphically illustrates how grace can reconcile a broken relationship and restore
the offender.

THE CAST OF CHARACTERS

The drama behind this little epistle is touching: a remarkable providence brought the lives of three men together—a runaway slave, the offended slave owner, and a godly apostle. These men were vastly different from each other except in one regard: they all were believers in Jesus Christ and therefore members of the same body (1 Cor. 12:12-14).

Before becoming a Christian, however, Onesimus (the slave) had run away from his master and fled to Rome. Rome was a haven for runaway slaves because they could easily mingle with the large population there and avoid detection.

In Rome, Onesimus somehow encountered the apostle Paul, who was under house arrest while awaiting trial on false charges of sedition. The details of their meeting are not given in Scripture, but it is clear that Onesimus became a Christian as a result of the apostle's ministry (Philem. 10).

Philemon was the slave owner whom Onesimus had wronged. He too had come to faith in Christ through Paul's ministry, possibly years before, during Paul's time in Ephesus (Acts 18-20; cf. 19:26). Philemon owned the home where the Colossian church met (Philem. 2; cf. Col. 4:17). He seems to have been a wealthy and influential man, at the opposite end of the social spectrum from Onesimus. Yet he was a devoted Christian, regarded by the apostle Paul as a beloved "fellow-worker" (Philem. 1).

Onesimus also became a treasured friend and fellow laborer to the apostle Paul, ministering personally to Paul during the apostle's imprisonment in Rome, when many other Christians were fearful of associating with Paul because of the stigma and potential persecution (cf. 2 Tim. 1:8; 4:10-16).

THE PLOT

Both Paul and Onesimus must have been very reluctant for the slave to return to his master. Paul even stated that sending Onesimus back was like sending his "very heart" (Philem. 12). Yet Onesimus needed to seek his master's forgiveness for the wrong he'd done.

Onesimus was guilty under Roman law of some serious crimes. He had defrauded his master by running away, a crime tantamount to stealing. It may well be that he had actually stolen money too, because Paul offered to reimburse Philemon for anything the slave owed (v. 18). It was a serious matter in Rome to be a fugitive slave. If Onesimus had been captured by slave-catchers, he might have been imprisoned, sold for ransom, or even killed.

Possibly for that very reason, Paul waited to send Onesimus back to Philemon until someone could escort him. That opportunity came when it was time to send Tychicus to Ephesus and Colossae with the epistles Paul wrote to the churches there. Paul's epistle to the Colossians introduced Onesimus to that church, which would henceforth be his home church. Paul called Onesimus "our faithful and beloved brother, who is one of your number" (Col. 4:9).

Tychicus' presence ensured some degree of safety for Onesimus on the journey back to Colossae; but from a human perspective, the return to Philemon's house held a significant personal risk for Onesimus. Under Roman law, Philemon had full power to punish a runaway slave any way he saw fit. Multitudes of Roman slaves were tortured and put to death for far more petty offenses. As a standard practice, runaway slaves were branded with an F (for the Latin *fugitivus*) on the forehead, to make it impossible for them to hide if they should run away again. At the very least, a runaway slave would be given a severe beating. (In the century before Paul's time, a famous slave revolt led by Spartacus had been suppressed, and from then on Roman law was especially harsh with slaves who rebelled against their masters.) Yet Onesimus returned willingly and apparently without hesitation to his master. That speaks of the genuineness of his faith.

THE BACKDROP

Slavery was the universal practice at the height of the Roman Empire, and issues related to slavery are interwoven in the drama of this epistle. So perhaps a word is in order about the biblical perspective on slavery.

First, the slavery countenanced in Scripture is an indentured slavery, meaning that the slave entered into slavery by contract with the slave owner—usually for a set period of time (cf. Exod. 21:2-6). There was nothing inherently oppressive or unjust about such a relationship. In fact, the slave-master relationship was supposed to work much like modern employer-employee relationships in which contracts are involved. When Scripture instructs slaves to obey their masters, it is tantamount to telling employees to submit to their bosses.

Some aspects of Roman slavery *could* actually be beneficial for the slave. Many slaves dressed, ate, and lived at a higher standard than poor freemen. Slaves might be physicians, teachers, artisans, musicians, or accountants. Many slaves who learned such trades could ultimately buy their freedom. Some slaves even owned property. Wise slave owners used such incentives to motivate their servants. Some slaves and their owners developed close bonds, almost like a family relationship. Slave owners often granted beloved slaves freedom in their wills.

But *most* Roman slavery was not so benign. Slavery throughout the Empire was continually beset with abuses and harsh practices that were inherently immoral. Many Roman slaves were acquired and held by forcible means, rather than being properly indentured. Slavery in Rome digressed to the point where slaves were regarded as mere property. In the worst situations, Roman slaves were deprived of the right to marry and were bred like animals. It was also not unheard of for slaves to be killed on a mere whim by their masters. There is no moral defense for anyone to claim such absolute power of life and death over a fellow human.

Why does not the Bible expressly declare slavery immoral? Because, in the first place, it was the *abuse* of slavery, not servitude per se, that was evil. There is nothing inherently immoral or unjust about one man's serving another. Indentured slavery, practiced without the abuses that often accompanied Roman slavery, was no more immoral than the modern relationship between a business owner and a contract worker.

Furthermore, all abuses of slavery *are* condemned in Scripture, either directly or by clear principles. For example, the man-stealing on which the slave trade in early America (and much of Roman slavery) was based is expressly condemned in Scripture (Exod. 21:16). The inhumanity and injustice often perpetrated by evil slaveholders is likewise denounced throughout Scripture (cf. Lev. 19:15; Isa. 10:1-2; Amos 5:11-14).

It would have been wrong for the early church to turn aside from her calling in order to conduct a campaign for social reform, civil rights, or the abolition of slavery. It is equally inappropriate for the church today to flirt with such causes. When social reform becomes the sole focus, the gospel message is inevitably obscured by the human-rights agenda, and the work of the church is thus compromised.

Instead, the early church undermined the abusive system of Roman slavery by reaching both slaves and slave owners with the Gospel. What occurred between Onesimus and Philemon is simply one example of how the master-slave relationship was transformed throughout the Empire as the Gospel spread. By urging Philemon to receive Onesimus as a "brother" (Philem. 16), Paul defined the relationship between Christian master and slave in a way that made abuses unthinkable.

THE LETTER

Paul's epistle to Philemon was no doubt sealed and given to Tychicus to carry on his journey, along with the epistles to the Ephesians and Colossians. The letter is a gentle prompting to Philemon, reminding him of his duty to forgive, and an appeal for extreme mercy toward Onesimus. It shows as clearly as anything in the New Testament the magnanimity of Paul's heart, and his love of mercy.

Forgiveness was clearly on Paul's mind as he penned all three of the letters Tychicus was carrying. The epistle to the Ephesians includes this: "Be kind to one another, tender-hearted, forgiving each other, just as God in Christ also has forgiven you" (4:32). And the Colossian epistle expands on the same thought: "As those who have been chosen of God, holy and beloved, put on a heart of compassion, kindness, humility, gentleness and patience; bearing with one another, and forgiving each other, whoever has a complaint against any one; just as the Lord forgave you, so also should you" (3:12-13).

Those verses sum up precisely the message Paul wanted to give Philemon in particular. Having developed a warm affection for Onesimus, he longed to see him reconciled to Philemon, whose friendship and support Paul also cherished.

The epistle to Philemon is unique in the Pauline writings for several reasons. First, it is the only inspired letter written to an individual who was not a pastor, and it is the only one of Paul's inspired writings dealing with purely personal issues. That is, it was not expressly given as instruction for the Church at large, though in effect it *does* instruct all Christians on the importance of forgiveness. And the fact that it was ultimately included in the canon of Scripture means it was distributed to the churches for everyone's edification. But that may have been Philemon's choice. Paul addressed the epistle only to him and his household.

Second, and even more remarkable, this is the only one of Paul's epistles where he downplays, rather than asserts, his apostolic authority. He does this with very good reason. His aim was to appeal to Philemon to forgive freely, not to pressure him into forgiving by the force of his authority—"that [Philemon's] goodness should not be as it were by compulsion, but of [his] own free will" (v. 14).

The epistle was *deliberately* an appeal, rather than an order, as Paul told his friend: "Though I have enough confidence in Christ to order you to do that which is proper, yet for love's sake I rather appeal to you" (vv. 8-9). Paul, conciously declining to assert authority over Philemon, appealed instead to their love for one another (v. 9), Philemon's sense of spiritual partnership with Paul (v. 17), and Philemon's own great debt to Paul, who had brought him to Christ (v. 19).

The letter is addressed not only to Philemon, but also to Apphia (who must have been Philemon's wife) and Archippus (no doubt their son; cf. Col. 4:17). Paul thus appealed to the whole family to set the example of forgiveness for the church that met in their home (v. 2).

THE APPEAL

Paul apparently knew Philemon well. The apostle had been God's chosen instrument to bring Philemon to Christ. The two were longtime friends and had ministered alongside one another. They had other close friends in common. For example, Epaphras, Philemon's former pastor in the Colossian church, was presently Paul's companion in Rome (v. 23). Paul had great confidence in Philemon's character, and that is why he made such a tender appeal to his friend rather than simply issuing a command with the weight of apostolic authority.

Philemon's reputation as a godly and loving Christian was evidently widespread. It had reached as far as Rome because Paul writes, "I hear of your love, and of the faith which you have toward the Lord Jesus, and toward all the saints" (v. 5).

Such love for the saints is characteristic of all true Christians. The apostle John wrote, "We know that we have passed out of death into life, because we love the brethren" (1 John 3:14). Love for one another is the natural, and expected, by-product of a knowledge of God: "Beloved, let us love one another, for love is from God; and everyone who loves is born of God and knows God. The one who does not love does not know God, for God is love" (1 John 4:7-8). Clearly, some measure of love for the brethren is present in every believer.

But Philemon's love was extraordinary. He was renowned for his great love of the brethren. Even Paul drew comfort and encouragement from what he had heard about Philemon's affection for the saints. He wrote, "I have come to have much joy and comfort in your love, because the hearts of the saints have been refreshed through you, brother" (Philem. 7).

In other words, showing love to the saints was the ministry for which Philemon was well-known. His hospitality and love for the people of God was a predominant feature of his character, and everyone could see it. Not only had he opened his home to the church at Colossae, but he also was especially devoted to the task of refreshing the hearts of his fellow believers (v. 7).

The Greek word translated "refreshed" in verse 7 is *anapauo*, a military term used to describe an army resting after a long march. Philemon's ministry among the saints had a rejuvenating and invigorating effect among the struggling and often-persecuted early church.

Nothing in the biblical record suggests that Philemon was an elder or teacher in the church. He seems to have been a layman with a ministry of support, hospitality, and encouragement. But the overflow of love from his heart was legendary.

Those very virtues were the basis of Paul's appeal on behalf of Onesimus. Although Onesimus had left Philemon's household as a runaway slave, he was returning as a brother in Christ. The slave-master relationship would be superseded by a whole new relationship. Onesimus and Philemon had become spiritual brothers, and Paul knew that Philemon would recognize the duty this placed on him, for in Christ "there is neither slave nor free man . . . for you are all one in Christ Jesus" (Gal. 3:28).

Here is the heart of Paul's appeal to Philemon:

Therefore, though I have enough confidence in Christ to order you to do what is proper, yet for love's sake I rather appeal to you—since I am such a person as Paul, the aged, and now also a prisoner of Christ Jesus—I appeal to you for my child, whom I have begotten in my imprisonment, Onesimus, who formerly was useless to you, but now is useful both to you and to me. And I have sent him back to you in person, that is, sending my very heart, whom I wished to keep with me, so that on your behalf he might minister to me in my imprisonment for the gospel; but without your consent I did not want to do anything, that your goodness should not be as it were by com-

pulsion, but of your own free will. For perhaps he was for this rea-
son parted from you for a while, that you should have him back for-
ever, no longer as a slave, but more than a slave, a beloved brother,
especially to me, but how much more to you, both in the flesh and in
the Lord.

—vv. 8-16

Paul's appeal to Philemon contrasts sharply with the approach he takes in all his other epistles. Here he does not appeal to doctrinal principles or divine law, but to Philemon's own love for the brethren (v. 9). Since Onesimus was now a brother in Christ, Paul knew Philemon would be naturally inclined to demonstrate love to him.

Paul used a similar approach with the Corinthians when he sought to encourage their giving. He appealed for each person to give with a willing heart: "Let each one do just as he has purposed in his heart, not grudgingly or under compulsion; for God loves a cheerful giver" (2 Cor. 9:7). A forceful appeal to duty would no doubt have been effective, but the reward for choosing obedience gladly is so much more rich, and Paul did not want to rob them of that reward. Likewise, with Philemon, Paul was so certain of his friend's willingness to do right that he saw no need to employ strong-arm tactics.

Was it Philemon's duty to forgive? Yes. To refuse forgiveness for Onesimus would have been disobedient to the clear teaching of Christ (cf. Luke 17:4; Matt. 6:15).

Withholding forgiveness is also a violation of the eternal moral law of God. Jesus, expounding on the sixth commandment ("You shall not murder," Exod. 20:13), taught that the Decalogue's prohibition against killing also rules out both anger and a vengeful heart:

"I say to you that every one who is angry with his brother shall be
guilty before the court; and whoever shall say to his brother, 'You
good-for-nothing [see margin],' shall be guilty before the supreme
court; and whoever says, 'You fool,' shall be guilty enough to go into

the hell of fire. If therefore you are presenting your offering at the altar,
and there remember that your brother has something against you,
leave your offering there before the altar, and go your way; first be rec-
onciled to your brother, and then come and present your offering."

                                                        − MATT. 5:22-24

Thus Christ not only condemned anger and spiteful words, but He also placed on every believer the duty to seek reconciliation when we know a brother is estranged by some offense we have committed. That entails a willingness to confess guilt when we have been wrong, and a willingness to forgive when we have been wronged. Whether we are the offender or the offended one, we should actively seek reconciliation, and that always involves a willingness to forgive.

Lest someone think this duty applies only to fellow believers, remember the Second Great Commandment: "You shall love . . . your *neighbor* as yourself" (Luke 10:27). In answer to the question "Who is my neighbor?" Jesus gave the Parable of the Good Samaritan, thus including even the most despised and outcast in the circle of those whom we are to love as we love ourselves.

Loving others as we love ourselves clearly implies the duty of forgiveness. This consists in a refusal to hold grudges, a refusal to retaliate when the offense is personal against us, and a willingness to extend full and complete forgiveness to all who seek it. It does not mean we should look the other way when we see someone in sin (see chapter 7). But in the case of a repentant brother, as Onesimus was, there is no justification whatsoever for withholding forgiveness. Philemon would have been sinning had he done so.

Consider this: a sin against us always involves a greater sin against God. David's adultery with Bathsheba, for example, was a sin against her. It was a sin against her husband, Uriah (whom David arranged to have killed). It was a sin against Uriah's family, now deprived of a beloved relative. It was a sin against David's family, who bore the consequences of his deed for generations. And it was a sin against the entire nation of Israel, for David was their trusted king, example, and spiritual leader.

Yet in Psalm 51, David's great prayer of repentance, he says (v. 4), "Against You, You only, I have sinned and done what is evil in Your sight"—as if the sins against other people were not even worth mentioning. They paled in comparison to David's sin against God, and he wanted to make sure God knew he understood that. It was not that David was hard-hearted or impervious to his sins against others. Those sins were enormous, involving the killing of Uriah, the stealing of his wife, the compromise of Israel's national purity, lies told to just about everyone, and a host of other wrongs. But as great as his sins were against other people, the sin against God was infinitely greater. And God was therefore the *first* one to whom David appealed for forgiveness. God was the only one who mattered eternally. If God forgave David, then David could seek the forgiveness of others and could seek to make restitution where possible. But since the offense against God was the greatest, it was the first thing that had to be dealt with.

If every offense against us involves a greater offense against God, and if God forgives the offender, who are we to *withhold* forgiveness? Whatever Onesimus' offense against Philemon, he had sinned even more seriously against God. If God had already forgiven him, Philemon was in no position to withhold *his* forgiveness. If God forgives the greater offense, it is sinful to refuse to forgive the lesser one. Are we more just, holy, or deserving than God? Are we a higher court, with a more demanding law? Obviously not. Then whom God has forgiven, we dare not condemn. Those who refuse to forgive or who seek their own revenge have in effect usurped the authority of God.

Philemon also had a duty to the entire church at Colossae to forgive Onesimus. Had he refused to forgive the newest member of that fellowship, the entire congregation would have suffered. The unity of the group would have been broken, and their testimony to the unbelieving community would have been hurt.

So looked at from virtually every angle, Philemon had a clear responsibility to forgive Onesimus. Yet rather than pressing that duty on his friend with the weight of apostolic authority, Paul gently appealed to Philemon as a beloved brother, knowing that Philemon's maturity in Christ was such that he would gladly forgive one who had seriously wronged him.

THE CHALLENGE

There is no historical record of precisely what wrongs Onesimus had committed against Philemon. We know, of course, that he had run away, leaving his obligations unmet, defaulting on the stewardship that had been entrusted to him, perhaps even stealing from Philemon in order to finance his flight (cf. v. 18). His running away no doubt left Philemon in something of a bind.

So despite Philemon's personal commitment to Paul, his love for the saints, and his Christian maturity, there was no reason for Paul to assume that forgiving Onesimus would come easy to him. Onesimus' return very well might stir some intense emotions within Philemon. Philemon had every human reason to be angry with Onesimus and to resent what the slave had done. Paul nonetheless had enough confidence in his friend's character to frame his appeal as a request rather than a command.

Imagine Philemon reading this letter. Onesimus was probably standing in front of him. Philemon might have been surprised and at first was probably none too pleased to see the slave who had caused him so much trouble. But as he read Paul's letter his heart must have been moved by the manner in which the apostle wrote.

Notice that the apostle refers to himself as "Paul, the aged . . . now also a prisoner of Christ Jesus" (v. 9). Paul was probably about sixty at the time this letter was written. But he is probably referring to something more than his chronological age. This may have been a subtle reminder to Philemon of all the things that had taken their toll on Paul over the years—imprisonments, lashings, beatings, stonings, starvation, shipwrecks, thirst, cold and exposure and the resulting sickness (cf. 2 Cor. 11:23-30). His frail body had been severely aged by such things, and he constantly felt the pain of it. Furthermore, he remained a prisoner. He knew his dear brother would not want to add to his woes. And so on Onesimus' behalf, he subtly reminded Philemon of his own sufferings. Surely Philemon could not turn down a request from a friend who had endured so much suffering on Christ's behalf.

THE ACT OF FORGIVENESS

Paul lays out Onesimus' case in a way that would touch Philemon's heart:

> *I appeal to you for my child, whom I have begotten in my imprisonment, Onesimus, who formerly was useless to you, but now is useful both to you and to me. And I have sent him back to you in person, that is, sending my very heart, whom I wished to keep with me, that in your behalf he might minister to me in my imprisonment for the gospel. . . . For perhaps he was for this reason parted from you for a while, that you would have him back forever, no longer as a slave, but more than a slave, a beloved brother, especially to me, but how much more to you, both in the flesh and in the Lord. If then you regard me a partner, accept him as you would me. But if he has wronged you in any way, or owes you anything, charge that to my account.*
>
> – vv. 10-18

That request to Philemon outlines three crucial aspects of forgiveness.

Reception

"Accept him" (v. 17). Paul petitioned Philemon to open his life and household to Onesimus and to take him back. Philemon may well have been naturally disinclined to do that. After all, Onesimus had wronged him once. Why should the disobedient slave be given another opportunity? Most slave owners would have simply branded the runaway slave's forehead, and then sold him or demoted him to the lowest level of responsibility.

Therefore, Paul gave Philemon several reasons to view Onesimus in a new light.

First, he was *repentant*. When Paul wrote, "I have begotten [him] in my imprisonment" (v. 10), he was talking about Onesimus' spiritual rebirth. Paul was saying he had personally led Onesimus to Christ. Onesimus was Paul's own child in the faith, as was Philemon himself (v. 19). Paul wanted Philemon to know that he was sure the slave was soundly converted.

The very fact that Onesimus returned with Paul's letter to Philemon was evidence of the reality of his repentance. His presence before Philemon was tantamount to saying he was willing to accept whatever punishment Philemon deemed fit. It is significant that Onesimus did not stay in Rome to hide behind Paul's apostolic authority while Tychicus took the letter to Colossae on his behalf. Rather, Onesimus, no doubt at Paul's encouragement, went back to face the man he had wronged and to personally seek his forgiveness. He would accept the consequences of his wrongdoing, and that meant he would bear whatever punishment Philemon decided was fair. All this was certainly "fruit in keeping with . . . repentance" (cf. Matt. 3:8).

Second, Onesimus was *transformed*. "If any man is in Christ, he is a new creature; the old things passed away; behold, new things have come" (2 Cor. 5:17). Onesimus, formerly a useless rebel, was now "useful" (v. 11). This is a reference to the slave's name (a common one for slaves), which means "useful." Paul assured Philemon that Onesimus' transformation was genuine. His entire life had been turned around by Christ. The useless one was now a precious brother, certainly useful to Paul, and potentially useful to Philemon.

Third, Onesimus was *proven faithful*. He had spent enough time in Rome with Paul to demonstrate his faithfulness to Christ. Paul's confidence in and love for the converted slave were firmly grounded. Onesimus had served Paul well and thus proved himself willing to share the reproach of Christ. Other more seasoned associates of Paul would turn away when the rigors of persecution became too much for them (2 Tim. 4:10). But Onesimus, even as a new believer, devoted himself to serving Paul.

There was an irony in all this. Having sinfully fled from his bond-service to Philemon, Onesimus by divine grace had become a bond-servant of Jesus Christ. The very service he had refused to Philemon, he now willingly devoted to the apostle Paul. And it came at an important time—when the aged apostle was in a state of dire need. In fact, Onesimus had become so useful to the imprisoned apostle that Paul said sending him back to Philemon was like sending his own heart (v. 12). Had he been able, Paul would have kept Onesimus in Rome by his own side. But he knew Onesimus needed to go back and reconcile the broken relationship with his master.

Paul also knew that Philemon himself would have been in Rome if possible to minister to Paul. So Paul assured Philemon that he regarded Onesimus' service to have been offered "in your behalf" (v. 13). But not wanting to presume any further on his dear friend's graciousness, Paul concluded that it was now time to send Onesimus back. The relationship between these two brethren needed to be reconciled. And so Paul appealed to one friend on behalf of another: "accept him" (v. 17).

Restoration

Paul suggested that all these events were orchestrated for a good reason by Divine Providence: "For perhaps he was *for this reason* parted from you for a while, that you should have him back forever, no longer as a slave, but more than a slave, a beloved brother, especially to me, but how much more to you, both in the flesh and in the Lord" (vv. 15-16, emphasis added).

Indeed, it is hard not to see the hand of God in the story of Onesimus. Providence orchestrated his meeting Paul in a place so distant from Colossae. Divine grace drew him to Christ and transformed his whole life and attitude. And now under the Holy Spirit's guidance, Onesimus was going back to seek reconciliation with the master whom he had defrauded. In the midst of it all, the apostle Paul gained a friend and loving servant, not to mention the encouragement and help he drew from Onesimus. And now Philemon was getting his servant back, having unknowingly loaned him to the dear friend whom he longed to help but had no earthly way of ministering to. Only God could wring so much good from an act of human sin! (Compare Gen. 50:20; Rom. 8:28.)

Paul asked Philemon not only to accept Onesimus, but also to restore him. More than merely restoring him to his former position as a slave, Paul asked Philemon to receive him as "more than a slave, a beloved brother" (v. 16). Some have misunderstood this expression, inferring that Paul was asking for Onesimus' emancipation. But there is no reason to read such a conclusion into Paul's request. As noted earlier, the apostles did not regard our Lord's Great Commission as a campaign to free slaves. Elsewhere Paul wrote:

> *Let each man remain in that condition in which he was called. Were you called while a slave? Do not worry about it; but if you are able also to become free, rather do that. For he who was called in the Lord while a slave, is the Lord's freedman; likewise he who was called while free, is Christ's slave.*
>
> —1 COR. 7:20-22

Nonetheless, Paul urged Philemon not to receive Onesimus as a *mere* slave, but also as a brother in Christ. Paul, familiar with Onesimus' commitment to Christ, knew the slave would be a rich source of joy, encouragement, and fellowship to Philemon.

Restitution

Paul now makes an astonishing proposal to Philemon: "If then you regard me a partner, accept him as you would me. But if he has wronged you in any way, or owes you anything, charge that to my account" (vv. 17-18). Paul was offering to make restitution on

Onesimus' behalf for whatever amount his wrongs had cost Philemon.

Restitution is fair and right; and when we seek another's forgiveness, an offer of restitution is always appropriate. The Old Testament civil laws demanded restitution in most cases where a wrong could be measured in terms of money or property. For intentional wrongs, the law demanded restitution with one-fifth interest (Num. 5:6-7).

Onesimus' running away had no doubt cost Philemon dearly. He certainly would have had to pay for someone to replace Onesimus. It is also possible that Onesimus' sin included embezzlement of money or property from Philemon. The slave was in no position to demand that Philemon forego restitution. He was also in no position to repay what he owed. So Paul graciously offered to pay on his behalf.

While restitution is always just and good, the kind of grace showed by Paul is even better. The most loving, magnanimous thing Philemon could do would be to forgive the slave's debt altogether. But Paul did not want to place Philemon under compulsion to forgive the offense. So he personally offered to make good on Onesimus' debt.

These verses are a wonderful illustration of how imputation works (see our earlier discussion). Paul asks Philemon to credit Onesimus with the apostle's own merit: "accept him as you would me" (v. 17). And he wants Onesimus' debt put to his account (v. 18). That is precisely how Christ justifies the believer. Having paid the debt of our sin, He imputes to us His own righteousness, and God receives us on that basis (Rom. 4:5).

Paul was modeling for Philemon the very sort of Christlike attitude he hoped to see his friend display toward the repentant slave. Nothing is more Christlike than assuming someone else's debt so reconciliation can take place. Paul was willing to suffer the temporal consequences of Onesimus' sin in the same way that Christ had willingly suffered the eternal consequences of all the sin of all the redeemed of all time.

Although Scripture does not record Philemon's response, it is likely that he saw the point of Paul's example and forgave Onesimus' debt entirely. In doing so, Philemon himself would have shouldered his offender's debt, which is precisely what Christ did in dying for our sins. That is why the act of forgiveness is the consummate expression of Christlikeness.

THE COST

Whether Philemon forgave the debt or not, Paul was so committed to seeing reconciliation take place that he reiterated his promise to repay the debt. In order to make it like an official contract, he signed the pledge in his own handwriting: "I, Paul, am writing this with my own hand, I will repay it" (v. 19). Paul normally dictated his letters, and then to insure their authenticity, he often wrote a brief closing greeting with his own hand (see Col. 4:18; 2 Thess. 3:17). In this case, early church tradition recorded that Onesimus was the one who acted as Paul's amanuensis. Then Paul dramatically closed the letter with this written I.O.U. Thus he underscored his great desire for the reconciliation of these two brothers and formally sealed his promise to Philemon with a binding, contractual guarantee.

Onesimus had no means to repay the debt himself. He was a mere slave, for one thing. Moreover, since his conversion in Rome, it seems he had devoted himself to the apostle Paul's service (cf. vv. 11-13; Col. 4:9), and that probably meant he had not acquired any kind of paying job. Paul, on the other hand, may well have had enough financial resources to pay the debt because the Philippian church had been so generous with him in his time of need (cf. Phil. 4:14-18).

However, as an aside, Paul reminded Philemon that he himself owed Paul an unpayable debt: "lest I should mention to you that you owe to me even your own self as well" (v. 19). By all rights, if Philemon put Onesimus' debt on Paul's account, the debt would *automatically* be canceled because Philemon owed Paul a far, far greater debt. Onesimus' debt to Philemon was measurable in numerical figures; Philemon's debt to Paul was an eternal, spiritual obligation. Paul, after all, was the one who had introduced Philemon to Christ. That was an incalculable debt that Philemon could *never* repay.

This is a perspective *every* Christian should have. We all owe our very existence to the immeasurable grace of God. That is a debt we cannot hope to repay. At no time are we justified in withholding grace from others. If our eternal offenses against God have been paid for by Christ, cannot we shoulder the burden of a temporal offense that someone else has committed against us? This principle is the very message of Jesus' parable about the unforgiving servant (see chapter 5).

There is no doubt that forgiveness is costly, and this episode illustrates that fact. But the most costly forgiveness of all was bought by the atoning sacrifice of Jesus Christ, and those who benefit from that great gift have every reason to forgive others, despite the cost. Whatever offense we bear from those who wrong us is comparatively paltry, no matter how great that offense may seem by human standards.

THE INCENTIVES

Paul, it seems, was confident of Philemon's willingness to forgive Onesimus' debt entirely. That may be what he referred to in verse 21 when he wrote, "I know that you will do even more than what I say." Nonetheless, Paul subtly suggested a few additional incentives for Philemon to forgive the prodigal slave.

Paul himself hoped to see the fruit of Philemon's forgiveness, and as an additional incentive for Philemon to be magnanimous, Paul informs him that he may shortly visit him in person: "At the same time also prepare me a lodging, for I hope that through your prayers I shall be given to you" (v. 22). It is possible, even likely, that when Paul penned this epistle, a trial date was set for him to appear before the imperial court, and it seems that Paul fully expected to be released. From Rome, he hoped to return to the churches he had founded in Asia Minor. This too would have an effect on Philemon's conscience. He could hardly be praying for Paul's return to Colossae unless he forgave Onesimus. He would not want his dear friend to show up and be disappointed in him. Such accountability to his spiritual father would move him to do the right thing for Onesimus.

The closing verses of Paul's epistle give a couple of other subtle incentives for Philemon to forgive. Paul writes, "Epaphras, my fellow prisoner in Christ Jesus, greets you, as do Mark, Aristarchus, Demas, Luke, my fellow-workers. The grace of the Lord Jesus Christ be with your spirit" (vv. 23-25).

First, by conveying greetings from five men known to Philemon, Paul reminded Philemon that all of them would be witnesses to his treatment of Onesimus.

Second, quietly included in that list of names is Mark. That refers to John Mark, author of the third Gospel. Mark was a cousin of Barnabas, and as a young man he had accompanied Paul and Barnabas on their first missionary journey. Along the way, he left the group and returned to Jerusalem (Acts 13:13). Mark's defection caused Paul to lose confidence in him. Later Barnabas wanted Paul to take John Mark on their second missionary journey, but Paul refused. Paul felt so strongly about the matter that he and Barnabas parted company over it (Acts 15:37-39). The apostle Peter evidently took Mark under his wing and helped bring him to maturity (1 Pet. 5:13). In time John Mark proved himself, even to the apostle Paul.

By now Paul had long since forgiven Mark. Mark ultimately became so much a part of Paul's ministry that shortly before Paul died, it was Mark whom he asked to be sent to him: "Pick up Mark and bring him with you, for he is useful to me for service" (2 Tim. 4:11).

The earlier tensions between Paul and Mark were widely known in the church. The episode even became a matter of record in the book of Acts. Luke, who wrote that account, was also known to Philemon; so he is included in the list of those whose greetings Paul conveyed in this epistle. So without Paul's even saying it, his own example of having forgiven Mark stood as yet another encouragement to Philemon that he should do the right thing with Onesimus.

THE OUTCOME

Did Philemon forgive Onesimus? Though Scripture does not expressly record how the incident turned out, there are several reasons to assume that Philemon's response was everything Paul hoped for. For one thing, Paul's epistle found its way into the New Testament canon. This was, after all, a private letter to Philemon, and it is highly unlikely that he would have allowed it to be circulated among the churches if he had chosen to reject Paul's advice.

Furthermore, if Philemon was the man of character Paul portrays him to be, it is unthinkable that he would have refused Paul's counsel. (If he was *not* the loving and godly man Paul described, then we would have a problem with the trustworthiness of Scripture.) Furthermore, if Philemon had refused to grant forgiveness to Onesimus, it is highly unlikely that the early church would have received the epistle into the canon without someone's protesting. So the very presence of this epistle in the canon is very strong evidence that Philemon did as Paul requested.

History records that Paul was released from prison just as he hoped (v. 22). We know that he traveled much in the remaining years of his life, and if he fulfilled his plans, he would have returned to Colossae to see for himself how well his two sons in the faith had reconciled with one another.

A few decades later, shortly after the turn of the first century, Ignatius, one of the early Church Fathers, wrote three epistles to the church at Ephesus. The first two of those epistles refer to the pastor at Ephesus as "Onesimus, a man of inexpressible love." Whether it was the same Onesimus is impossible to tell. If so, he would have been an old man, probably at least in his seventies by then. If this was a different and younger Onesimus, he may have been someone named for the old slave who had made himself useful to the apostle Paul.

Only heaven will reveal the full truth about the end of the story. And there we will learn, I'm certain, that the fruits of one act of forgiveness are unimaginably far-reaching. In this case, before Philemon ever forgave, the seeds were sown for a rich harvest of spiritual fruit because Paul's brief letter of appeal to Philemon found its way into the New Testament, where it continues to challenge us all to forgive others as Christ forgave us.

And for Paul and Philemon and Onesimus, the reconciliation of this broken relationship would have been one of those sublime moments when everyone came out triumphant—Paul because he shared in the joy of reconciling two dear friends, Onesimus because he was forgiven an unpayable debt, and Philemon because he received the eternal blessings that come to the one who forgives.

FIVE

FORGIVING ONE ANOTHER

As those who have been chosen of God, holy and beloved,
put on a heart of compassion, kindness, humility, gentleness and patience;
bearing with one another, and forgiving each other, whoever has
a complaint against any one; just as the Lord
forgave you, so also should you.

– COL. 3:12-13

For a Christian to be willfully unforgiving is unthinkable. We who have been forgiven by God Himself have no right to withhold forgiveness from our fellow sinners. In fact, Scripture plainly commands us to forgive in the same manner as we have received forgiveness: "Be kind to one another, tender-hearted, forgiving each other, just as God in Christ also has forgiven you" (Eph. 4:32).

Since God *commands* us to forgive others, refusing to do so is an act of direct disobedience against Him. Let me say it plainly: refusing to forgive is a horrible sin.

Forgiveness reflects the character of God. Unforgivingness is therefore ungodly. That means unforgivingness is no less an offense to God than fornication or drunkenness, even though it is sometimes deemed more acceptable. Certainly it is more frequently found in the open among the people of God than the sins we typically regard as heinous. But Scripture is clear that God despises an unforgiving spirit.

As God's children, we are to mirror His character. At salvation we are given a new nature that bears God's spiritual likeness (Eph. 4:24). So forgiveness is an integral part of the Christian's new nature. An unforgiving Christian is a contradiction in terms. When you see a professing Christian who stubbornly refuses to relinquish a grudge, there's good reason to question the genuineness of that person's faith.

Yet to face the issue squarely, we must all admit that forgiveness does not come easily, even as Christians. Often we do not forgive as speedily or as graciously as we should. We're all too prone to nurse offenses and withhold forgiveness.

As we have seen, forgiveness is costly. Forgiveness requires us to set aside our selfishness, accept with grace the wrongs others have committed against us, and not demand what we think is our due. All of that runs counter to our natural, sinful inclinations. Even as new creatures, we retain a remainder of sin in our flesh. Sinful habits and desires continue to plague us. That is why Scripture commands us to put off the old man and clothe ourselves with the new (Eph. 4:22-24; Col. 3:9-10). And the new man is characterized by forgiveness. Notice that in both places where the apostle Paul employs such terminology, he highlights forgiveness as an essential garment for "the new self" (Eph. 4:32; Col. 3:13).

Forgiveness is so important to the Christian's walk that it was never far from the focus of what Christ taught. His sermons, His parables, His private discourses, and even His prayers were all filled with lessons about forgiveness. In fact, this was so much a running motif in Jesus' earthly sermons and sayings that one would have to be willfully blind to miss the point.

For example, as we have seen, at the heart of the Lord's Prayer is this petition: "Forgive us our debts, as we also have forgiven our debtors" (Matt. 6:12). Both the context and the cross-reference in Luke 11:4 indicate that the "debts" referred to here are *spiritual* debts; "debtors" are those who have committed transgressions against us.

It is significant that of all the phrases in the Lord's Prayer, it was *this* phrase that Christ saw fit to explain in the most detail. Immediately after the prayer's amen, He turned to the disciples and said, "For if you forgive men for their transgressions, your heavenly Father will also forgive you. But if you do not forgive men, then your Father will not forgive your transgressions" (vv. 14-15).

That has always been a difficult passage for expositors. At first glance it seems to make God's forgiveness revokable. Some have cited this verse to argue that if we refuse forgiveness to those who offend us, God will *withdraw* His forgiveness from us, implying that a Christian who does not forgive can lose his or her salvation.

But as we saw in chapter 3, the forgiveness spoken of here is not the *judicial* forgiveness of justification. It is the daily, *parental* forgiveness we are to seek when our sin has grieved our heavenly Father. One interpretive key is the prayer's address: "Our Father." This is a prayer for parental, not judicial, forgiveness. What Jesus is actually saying here is tantamount to: "If you refuse to forgive, your heavenly Father will discipline you severely for *your* sin of unforgivingness."

A well-known parable found elsewhere in Matthew's Gospel perfectly illustrates the point. Usually known as the Parable of the Unforgiving Servant, this often-misunderstood passage and its context contains some of Scripture's richest truth about forgiving one another.

PETER'S QUESTION

The parable was Jesus' response to a question raised by Peter. Having heard so much on the subject from Jesus, the disciples could not have missed the importance He placed on forgiveness. But they no doubt all had questions about how far He expected them to go in forgiving one another. As usual, Peter was the spokesman for them all.

Christ's teaching about forgiveness must have seemed radical to the disciples. What He taught contrasted markedly with what the rabbis of His time believed. We already mentioned in chapter 2 how the rabbis had twisted the eye-for-an-eye provision in the Old Testament and were using it as justification for personal vengeance.

Obviously, forgiveness was not necessarily regarded as a high virtue by most of the influential religious teachers of Jesus' day. In fact, the rabbis usually portrayed forgiveness as optional. The rabbis *did* acknowledge that the Old Testament permitted and even encouraged forgiveness in some cases. However, they strictly limited to three the number of times any person could be forgiven for the same offense.

They believed they had biblical authority for that view. They drew support for it from the book of Amos, where God pronounced doom on the enemies of Israel with these words: "For three transgressions of Damascus, and for four I will not revoke its punishment" (1:3). In that same chapter God pronounced similar judgments against Gaza, Tyre, Edom, and Ammon, always with the words, "For three transgressions . . . and for four" (cf. vv. 6, 9, 11, 13). In other words, each of those hostile nations was permitted three offenses that God overlooked, and He judged them for the fourth offense.

The rabbinical scholars reasoned that if God forgives men only three times, it would be presumptuous and even wrong for mere creatures to forgive their fellow creatures any more than that. So they set a limit on the number of times forgiveness could be extended.

No doubt because of the stress on grace and forgiveness throughout Christ's teachings, the apostles knew that He was calling them to a higher standard. Since Christ Himself had never quantified the number of times forgiveness is to be granted, Peter wanted to get some clarification. Matthew 18:21 says, "Then Peter came and said to Him, 'Lord, how often shall my brother sin against me and I forgive him? Up to seven times?'"

Peter no doubt thought he was being magnanimous. He doubled the rabbinical prescription, then rounded the number up to a perfect 7, possibly thinking the Lord might commend him for his generosity.

Jesus' reply undoubtedly stunned Peter and all the other disciples.

JESUS' ANSWER

Jesus said to him, "I do not say to you, up to seven times, but up to seventy times seven" (vv. 22).

The fleshly mind immediately protests what seems an unreasonable standard. Doesn't forgiveness have a limit? Common sense would seem to suggest that repeat offenders should not be granted pardon indefinitely. At what point does grace become gullibility? Seventy times seven is 490! No one can possibly even keep count of such a high number of offenses!

But that is precisely the point! Keeping count has nothing to do with true forgiveness. If an offense is sincerely forgiven, it cannot be held against the offender. The rabbinical system in effect required the offended party to remember and record supposedly forgiven offenses and stop forgiving after the third time. Jesus' teaching on forgiveness permits no such score-keeping. "Seventy times seven" set the standard so high that it would be pointless to keep an account of the injuries we have borne. But that is fitting, because the sort of love Christians are called to exemplify "does not take into account a wrong suffered" (1 Cor. 13:5).

The person who keeps track of wrongs, thinking he can stop forgiving when the tally reaches 490, has utterly missed the point of Jesus' words. Our Lord was not setting a numerical limit on forgiveness, but quite the opposite. He simply took Peter's number and multiplied it by seventy! For all practical purposes, He made it impossible to tabulate offenses the way Peter was thinking. In effect, He eliminated any limit on forgiveness whatsoever.

Jesus' words may contain an allusion to an Old Testament reference. Early in the book of Genesis, we encounter a man in Cain's lineage named Lamech. (This is a different Lamech from the man who was Noah's father.) Scripture says very little about Lamech, but what is recorded indicates that he was an angry man who loved vengeance. He killed someone, apparently in self-defense. Knowing that God had sworn to avenge Cain sevenfold, Lamech arrogantly believed he deserved seventy times as much vengeance. Scripture records that he devised a saying that, in Hebrew, reads like a song or a poem: "Hear my voice; ye wives of Lamech, hearken unto my speech: for I have slain a man to my wounding, and a young man to my hurt. If Cain shall be avenged sevenfold, truly Lamech seventy and sevenfold" (Gen. 4:23-24, KJV).

Lamech's boast typifies the tendency of sinful humanity. The sinful mind loves vengeance and thinks seventy times seven is a fitting ratio by which to measure revenge. Instead, Christ taught that seventy times seven is the measure by which we ought to forgive. In other words, we should always return good for evil in precisely the same abundant measure that we might otherwise be sinfully inclined to return evil for evil (cf. Rom. 12:17; 1 Thess. 5:15; 1 Pet. 3:9).

On another occasion Jesus said, "Be on your guard! If your brother sins, rebuke him; and if he repents, forgive him. And if he sins against you seven times a *day*, and returns to you seven times, saying, 'I repent,' forgive him" (Luke 17:3-4, emphasis added).[1] Again, the point is not to set a numerical limit, such as seven times in one day, but to underscore the freeness and frequency with which we are to forgive.

Someone might ask, Who in the world would commit the same offense seven times in one day and then profess repentance after each time? Here's the point: this sort of behavior is precisely how *we* sin against *God*. We sin; then we express sorrow for our sin and seek God's forgiveness; then we turn around and commit precisely the same sin again. Anyone who has ever been in bondage to a sinful habit knows precisely what the routine is like.

Does God forgive under such circumstances? Yes, He does. And since His forgiveness sets the criterion by which we are to forgive, the standard is set blessedly high. What may seem at first like an impossibly unfair and unattainable standard is in fact wonderful news for anyone who has ever needed to seek the forgiveness of God for repeat offenses. Jesus is teaching here that the forgiveness we extend to others should be as boundless as the mercy of God we desire for ourselves. That shatters all the limits anyone would try to place on human forgiveness.

All of this is underscored by the parable Jesus gave in reply to Peter's question. The main characters in the parable are a gracious king, a servant deeply in debt to the king, and another slave who owed the first servant a smaller debt.

THE KING'S FORGIVENESS

The parable begins by describing an incredible act of forgiveness on the part of the king:

> *"For this reason the kingdom of heaven may be compared to a king who wished to settle accounts with his slaves. And when he had begun to settle them, there was brought to him one who owed him ten thousand talents. But since he did not have the means to repay, his lord commanded him to be sold, along with his wife and children and all that he had, and repayment to be made. The slave therefore falling down, prostrated himself before him, saying, 'Have patience with me, and I will repay you everything.' And the lord of that slave felt compassion and released him and forgave him the debt."*
>
> — MATT. 18:23-27

This debtor to the king was very likely a man of high rank, even though he is referred to as a servant. Ancient kings employed provincial governors called satraps. One of the responsibilities of the satrap was to collect taxes. This indebted servant might have been one of these provincial governors, and the settling of accounts referred to in verses 23-24 was the time appointed for the satrap to bring the tax money from his region to the king.

This man was deeply in debt. Such a massive debt was no doubt because of some embezzlement or other dereliction of duty on the servant's part. Moreover, if he had taken all the tax money by theft or embezzlement, he had utterly squandered it, because he had no means by which to repay what he owed.

Ten thousand talents was an unbelievably large amount of money for one individual to owe. A talent was the largest measure of money in the Roman world. This refers to the Attic talent, in use at that time throughout the Empire. One such talent was worth 6,000 denarii, and a denarius was considered a fair wage for a day's work (cf. Matt. 20:2). In fact, a denarius was a soldier's wage for a day. So 6,000 denarii, one talent, was a considerable sum of money (about seventeen years' wages), and 10,000 talents were equal to seventeen years' wages for 10,000 men. This was an unfathomable amount of personal debt. In today's terms this would be millions, possibly billions, of dollars. To put it in perspective, records from the first century reveal that the total annual revenue collected by the Roman government from the entire land of Palestine averaged about 900 talents. Furthermore, Solomon's temple was world-renowned for the massive amounts of gold it contained. All that gold, according to the Old Testament, amounted to just over 8,000 talents (1 Chron. 29:4-7)—less than this one man owed!

The Greek expression translated "ten thousand" does not necessarily even signify a precise amount. This was the largest number expressible in the Greek language. It is the word from which we derive the English term *myriads*, and it was often used exactly the way we employ its English counterpart—to represent any uncountable number. In the *New American Standard Bible* translation the same word is translated "myriads" in Revelation 5:11; in 1 Corinthians 4:15 it is rendered "countless."

So this man owed the king a debt that, for all practical purposes, was unpayable. Since he had no means by which to finance such a massive liability, the king commanded that he, his family, and all his possessions be sold, with the proceeds to be paid against the debt.

Obviously, this debt was so large that the sale of the man and his family would not have covered even the smallest fraction of what was owed. Nonetheless, it was the king's right to demand such a penalty for this man's misdeeds.

The servant's state was utterly hopeless. His only hope lay in the king's goodness. So he began to plead for mercy. Jesus said, "falling down, [he] prostrated himself" before the king (v. 26). This was far more than the usual homage given a king. It signified the man's utter, abject despair. He was literally throwing himself before the king in a plea for mercy. He offered no defense because he had none. He fully admitted his guilt and simply petitioned for mercy.

"Have patience with me, and I will repay you everything," he cried (v. 26). The promise was no doubt sincere, but the burden of such a debt was more than a hundred men could ever repay, and the monarch knew it.

At this point the average monarch might be expected to deal mercilessly with the slave. The gross abuse of his position, the waste of a fortune, the size of the deficit, combined with the servant's foolish pledge to pay it back, is the stuff that would exasperate a typical king. The servant certainly deserved no mercy.

But this was no typical sovereign. In an incredible gesture of pardon, he freely forgave the man's debt. No repayment plan was instituted; the king was willing to absorb the loss himself, simply for the sake of showing mercy to a helpless servant. This is an amazing, unearthly compassion. It is the very picture of what God does on behalf of every sinner who repents.

The servant perfectly symbolizes the lost sinner, saddled with a monstrous, unpayable debt—the overwhelming burden of sin's guilt. The debtor's prison pictures hell, where condemned sinners will spend eternity paying for the unpayable. And the king pictures a loving and compassionate heavenly Father, a God of unfathomable mercy and grace who is always willing and eager to forgive.

This king's forgiveness is astonishingly generous. Consider all that his pardon involved. In order to forgive this massive amount of money, he had to regard it as a legitimate loan, though the facts make clear that this was a case of embezzlement and waste. Even in the best case, the debt resulted from unconscionable malfeasance combined with inconceivable extravagance. In fact, the man may well have been guilty on all counts. Yet the king graciously forgave not only the debt, but also whatever wickedness had helped accrue such monstrous debt. He did not chide the man or punish him for his crookedness. He simply, compassionately forgave him.

One wonders how any king could be so compassionate with such a wicked subject. But remember, this is precisely the picture of what God does for the repentant sinner. He not only forgives sin's guilt, but He elevates the sinner to a position of incomprehensible, utterly undeserved favor!

THE SERVANT'S UNFORGIVINGNESS

You would think that someone so freely forgiven would appreciate the importance of showing compassion to others. But the behavior exhibited by the forgiven slave is shocking: "That slave went out and found one of his fellow-slaves who owed him a hundred denarii; and he seized him and began to choke him, saying, 'Pay back what you owe'" (v. 28).

A hundred denarii represented about 100 days' wages. That is not an insignificant sum considered by itself, but compared to the amount the first servant had been forgiven, it was nothing. Jesus' wording indicates that the forgiven servant went out immediately from his encounter with the gracious king, and practically the first thing he did was find this other servant who owed him money. He then began to demand immediate repayment, punctuating his demands with the harshest conceivable threats, and even physical brutality.

Think for a moment about the situation this parable presents. The debt owed to this man by his fellow servant was a legitimate debt. From a legal standpoint, he did have a rightful claim on what was owed to him. Technically, he was completely within his rights to demand repayment. But do not our moral senses naturally and rightfully recoil at his behavior?

We see his act as morally repugnant, because it is. The first servant's very existence depended on an incomprehensible act of mercy that had been shown to him. Did he not therefore have a duty to love mercy and to extend it to others as well?

The totally undeserved forgiveness he had received from the king should have made him profoundly grateful, and also profoundly merciful. His unmerciful actions toward his fellow slave were therefore an insult to the king who had forgiven him. The extraordinary mercy he had received ought to have been the thing that filled his heart and mind. Instead, he was obsessed with regaining the paltry sum owed him by a fellow servant. His actions betrayed a lack of gratitude. It was as if he had already forgotten the great mercy that had been shown to him.

The slave's behavior is grotesque. It reads like a caricature of the worst kind of villainy. It seems unreal, inhuman. Who could ever behave this way?

That was exactly the point Jesus wanted to make with the disciples. He purposely portrayed the servant in a way that would shock them. If the slave's behavior seems unreasonable and totally irrational, it is supposed to. Our Lord was underscoring the absurdity of an unforgiving Christian. This is bizarre, unconscionable behavior. No sensible person could ever be expected to act this way.

But it is exactly what occurs every time a Christian is unforgiving.

Notice that the servant who owed the lesser debt made precisely the same plea the original servant had made to the king: "Have patience with me and I will repay you" (v. 29). The forgiven servant *should* have been moved by this echo of his own despair. After all, only a very short time before he had been in a far worse predicament, and those were his very words! If anyone in the world should have understood the plight of the second servant, it was this man who had already been forgiven for so much.

But he turned a deaf ear to his fellow servant's plea. With astonishing coldheartedness, he "threw him in prison until he should pay back what was owed" (v. 30).

Debtors' prisons were common in that time. The debtor was imprisoned and given some menial labor to do, for which he was paid a pittance. Those wages went toward the payment of the debt, and the prisoner was not released until the debt was paid. It was a questionable way to deal with debtors, however, because imprisoning them cut their earning power, imposed further hardships on their families, and in many cases made repayment practically impossible. The creditor therefore often came out on the losing end. So imprisonment was usually a last resort used for only the most recalcitrant debtors.

It was for those reasons extremely unwise and unduly severe to have a debtor thrown in prison who was willing to repay. Even if the first servant had decided to insist on repayment of what was owed to him, he did not need to have the second servant imprisoned. Such punishment was unreasonable, overly harsh, and irrational. It perfectly pictures the absurdity of a Christian with a vengeful heart.

THE OTHER SERVANTS' OUTRAGE

Notice who was most offended by the servant's harsh treatment of the debtor: his fellow servants. "When his fellow-slaves saw what had happened, they were deeply grieved and came and reported to their lord all that had happened" (v. 31).

These servants obviously knew about the great debt the first man had been forgiven. And they were rightfully indignant when they saw his response to a fellow servant in need. In effect, the unforgiving servant had placed himself above the king. His actions suggested that he believed he had a right to extract vengeance in a situation identical to the one in which he had asked the king to show him mercy. This was unspeakably wicked. It is no wonder that his fellow servants were outraged.

The other servants' involvement pictures how the sin of one individual affects the entire body. One unforgiving person in the church can cause offense to the entire flock, and it is right that Christians should get involved in dealing with such an obvious offense. In fact, the broader context of Matthew 18 includes Jesus' instructions on how discipline is to be handled in the church (see chapter 7 for a fuller discussion of the process of church discipline).

THE KING'S ANGER

Understandably, the king also was outraged when he heard the report of what had happened:

> "Then summoning him, his lord said to him, 'You wicked slave, I forgave you all that debt because you entreated with me. Should you

not also have had mercy on your fellow-slave, even as I had mercy on you?' And his lord, moved with anger, handed him over to the torturers until he should repay all that was owed him."

– vv. 32-34

The king's response was so severe that it causes many people to conclude that the unforgiving servant in this parable cannot possibly represent a true believer. They assume punishment this harsh must represent hell; and since no genuine believer is ever subject to the threat of hell, this man must represent an unregenerate person.

Others cite the parable as an argument in favor of the view that disobedient Christians can lose their salvation.

This is admittedly a difficult passage. It is possible to read verse 34 ("handed him over to the torturers until he should repay all that was owed him") to mean that the unforgiving servant was saddled with the same debt that had already been forgiven. But that introduces some obvious difficulties into the imagery of the parable. Does this suggest that God will withdraw His judicial forgiveness—justification—from those who fail to forgive others? Certainly not. That would ultimately make justification hinge on the sinner's own works. It would also suggest that God Himself is vacillating—granting "forgiveness" but withdrawing it later. Scripture plainly says He will not do that. When God forgives us, He removes our sins as far from us as the east is from the west (Ps. 103:12). He blots out our sins and promises to remember them no more (Isa. 43:25; Jer. 31:34; Heb. 8:12). He does not forgive and then rescind His forgiveness.

Could it be that the unforgiving servant represents a professing believer who was actually never regenerate to begin with? This is a popular view. Those who advocate this interpretation say the unforgiving servant pictures someone who hears the Gospel and embraces it externally, but who never really receives the forgiveness offered in the Gospel. That is a more viable interpretation, but it still suggests that the servant's response, rather than the king's decree, is the key issue in justification. It makes forgiveness conditional on the sinner's subsequent behavior.

An important rule of thumb when interpreting parables is to look for the parable's central meaning and to resist the temptation to try to press too much meaning out of peripheral details. The meaning of this parable is expressed plainly by Christ in verse 35: "So shall My heavenly Father also do to you, if each of you does not forgive his brother from your heart." This whole parable is virtually a commentary on Jesus' earlier words in Matthew 6:14-15: "For if you forgive men for their transgressions, your heavenly Father will also forgive you. But if you do not forgive men, then your Father will not forgive your transgressions."

Remember also that this parable is a lesson for Peter and the other disciples. Jesus did not aim the message of the parable at interested but uncommitted hearers. He clearly made it a warning to those in the innermost circle of His followers (v. 35). The lesson it contains is for already-regenerate people—believers, not merely pretenders.

Therefore, the first servant must represent a truly regenerate, yet unforgiving believer. The severity of the king's punishment here is actually illustrative of how God will discipline unforgiving believers. It is sometimes necessary for a parent to deal harshly with a persistently rebellious child; and God Himself will employ harsh measures when necessary to correct a disobedient Christian. The harshness of His discipline is a measure of His love for His people and His concern for their purity. As we saw in chapter 3, it is not true that God's discipline is always mild and friendly; often it is prompted by the severest kind of fatherly displeasure. And some of His most severe discipline is given to believers who refuse to show mercy to others.

Notice how the king addressed the unforgiving servant: "You wicked slave." Would God refer to one of His own children as "wicked"? He certainly is not blind to their wickedness (cf. 2 Chron. 7:14). And this slave was behaving in a way that was undeniably wicked. Sin is wicked, whether committed by a believer or unbeliever. In fact, unforgivingness is *more* wicked in a believer because the believer's refusal to forgive is a slight against the very grace on which he depends for redemption. In a case like this, it would not be any more inappropriate for God to call a believer "wicked" than it was for Christ to address Peter as "Satan" (Matt. 16:23).

Notice also that the punishment administered, though extremely severe, seems to picture only the harshest kind of discipline, not eternal condemnation. The king "handed him over to the torturers"—not the executioners—"until he should repay all that was owed him" (v. 34).

Look at that verse closely. What was now owed to the king? Since the earlier debt was already legally forgiven, the remaining debt was primarily this man's duty to show the same kind of mercy to others. The "torturers" represent the rod of God's discipline. The lesson of the parable is this: Christians who refuse to forgive others will be subject to the severest kind of discipline until they learn to forgive as they have been forgiven.

"All that was owed him" also represents the temporal consequences of sin. Again, justification erases the guilt of our sin in the eternal court of God, but it does not necessarily guarantee an escape from sin's consequences in this life. This parable seems to suggest that as a means of His loving discipline, God might actually magnify the temporal consequences of sin. Though the *guilt* of sin is forgiven so that it will never be an issue in eternal judgment, God may permit the *consequences* of sin to be even more severe, in order to motivate a sinning believer to obey. Because unforgivingness is so completely foreign to what Christians should be, Christ applies this threat particularly to that sin: "So shall My heavenly Father also do to you, if each of you does not forgive his brother from your heart" (v. 35).

Christians *ought* to be the most forgiving people on earth, because they have been forgiven as no one else has. Therefore, those who refuse to forgive are worthy of the most severe kind of discipline from the hand of a loving Father.

James 2:13 gives an inexorable principle of divine justice: "Judgment will be merciless to one who has shown no mercy." For the unsaved, the prospects of this principle are fearsome indeed. Those who have been merciless will have no mercy in the eternal court of God. They will suffer eternal torment entirely without mercy.

But there is an application of this principle for the believer as well. Christians who fail to show mercy will be subject to divine chastisement without much mercy. That is the whole message of this parable. I am convinced that multitudes of Christians who suffer from stress, depression, discouragement, relationship problems, and all sorts of other hardships experience these things because of a refusal to forgive. Forgiveness from the heart would liberate the person immediately from such "torturers"—and glorify God in the process.

In fact, the corollary of the James 2:13 principle is one of the Beatitudes: "Blessed are the merciful, for they shall receive mercy" (Matt. 5:7). Divine mercy is promised to those who show mercy. On this subject, Scripture speaks with extraordinary clarity.

Notice that Jesus speaks of forgiveness "from your heart" (Matt. 18:35). Genuine forgiveness is not feigned or grudging, but is given as freely as we ourselves desire to be forgiven. It involves a deliberate refusal to hold the guilt over the head of the offender. It means ending the bitterness, laying aside anger, and refusing to dwell on the offense that has been forgiven. It is a complete letting go of any thought of retaliation or reprisal. It is, as nearly as possible, the human equivalent of what God promises—to remember the sin no more (cf. Jer. 31:34).

Such forgiveness does not come easy, particularly when it deals with the kinds of sins that destroy lives and relationships. When we're talking about a personal slight or an unkind word, it's relatively easy to forgive. But what if the offense is more serious? Where do people find the strength to forgive when they discover a spouse has cheated, or when a drunk driver causes the death of a loved one? Is it humanly possible to forgive such offenses?

It may not *seem* humanly possible, and it certainly does not lie within the power of fallen human nature alone to forgive such things from the heart. But it certainly is possible for redeemed people, under the influence of the Holy Spirit's power, to forgive even the most serious offenses. In the chapter that follows we will look more intently at some of these issues and will delve into some of the most important practical issues regarding how we should forgive one another.

SIX

❧

JUST AS GOD HAS FORGIVEN YOU

Forgiving each other,
just as God in Christ also has forgiven you.

– EPH. 4:32

It was Monday, December 1, 1997. About a dozen students were huddled to pray—as they did every morning—in the hallway outside the administration office at Heath High School in Paducah, Kentucky. Classes would start in a few minutes, so someone closed in prayer.

The final amen still hung in the air. Students had not yet begun to move away to their classes. Suddenly the sound of gunshots shattered the peace of the moment. A fourteen-year-old freshman had walked up to the group with a .22 caliber automatic pistol and was firing into the prayer circle, calmly shooting students one at a time.

When it was over, three students were dead and five others seriously wounded. The story made headlines for weeks. What was so astonishing was that by all accounts, the students in the prayer circle had done nothing to provoke the boy who did the shooting. In fact, several of them had previously befriended him. The secular media were at a loss to explain how anyone so young could commit such a heinous act of pure evil.

Another aspect of the story also caught the media's eye—the amazing forgiveness immediately extended by the survivors and their loved ones. Many relatives of the victims were interviewed by the press in the days and weeks following the shooting. Despite the utter senselessness of the crime, no one spoke with bitterness or a desire for vengeance. Churches in Paducah, while ministering to the victims and their loved ones, also reached out to the shooter and his family. One of the injured girls was fifteen-year-old Melissa Jenkins. As she lay in the hospital less than a week after the shootings, fully aware that the damage to her spinal cord was so severe she would be a paraplegic for the rest of her life, she sent a message through a friend to the boy who had deliberately shot her: "Tell him I forgive him."

How can someone who has been so grievously wounded forgive so freely and so quickly? Apart from Christ, it is well nigh impossible. "But we have the mind of Christ" (1 Cor. 2:16). The Holy Spirit indwells and empowers us. Therefore, Christians are capable of superhuman acts of forgiveness.

My own brother-in-law went to a jail to express his forgiveness and offer the forgiveness of God to the drug addict who had murdered his son in a market holdup.

One of the earliest examples of this sort of forgiveness is Stephen, the first martyr. While he was being stoned, with large rocks battering his body, breaking his bones, causing him to bleed and ultimately die—in the midst of all that trauma he found strength to pray for his killers. "Falling on his knees, he cried out with a loud voice, 'Lord, do not hold this sin against them!' And having said this, he fell asleep" (Acts 7:60). Despite the violence of the moment, his death was so peaceful that Scripture portrays him as simply drifting into a tranquil slumber.

The natural tendency in such situations is to pray for vengeance. In fact, the death of the Old Testament prophet Zechariah makes an interesting contrast with that of Stephen. Like Stephen, Zechariah was stoned, but notice the marked difference in his dying prayer:

> So they conspired against him and at the command of the king they stoned him to death in the court of the house of the LORD. Thus Joash the king did not remember the kindness which his father

Jehoiada had shown him, but he murdered his son. And as he died
he said, "May the LORD see and avenge!"

$-$2 CHRON. 24:21-22

We cannot fault Zechariah for praying for vengeance. He recognized, of course, that vengeance belonged to God, and he properly left the matter with God. His praying this way should not be regarded as a sin.

In fact, there's a legitimate sense in which all martyrs are entitled to plead for vengeance against their persecutors. Revelation 6:10 gives us a look behind the curtains of the cosmic drama. There we learn that the perpetual cry of the martyrs of all ages is, "How long, O Lord, holy and true, will You refrain from judging and avenging our blood on those who dwell on the earth?"

There is certainly no sin in crying for justice like that. God *will* avenge His people, and when His vengeance is finally administered, no one will be able to complain that it is unjust. In fact, we will simply marvel at the long-suffering of God that restrained vengeance for so long.

But for now, in the bright light of the New Covenant, while the fullness of divine vengeance is restrained and the Gospel is being proclaimed to the world, there is a higher cause than vengeance to plead for—forgiveness and reconciliation with those who persecute us. Jesus said, "Love your enemies, do good to those who hate you, bless those who curse you, pray for those who mistreat you" (Luke 6:27-28). Christ Himself gave us the example to follow when, as He died at the hands of evil men, He prayed for their forgiveness. Stephen obviously got the message.

What about justice? It is natural, and even right, to want to see justice fulfilled and divine vengeance administered. But for the Christian there is another priority. Justice will come, but in the meantime our thoughts and actions toward others are to be driven by mercy. As Christians, we should be obsessed with forgiveness, not vengeance.

THE VOICE OF THE BLOOD

There is a clear illustration of this in the book of Hebrews. The writer of that Bible book makes several references to Abel, Adam's second-born, who was killed unjustly by his own elder brother. Abel is listed in Hebrews 11 as the first member of the famous "Hall of Faith" found in that chapter. Hebrews 11:4 says this about Abel: "By faith Abel offered unto God a more excellent sacrifice than Cain, by which he obtained witness that he was righteous, God testifying of his gifts: and by it he being dead yet speaketh" (KJV).

That phrase "he being dead yet speaketh" is a familiar one, but have you ever realized what it refers to? It is an allusion to Genesis 4:10, where God said to Cain, "What have you done? The voice of your brother's blood is crying to Me from the ground." Though Abel was dead, he still spoke through his innocent blood, crying out for vengeance.

Those were figurative terms, of course. Abel's blood did not literally cry out. But the violent and unjust manner of his death—brutal murder at his own brother's wicked hand—fairly screamed for vengeance. Justice needed to be done. A crime had been committed for which severe punishment was in order. Abel's blood, spilled on the ground, was a testimony against Cain. In metaphorical terms, Abel's blood was crying for retribution against Cain.

Abel was the first martyr, and the blood of every martyr since then has joined the cry for justice against the persecutors of God's people. In that sense, they *all* still speak, though they are dead. They are the very ones pictured in Revelation 6:10, under the altar, calling for God to glorify Himself in the accomplishment of justice.

But Hebrews 12:24 makes an interesting contrast. There the writer mentions *Jesus'* blood, "which speaks better than the blood of Abel." The meaning is clear: whereas Abel's blood (and the blood of other martyrs) screams for vengeance, Christ's blood pleads for mercy.

Jesus' blood, shed as an atonement for sins, appeals for *forgiveness* on behalf of sinners. This is a remarkable truth. All the blood of all the martyrs of all time cries out for justice and vengeance and retribution. But Christ's blood "speaks better."

Again, there is nothing wrong with desiring justice. Justice honors God. It is certainly legitimate to want to see wrongs made right and evildoers recompensed for their wickedness. But the longing for forgiveness is better still. Christians are to be characterized by a desire for mercy, compassion, and forgiveness—even for their enemies.

How do we develop such a state of mind? How can a Christian, badly hurt by the offenses of another, learn to forgive "from [the] heart" the way Jesus commanded (Matt. 18:35)? What about the commands in Scripture to confront those who sin against us? How do we know when to confront and when to overlook an offense?

Furthermore, how can we forgive those who have not repented? Doesn't God himself withhold forgiveness from the unrepentant? If we are to forgive in the same way we have been forgiven, don't we first need to require the repentance of the offender?

Those are all essential questions. Does the Bible offer answers? I believe it does. Let's begin by exploring what Scripture means when it commands us to forgive in the same way God forgives.

GOD'S FORGIVENESS/OUR FORGIVENESS

How can forgiveness between fellow sinners be compared to the forgiveness of an offended deity? There must be some similarities, because Scripture instructs us to forgive in the same manner as we have been forgiven. This idea occurs in two verses we have quoted repeatedly: Ephesians 4:32 ("forgiv[e] each other, just as God in Christ also has forgiven you") and Colossians 3:13 ("just as the Lord forgave you").

Some take the position that this teaches forgiveness should always be conditional. Their rationale goes like this: God forgives only those who repent. Therefore, if we are going to forgive in the same manner as we have been forgiven, we should withhold forgiveness from all who are unrepentant. Some fine teachers hold this view. For example, Jay Adams writes:

> It should go without saying that since our forgiveness is modeled after God's (Eph. 4:32), it must be conditional.

Forgiveness by God rests on clear, unmistakable conditions. The apostles did not merely announce that God had forgiven men. . . . Paul and the apostles turned away from those who refused to meet the conditions, just as John and Jesus did earlier when the scribes and the Pharisees would not repent.[1]

There is some merit in Adams's position. There are times when forgiveness must be conditional, and we shall discuss that issue before the close of this chapter. I have great respect for Adams and have recommended his book on forgiveness as a helpful study of the subject. On this issue, however, I must disagree with the position he takes.

To make conditionality the gist of Christlike forgiving seems to miss the whole point of what Scripture is saying. When Scripture instructs us to forgive in the manner we have been forgiven, what is in view is not the idea of *withholding* forgiveness until the offender expresses repentance.

Listen carefully to what these verses are saying:

• *Matthew 6:12, 14-15*: "And forgive us our debts, as we forgive our debtors. . . . For if ye forgive men their trespasses, your heavenly Father will also forgive you: but if ye forgive not men their trespasses, neither will your Father forgive your trespasses" (KJV).

• *James 2:13*: "For judgment will be merciless to one who has shown no mercy; mercy triumphs over judgment."

• *Matthew 18:35*: "So likewise shall my heavenly Father do also unto you, if ye from your hearts forgive not every one his brother their trespasses" (KJV).

• *Luke 6:36-38*: "Be merciful, just as your Father is merciful. And do not pass judgment and you will not be judged; and do not condemn, and you shall not be condemned; pardon, and you will be pardoned. Give, and it will be given to you; good measure, pressed down, shaken together, running over, they will pour into your lap. For whatever measure you deal out to others, it will be dealt to you in return."

The emphasis is on forgiving freely, generously, willingly, eagerly, speedily—and from the heart. The attitude of the forgiver is where the focus of Scripture lies, not the terms of forgiveness.

Most of those who hold that all forgiveness is conditional portray forgiveness as a formal transaction in which the forgiven one must repent and the offended party promises in return never to bring up the sin again. If this transaction has not occurred, they say, real forgiveness has not yet taken place. In some cases the offender may repent and ask forgiveness without prompting, and forgiveness should be granted on the spot. But in most cases, particularly when the offender is ignorant of having committed a wrong, the offended party must first confront the offender and formally solicit repentance before he or she can forgive. In short, no act of forgiveness can occur until the offender asks for forgiveness.

Sadly, I have seen people who hold this opinion become obsessive confronters and ultimately make themselves odious to friend and foe alike. Others nurse grudges, refuse to relinquish bitterness, and even sever friendships over relatively petty offenses, justifying such attitudes because they are convinced they have no duty to forgive until the offender repents.

While it is often true that forgiveness involves a two-way transaction, it is not true of *all* forgiveness. There are times when forgiveness should be unconditional and unilateral, and there are other times when forgiveness must be withheld until the offender repents. The biblical principles governing these different kinds of forgiveness are clear.

CONDITIONAL FORGIVENESS/ UNCONDITIONAL FORGIVENESS

It is obvious from Scripture that sometimes forgiveness must be conditional. For example, in certain cases the offender is to be confronted and ultimately even excommunicated from the church if he or she refuses to repent (Luke 17:3; Matt. 18:15-17). We will closely examine the biblical process for church discipline in chapter 7.

But does *every* offense call for confrontation, possibly leading to

formal church discipline? Is there no place for simply granting unilateral forgiveness for petty offenses? Is there no time when the
offended party should simply overlook a transgression, choosing to
suffer wrong and forgive without being asked or without formally
confronting the offender?

Obviously, these questions have important practical ramifications. If you had a friend who scrupulously tried to confront you
every time you committed a petty offense, wouldn't the friendship
grow tedious pretty quickly? And if marriage partners saw it as their
solemn duty to confront each other for every offense, wouldn't such
a mind-set make the marriage relationship practically impossible to
endure?

It is a mistake to assume that verses like Luke 17:3 ("If your
brother sins, rebuke him") and Matthew 18:15 ("If your brother
sins against you, go and show him his fault," NIV) are absolute pre-
scriptions for every kind of transgression. If we were obligated to
confront one another for every paltry misdeed, we would be doing
little else.

Indeed, Scripture gives us another principle for dealing with the
vast majority of petty infractions: overlook the offense. Forgive unilaterally, unconditionally. Grant pardon freely and unceremoni-
ously. Love demands this. "Keep fervent in your love for one
another, because love covers a multitude of sins" (1 Pet. 4:8).
"Hatred stirs up strife, but love covers all transgressions" (Prov.
10:12). "He who covers a transgression seeks love" (Prov. 17:9).
Love "does not take into account a wrong suffered . . . [but] bears
all things, believes all things, hopes all things, endures all things" (1
Cor. 13:5-7). The *New International Version* renders 1 Corinthians
13:5 this way: "[Love] keeps no record of wrongs."

Jay Adams recognizes the Christian's duty to overlook petty
offenses, citing some of these same texts. "But," he writes, "it is not
. . . forgiveness."[2] Having defined forgiveness as a two-way transaction, he has no room in his system for unilateral or unconditional
forgiveness. So he draws a distinction between forgiveness and
overlooking another's transgression. If true, that would mean all the

petty offenses we choose to overlook (or "cover," in biblical terminology) are not really to be regarded as forgiven.

But the Bible itself makes no such distinction. Covering
another's transgression is the very essence of forgiveness. Speaking
of God's forgiveness, Psalm 32:1 equates the concepts of forgiveness
and the covering of sin: "How blessed is he whose transgression is
forgiven, whose sin is covered!" This is a Hebrew parallelism,
employing two different expressions to designate the same concept.
To cover someone else's sin is the very essence of forgiveness.

Psalm 85:2 draws the same parallel: "You forgave the iniquity of
Your people; You covered all their sin."

James 5:20 also equates forgiveness with the covering of sin:
"He who turns a sinner from the error of his way will save his soul
from death, and will cover a multitude of sins."

So when 1 Peter 4:8 says, "Love covers a multitude of sins," it is
describing forgiveness.

Furthermore, Scripture also teaches that forgiveness can be
unilateral and unconditional. Mark 11:25-26 clearly speaks of this
kind of forgiveness and even makes it a condition for receiving
God's forgiveness:

> "Whenever you stand praying, forgive, if you have anything against
> anyone; so that your Father also who is in heaven may forgive you
> your transgressions. But if you do not forgive, neither will your
> Father who is in heaven forgive your transgressions."

That describes an immediate forgiveness granted to the offender
with no formal meeting or transaction required. It necessarily refers
to a pardon that is wholly unilateral, because this forgiveness takes
place *while the forgiver stands praying*.[3] "Forgive" is the clear command
of that verse, and it is to take place on the spot. There is no mention
of confrontation. There is no command to seek the offender's
repentance. The forgiveness of Mark 11:25 is therefore different
from the forgiveness of Luke 17:3. *This* forgiveness is to be granted
unconditionally and unilaterally.

UNCONDITIONAL FORGIVENESS: WHAT DOES IT MEAN?

What does unilateral forgiveness entail? If there's no transaction, no seeking of forgiveness, no formal granting of pardon, no words exchanged between the two parties, then what exactly is accomplished by this sort of forgiveness?

Its chief effects are wrought in the heart of the forgiver. This kind of forgiveness involves a deliberate decision to cover the other person's offense. "Forgive" in Mark 11:25 is an imperative, a command. The forgiveness called for here is necessarily a volitional matter. In other words, it is a choice, not a feeling or an involuntary response.

It is, as Matthew 18:35 suggests, *from the heart*; but even that does not place forgiveness primarily in the realm of feeling. "Heart" in Scripture normally designates the seat of the intellect (cf. Prov. 23:7; Luke 9:47). So this speaks of a deliberate and rational decision. It is a choice made by the offended party to set aside the other person's transgression and not permit the offense to cause a breach in the relationship or fester in bitterness.

In effect, the person who chooses to forgive resolves not to remember the offense, refuses to hold a grudge, relinquishes any claim on recompense, and resists the temptation to brood or retaliate. The offended party simply bears the insult. The offense is set aside, lovingly covered for Christ's sake. For petty and unintentional offenses, this is the proper and loving way to forgive—unilaterally, without confrontation and without stirring any strife.

This, I believe, is what Scripture refers to most often when it calls us to forgive one another. The heavy emphasis on forgiveness in Scripture is not meant to make us more confrontational, but quite the opposite. When Scripture calls us to have an attitude of forgiveness, the emphasis is always on long-suffering, patience, benevolence, forbearance, kindness, and mercy—not confrontation.

To deny that forgiveness can ever be unilateral is in my view a potentially serious mistake. It places too much stress on confrontation. And that tends to produce more conflict than it avoids. People who insist on confronting every wrong often simply stir strife—the antithesis of what Jesus' teaching on forgiveness was intended to produce. Real love should *cover* the vast majority of transgressions, not constantly haul them out in the open for dissection (1 Pet. 4:8).

TO CONFRONT OR NOT TO CONFRONT?

All of this calls for some careful distinctions. Obviously there are times when confrontation is essential. How do we identify those situations? Are there clear biblical principles that teach us when to confront and when to forgive unilaterally?

I believe there are. Here are some guidelines to help you in drawing the distinction:

Whenever possible, especially if the offense is petty or unintentional, it is best to forgive unilaterally. This is the very essence of a gracious spirit. It is the Christlike attitude called for in Ephesians 4:1-3:

> *Therefore I, the prisoner of the Lord, entreat you to walk in a manner worthy of the calling with which you have been called, with all humility and gentleness, with patience, showing forbearance for one another in love, being diligent to preserve the unity of the Spirit in the bond of peace.*

That calls for a gracious tolerance ("forbearance ") of others' faults. This is necessary for the sake of maintaining peace.

In other words, believers are supposed to have a sort of mutual immunity to petty offenses. Love "is not easily angered" (1 Cor. 13:5, NIV). If every fault required formal confrontation, the whole of our church life would be spent confronting and resolving conflicts over petty annoyances. So for the sake of peace, to preserve the unity of the Spirit, we are to show tolerance whenever possible.

This, then, is the governing rule: Unless an offense *requires* confrontation, unconditional, unilateral forgiveness should cover the transgression. The offended party, in suffering the offense, is following in the footsteps of Christ (1 Pet. 2:21-25). This is the very attitude Christ called for in Matthew 5:39-40: "Whoever slaps you on your right cheek, turn the other to him also. If anyone wants to sue you and take your shirt, let him have your coat also."

If you are the only *injured party, even if the offense was public and flagrant, you may choose to forgive unilaterally.* Examples of this abound in Scripture. Joseph, for example, was the victim of a grievous wrong at the hands of his brothers. They plotted to kill him, then sold him into slavery.

But he held no grudge. Years later, when famine drove the wicked brothers to Egypt in search of food, Joseph recognized them and freely forgave them, without any expression of repentance on their part. Before they even realized who he was, he was moved to tears with compassion for them. Finally revealing his true identity to them, he said, "I am your brother Joseph, whom you sold into Egypt. And now do not be grieved or angry with yourselves, because you sold me here, for God sent me before you to preserve life" (Gen. 45:4-5). His forgiveness was unconditional, unilateral, not predicated on any expression of remorse from them.

In fact, as far as we know from Scripture, the closest these brothers ever came to formally declaring their repentance was after Jacob died. Once their father was no longer there to stay Joseph's hand, they imagined their offended brother might unleash vengeance against them. The brothers, knowing the gravity of their sin, were evidently unable to believe that his charity toward them was well-meant. They feared he might still secretly harbor a wish for vengeance. So they told Joseph that it was *their father's* wish that he grant them forgiveness (Gen. 50:16-17). They did not formally admit their wrong and express repentance, though it is quite clear that they were humbled men by now.

But all their pleading was wholly unnecessary. Joseph had forgiven them long before. Having seen undeniable evidence that the hand of Divine Providence was working good in his life through the evil that was done to him, Joseph had long since forgiven his brothers fully, freely, and unconditionally. His perspective? "You meant evil against me, but God meant it for good" (Gen. 50:20). The knowledge that God had a good purpose for his sufferings made it impossible for Joseph to harbor a grudge.

There are also other examples of unilateral forgiveness in Scripture, even when the offense was public and pronounced. For example, on at least one significant occasion David unilaterally and unconditionally forgave the most humiliating kind of public insult.

It occurred during Absalom's rebellion against David. David was forced to flee Jerusalem so that his defiant son would not destroy the city in his zeal to overthrow David's throne. During that agonizing and painful exodus from Jerusalem, a worthless character named Shimei publicly taunted the already heartbroken David, trying to humiliate him further. Second Samuel 16:5-8 records what happened:

> *[Shimei] came out cursing continually as he came. And he threw stones at David and at all the servants of King David; and all the people and all the mighty men were at his right hand and at his left. Thus Shimei said when he cursed, "Get out, get out, you man of bloodshed, and worthless fellow! The LORD has returned upon you all the bloodshed of the house of Saul, in whose place you have reigned; and the LORD has given the kingdom into the hand of your son Absalom. And behold, you are taken in your own evil, for you are a man of bloodshed!"*

Abishai, one of David's companions, wanted justice on the spot: "Why should this dead dog curse my lord the king? Let me go over now, and cut off his head" (v. 9).

But David's response was a godly forbearance:

> *"If he curses, and if the LORD has told him, 'Curse David,' then who shall say, 'Why have you done so?' . . . Behold, my son who came out from me seeks my life; how much more now this Benjamite? Let him alone and let him curse, for the LORD has told him. Perhaps the LORD will look on my affliction and return good to me instead of his cursing this day."*

Shimei continued to run along the hillside next to David, cursing and throwing rocks and dirt at the king, but David bore the insults with grace and forbearance—though under the circumstances it would have been perfectly appropriate for David, a sitting king, to demand that the mocker be punished.

Later, after David was victorious over the rebels, Shimei made a show of remorse, begging David's mercy. David, still over the protest of his men, reaffirmed his forgiveness to Shimei (2 Sam. 19:18-23). Having already forgiven the initial offense unilaterally, David now forgave Shimei formally.

Stephen's prayers for those who stoned him are another example of unilateral, unconditional forgiveness. The fact that Stephen prayed for God's mercy for his murderers shows that he had already forgiven them. It is true that *God's* forgiveness was not to be granted apart from their repentance; but Stephen himself had already made a deliberate, conscious choice to relinquish the right to retribution. He had forgiven them in his heart.

This brings up an important point. Even after we have forgiven offenders for their transgressions against us, God Himself may exact justice for their sins against *Him*. We can forgive an offense against us. But we cannot grant forgiveness for sin against God. "Who can forgive sins, but God alone?" (Luke 5:21). To forgive someone does not convey some priestly absolution, clearing them of sin before God. Those whom we forgive must still give account to God.

For example, Stephen's forgiving his killers did not assure that their sins would go unpunished if they did not also seek *God's* forgiveness. In the case of Saul of Tarsus (who stood by the garments of Stephen's killers, consenting to the martyr's death, Acts 7:58; 8:1), his offense was completely blotted out when he fully repented. We are never told what became of those who threw the stones, but if they never embraced Christ as Lord and Savior, they will suffer the wrath of God for the sin of killing Stephen. Stephen forgave the offense against him; the sin against God still had to be reckoned with.

Shimei is another case in point. David kept his promise not to kill Shimei, but Shimei remained an unregenerate and worthless man to the end of his life. Knowing this, on his deathbed David instructed Solomon how to deal with Shimei: "Do not let him go unpunished, for you are a wise man; and you will know what you ought to do to him, and you will bring his gray hair down to Sheol with blood" (1 Kings 2:9).

This is a difficult command to explain, until we realize that David, as the divinely appointed king, was responsible to see that God's glory was not besmirched in Israel. He had kept his promise to Shimei: he did not kill him for his insult. As far as David was concerned, the personal offense against him was forgiven. But Shimei's act also involved the most wretched kind of blasphemy against God. And since Shimei remained in wanton rebellion against God, divine justice still had a claim on him. For the sake of the nation's purity, this needed to be dealt with. It was now time for the account to be settled—for the sake of *God's* glory, not David's. David could overlook a personal transgression against him; he could not ultimately overlook a public act of overt hostility to God. As Puritan commentator Matthew Henry wrote, David's instructions to Solomon "proceeded not from personal revenge, but a prudent zeal for the honour of the government and the covenant God had made with his family, the contempt of which ought not to go unpunished."[4] Surely that is why David waited until he was on his deathbed to order that Shimei be punished. This way, no one could say that David did it to preserve his own honor.

And Solomon wisely honored David's forgiveness of Shimei's insult. Instead of summarily executing him for that past offense, Solomon imposed a restriction on Shimei, forbidding him ever to set foot outside the city of Jerusalem. As long as he stayed in the city, under the king's supervision, he could move about freely in perfect safety. But the day he set foot across the Kidron Valley, he would be killed. Shimei agreed to the terms, which were gracious (1 Kings 2:36-38). But because he was a wicked man, Shimei broke his word. He left the city in search of some runaway slaves, and when Solomon found out, he summoned him and said:

"Did I not make you swear by the LORD and solemnly warn you, saying, 'You will know for certain that on the day you depart and go anywhere, you shall surely die'? And you said to me, 'The word which I have heard is good.' Why then have you not kept the oath of the LORD, and the command which I have laid on you? . . . You know all the evil which you acknowledge in your heart, which you did to my father David; therefore the LORD shall return your evil on your own head."

— vv. 42-44, emphasis added

In other words, Shimei's death was the Lord's, not David's, reprisal for Shimei's sin. David forgave the man and kept his promise not to retaliate. But in the end, given Shimei's refusal to repent, God Himself demanded justice.

Our forgiving an offense does not guarantee that the offender will receive judicial forgiveness from God. God, who knows the heart, always judges righteously. Our part is to be gracious, bear the wrong, and pray for the offender's full repentance. God Himself will see to it that justice is done if the offender fails to seek divine forgiveness.

WHEN UNCONDITIONAL FORGIVENESS IS NOT AN OPTION

There are times when it is necessary to confront an offender. In such cases, unconditional forgiveness is not an option. These generally involve more serious sins—not petty or picayune complaints, but soul-threatening sins or transgressions that endanger the fellowship of saints. In such situations Luke 17:3 applies: "If your brother sins, rebuke him; and if he repents, forgive him." In such cases, if a brother or sister in Christ refuses to repent, the discipline process outlined in Matthew 18 applies (see chapter 7).

Here are some guidelines for determining when such confrontation is necessary:

If you observe a serious offense that is a sin against someone other than you, confront the offender. Justice does not permit a Christian to cover a sin against someone else. I can unilaterally and unconditionally forgive a personal offense when I am the victim, because it is I who then bears the wrong. But when I see that someone else has been sinned against, it is my duty to seek justice. (The only exception to this would be when the offended person himself chooses to ignore a personal slight or insult. This was the case when David forbade Abishai to wreak vengeance against Shimei.)

While we are entitled, and even encouraged, to overlook wrongs committed against us, Scripture everywhere forbids us to overlook wrongs committed against another.

- *Exodus 23:6*: "You shall not pervert the justice due to your needy brother in his dispute."
- *Deuteronomy 16:20*: "Justice, and only justice, you shall pursue."
- *Isaiah 1:17*: "Learn to do good; seek justice, reprove the ruthless, defend the orphan, plead for the widow."
- *Isaiah 59:15-16*: "Yes, truth is lacking; and he who turns aside from evil makes himself a prey. Now the LORD saw, and it was displeasing in His sight that there was no justice. And He saw that there was no man, and was astonished that there was no one to intercede."
- *Jeremiah 22:3*: "Thus says the LORD, 'Do justice and righteousness, and deliver the one who has been robbed from the power of his oppressor. Also do not mistreat or do violence to the stranger, the orphan, or the widow; and do not shed innocent blood in this place.'"
- *Lamentations 3:35-36*: "To deprive a man of justice in the presence of the Most High, to defraud a man in his lawsuit—of these things the LORD does not approve."

It is not our prerogative to "forgive" someone for an offense against another. Therefore, those who witness such an offense have a duty to confront the offender with his or her transgression.

When ignoring an offense might hurt the offender, confrontation is required. Sometimes choosing to overlook an offense might actually injure the offender. In such cases it is our duty to confront in love.

Galatians 6:1-2 says, "Brethren, if a man be overtaken in a fault, ye which are spiritual, restore such a one in the spirit of meekness; considering thyself, lest thou also be tempted. Bear ye one another's burdens, and so fulfil the law of Christ" (KJV).

The word translated "overtaken" in that passage literally means "caught." It can signify two things. It might mean that the person was discovered in some secret transgression. Or it could mean that the person is ensnared in some sinful habit. Either way, confrontation is necessary. Overlooking the sin is not an option. Love for the sinning brother requires that you confront and seek to restore. This is an essential part of bearing one another's burdens (v. 2).

Sins that require confrontation because of their potential for harm to the sinning person include serious doctrinal error, moral failure, repeated instances of the same offense, sinful habits or destructive tendencies, or any other transgression that poses a serious danger to the offender's spiritual well-being.

In all such cases, confrontation should be motivated by love and a desire for the offender's good. Such confrontation should never be used to gratify a thirst for personal vengeance, to punish the offender, or to fulfill any other self-aggrandizing purposes. That is why Galatians 6:1 expressly says those who are "spiritual" should deal with the sinning individual.

Ironically, these are the circumstances in which confrontation is the hardest. We are easily tempted to confront the sins we should overlook and to overlook the ones we should confront. But whether the situation calls for forbearance or confrontation, the primary motivation should always be love for the offender (as well as for the offended).

When a sin is scandalous or otherwise potentially damaging to the body of Christ, confrontation is essential. Some sins have the potential to defile many people. Hebrews 12:15 warns of such dangers: "See to it that no one comes short of the grace of God; that no root of bitterness springing up causes trouble, and by it many be defiled."

The responsibility is incumbent on every member of the body not only to "stimulate one another to love and good deeds" (Heb.

10:24), but also to exhort one another, so that no one becomes hard-ened through "the deceitfulness of sin" (Heb. 3:13).

The apostle Paul rebuked the Corinthians for their failure to confront and deal with scandalous sin within the flock. One of their members was having sexual relations with "his father's wife" (1 Cor. 5:1)—probably his stepmother; the sin carried such a stigma in the culture that it was tantamount to incest. Such sins did "not exist even among the Gentiles." Even the rankest pagans in Corinth were scandalized by the sin in that church.

Paul rebuked them: "Ye are puffed up, and have not rather mourned" (v. 2, KJV). "Puffed up" is from a Greek expression that literally means "inflated." It speaks of pride. Perhaps, as is true of many today, the Corinthians' pride was in their tolerance. They may have been boasting in the very fact that they were not so "narrow-minded" as to make an issue out of this man's misdeeds.

Paul rebuked them harshly: "Your boasting is not good. Do you not know that a little leaven leavens the whole lump of dough?" (v. 6). He ordered them to excommunicate the offender, who, he said, needed to be "removed from [their] midst" (v. 2).

> *I, on my part, though absent in body but present in spirit, have already judged him who has so committed this, as though I were present. In the name of our Lord Jesus, when you are assembled, and I with you in spirit, with the power of our Lord Jesus, I have decided to deliver such a one to Satan for the destruction of his flesh, so that his spirit may be saved in the day of the Lord Jesus.*
>
> – vv. 3-5

Open sin is *always* a scandal in the church and must be dealt with. It is not our prerogative to "forgive" those intent on living lives of flagrant disobedience. The entire church suffers when this sort of sin is permitted to exist. Such sin is like leaven, working its way through a lump of dough. Covering such sins, overlooking the evil, is never the right thing in such situations. This sort of sin must be rebuked, and in chapter 7 we will carefully examine the process by which this is to be done.

Any time an offense results in a broken relationship, formal forgiveness is an essential step toward reconciliation. Any sort of offense that causes a breach in relationships simply cannot be overlooked. Both the offense and the breach must be confronted, and reconciliation must be sought.

Reconciliation is always the goal when we confront someone about a wrong done. Once again, if your confronting aims at punishing the offender, or if it is simply a means of castigation and censure, you are confronting with the wrong aim in mind. The goal of all righteous confrontation is the repair of a broken relationship and the restoration of the offender.

Whenever there is a broken relationship between Christians, *both* parties have a responsibility to seek reconciliation. If you are the offended party, Luke 17:3 applies: "If your brother sins, rebuke him." You are the one who must go to him. If you are the offender, Matthew 5:23-24 applies: "If . . . you are presenting your offering at the altar, and there remember that your brother has something against you, leave your offering there before the altar, and go your way; first be reconciled to your brother, and then come and present your offering."

A rift in the relationship between Christians rules out the possibility of the kind of forgiveness that simply overlooks a fault. Whether harsh words have been exchanged or an icy silence prevails, if both sides know that a breach exists, the only way to resolve matters is by the formal granting of forgiveness. Sometimes the wrong is one-sided. Other times it involves admission of wrong and the seeking of forgiveness on both sides.

In any case, reconciliation is essential. If you have committed the offense, it is sinful not to make it right. If you are the offended party, you also have a duty to seek reconciliation—to try to win your brother. There is never any excuse for a Christian on either side of a broken relationship to refuse to pursue reconciliation. The only instance where such a conflict should remain unresolved is if all the steps of discipline in Matthew 18 have been exhausted and the guilty party still refuses to repent.

But even then, you are to hold no bitterness in your heart, and you are to love that offender as you love your enemies, with a longing for their spiritual well-being and restoration to fellowhship. "Yet do not regard him as an enemy, but admonish him as a brother" (2 Thess. 3:15). Though no formal transaction of forgiveness is possible, the heart holds no ill will, and reconciliation remains the goal.

Furthermore, if you are the guilty party, you have a responsibility to pursue reconciliation *quickly*. This is repeatedly emphasized in Scripture. For example, Matthew 5:23-24 (cited above) suggests that if you are in the middle of an act of worship and you remember that you have offended a brother, you are to leave your gift at the altar, and *"first* be reconciled to your brother." In such a case reconciliation of a broken relationship takes precedence over worship!

That makes reconciliation a very high priority indeed, for it even takes precedence over worship offered to the Lord. My book on the subject of worship was titled *The Ultimate Priority* because worship is normally the supreme priority in the Christian's life. But there is this one exception: when you know you have offended a brother or sister. *Then* the first priority is the reconciling of the broken relationship.

Matthew 5 continues:

> *"Make friends quickly with your opponent at law while you are with him on the way, in order that your opponent may not deliver you to the judge, and the judge to the officer, and you be thrown into prison. Truly I say to you, you shall not come out of there, until you have paid up the last cent."*
>
> — vv. 25-26

In such cases, especially if you have committed a wrong, your duty is to seek reconciliation without delay. Those who delay or impede the reconciliation process will reap additional punishment. The allusion is to divine chastisement, and the verse implies that God

Himself will enforce the penalty due to those who defer such an urgent duty.

SUFFERING WRONG RATHER THAN CAUSING REPROACH

The presumption in Matthew 5:22-26 seems to be that the party who is being handed over to the judge is the guilty party. Since he has committed the wrong, it is therefore incumbent on him more than on anyone else to seek to remedy the wrong speedily.

But sometimes it may be even appropriate for the one who has been wronged simply to suffer the wrong, especially if necessary to avoid the dishonor of bringing a dispute before a secular court.

In the church at Corinth, for example, there were believers who, refusing to settle their differences among themselves, were suing one another in pagan courts (1 Cor. 6:1). Paul reminded them that it is better to suffer wrong or be defrauded than to bring a lawsuit against another believer before a pagan judge. That is the most-notable example of Christian forgiveness, even when there is not reconciliation.

Sadly, I have known of several Christians who were willing to violate that clear command. They always seem convinced that somehow *their* case is the exception to Paul's rule. Give them an opportunity to explain why they feel they are within their rights to sue a fellow Christian and inevitably they will explain how they are about to be wronged through some great injustice that only a court can remedy. Surely God does not countenance such gross injustices, they typically plead, saying He cannot wish that *this* wrong be overlooked, and so on.

Paul recognizes that the other person may be wrong. But he plainly says it is better to be defrauded than to sue another Christian (1 Cor. 6:7). Lawsuits where a Christian takes another Christian before a secular judge are never justifiable.

But what if the offender stubbornly and deliberately refuses to acknowledge the wrong? The church, rather than a secular court, should act as arbiter. Ultimately in such cases, the church may need to institute discipline against the offending member (1 Cor. 6:2).

I'm convinced that if church discipline were more consistently practiced, there would be fewer such conflicts between Christians, and genuine love and harmony would prevail more in the church.

An appalling number of churches refuse to obey the biblical instructions to discipline sinning members. What should someone do who has exhausted every avenue of appeal in the church and still feels an injustice has been done? In such cases, 1 Corinthians 6:7 applies: suffer the wrong for the sake of Christ. If the church you attend is wantonly disobeying Christ's clear instructions about how to deal with sin within the fellowship, you may need to seek a church where Scripture is more faithfully obeyed.

But some injustices will never be made right this side of eternity. It is clear that the Christian's duty in such cases is to suffer the wrong gracefully, magnanimously, and willingly for the sake of Christ. God Himself will ultimately right all such wrongs. Meanwhile, we must refuse to harbor a grudge. We must never allow a spirit of resentment to stain our character. We must seek to be like Joseph, willing to see the hand of God working good, even in the most unjust circumstances.

WHEN IT IS HARD TO FORGIVE

Forgiveness certainly does not come naturally to fallen creatures. We tend to be driven too much by our feelings. Those who indulge themselves in bitter feelings will find forgiveness does not easily germinate in such soil. Instead, the root that springs up is a defiling influence. It is hurtful not only to the bitter person, but to many others as well (Heb. 12:15).

Forgiveness is often frustrated by negative emotions, lingering resentment, and unquenched anger. Some imagine, wrongly, that they cannot forgive if they do not "feel" like forgiving.

But as we already noted briefly, forgiveness is not a feeling. Those who insist on being driven by passion will find forgiveness very hard indeed, because forgiveness often involves a deliberate choice that runs contrary to our feelings. Bitter emotions tell us to dwell on an offense. In contrast, forgiveness is a voluntary, rational decision to set the offense aside and desire only the best for the offender.

"But I cannot do that," someone says. "I *try* to set it aside, but everywhere I go, something reminds me, and I find myself thinking about it and getting upset all over again."

Such thoughts are temptations to sin. Brooding over an offense is no less a sin than lust or covetousness or any other heart-sin. A willful choice must be made to turn away from that kind of thinking. Instead we must deliberately cover the offense and refuse to succumb to angry and vengeful thinking, whether we feel like it or not.

Those who forgive even when it's hard invariably find that the proper emotions will follow. "Love your enemies, do good to those who hate you, bless those who curse you, pray for those who mistreat you" (Luke 6:27-28)—those are all willful, deliberate, rational acts, not emotional reflexes. Obey Christ's commands to do such things, and your anger will eventually give way to meekness, frustration will be overcome by peace, and anxiety will succumb to calm.

Forgiveness results in the lifting of many burdens. To grant someone forgiveness when he or she repents is to lift the burden of guilt from that person. But to forgive when forgiveness is unilateral and unconditional liberates the forgiver to enjoy the even greater mercies given in return by a generous heavenly Father, who promises to pour into our laps a "good measure, pressed down, shaken together, running over" (Luke 6:38).

SEVEN

>>>

If Your
Brother Sins

If your brother sins, rebuke him;
and if he repents, forgive him.

—Luke 17:3

There are times when sin has to be dealt with through confrontation. And if the guilty party refuses to repent, the ultimate result may mean excommunication from the church. This is true chiefly when the offender's sin has a potential to continue working injury, or when the offense brings a public reproach on the name of Christ.

The process Scripture outlines for dealing with sin in the flock is called "church discipline." That's a fitting name for it, because as with parental discipline, the main goal is correction. Church discipline is successful when it brings about repentance and reconciliation. When it is unsuccessful, it ends in excommunication. But excommunication is never the desired goal; restoration is.

The mere subject of church discipline is enough to stir strong feelings among Christians. Not long ago we dealt with the subject on our radio broadcast. I was amazed at the letters we received from people who strongly felt that all forms of church discipline are inherently unloving. One listener, who admitted she heard only part of a broadcast, wrote:

The whole process of church discipline sounds incredibly controlling and uncharitable. I cannot believe that any church would ever threaten to excommunicate its own members for what they do in their private lives. And I cannot imagine a church making a public pronouncement about someone's sin! What people do on their own time is their business, not the whole church's. And the church is supposed to be where people can come to learn how to overcome sin. How can they do that if they have been excommunicated? If we shun our own members, we're no better than the cults. I cannot imagine that Christ would ever excommunicate someone from His church. Didn't he seek out sinners and avoid those who were holier-than-thou? After all, it's not the people who are whole that need a physician. I'm glad my church does not excommunicate members who sin. There'd be none of us left! I thought the gospel was all about forgiveness!

Those comments reflect several common and widespread misunderstandings about the subject.

First of all, church discipline is not antithetical to forgiveness. In fact, Jesus' instructions for the discipline process outline exactly *how* forgiveness should work when a believer's sin has implications for the whole flock.

Second, biblical discipline is not about micromanaging people's lives. As we saw in the previous chapter, the kind of offenses that require confrontation and biblical discipline are not unintentional transgressions, minor peccadilloes, petty annoyances, or matters of simple preference, but serious violations of clear biblical principles—sins that hurt other believers, destroy the unity of the flock, or otherwise sully the purity of the church. In such cases, sin *must* be dealt with. Such sins cannot be covered up. They are like leaven, and left alone their evil effects will eventually permeate the whole church (1 Cor. 5:6).

Third, proper discipline is not out of harmony with the Spirit of Christ. Christ Himself prescribed this method of dealing with sin in the flock. If your opinion of Christ is that He would never countenance the excommunication of a sinning church member, you have a distorted understanding of Christ.

Fourth, correctly applied discipline is not incompatible with love. In fact, just the opposite is true. In earlier chapters we discussed the fact that God lovingly disciplines believers who sin. The Matthew 18 process recognizes the legitimate role of the church as an instrument of both loving exhortation and, on occasion, divine chastening. Properly applied church discipline therefore pictures God's love for His children (cf. Heb. 12:7-11).

Fifth, the public aspect of discipline is a final resort, not the first step. The point of reporting a person's offense to the church is not to get church members to "shun" the sinning individual, but precisely the opposite: to encourage them to pursue that person in love, with the aim of restoration.

The permissiveness that results when discipline is neglected inevitably leads to chaos. This is as true in the church as it is in a family. No adult enjoys being around children who are never disciplined. In the same way, a church that is lax on dealing with sin in the body ultimately becomes intolerable to all but the most immature believers. Failing to practice church discipline therefore insures that the flock will be spiritually stunted. It is also a sure way to incur God's displeasure (Rev. 2:14, 20).

Jesus' instructions about church discipline in Matthew 18 are clear and unequivocal. This issue is therefore a good test of whether a church is serious about obedience to Christ. People often ask me what to look for in a church. Consistent, proper discipline is near the top of my list. One thing is certain: a church that does not discipline sinning members is going to have perpetual and serious problems.

THE PLACE

Matthew 18 begins with a long discourse from Christ about the childlikeness of the believer. At the start of His discourse, He took a child and set him in the midst of the disciples as an object lesson. The discourse that ensued includes numerous references to "little ones"—by which He means *believers*, not literal children (cf. vv. 6, 10, 14). He was comparing believers to children because of their simple trust, their loving obedience, their need for protection, and their need for discipline.

The section outlining the discipline process covers only three verses:

> *"If your brother sins, go and reprove him in private; if he listens to you, you have won your brother. But if he does not listen to you, take one or two more with you, so that by the mouth of two or three witnesses every fact may be confirmed. If he refuses to listen to them, tell it to the church; and if he refuses to listen even to the church, let him be to you as a Gentile and a tax-gatherer."*
>
> —vv. 15-17

Notice that He uses the expression "the church" twice in verse 17. The Greek word is *ekklesia*, literally meaning "called-out ones." The word is sometimes employed to speak of any assembly of people. An example of this would be Acts 7:38, which refers to the congregation of Israel during the Exodus as "the church in the wilderness" (KJV). Some argue that since the discourse in Matthew 18 preceded Pentecost, Christ could not have been speaking of the New Testament church. But Christ had already introduced the concept of the church to his disciples, ("I will build my church; and the gates of Hades shall not overpower it," Matt. 16:18). So the instructions in Matthew 18 were given in anticipation of the New Testament body. It is hard to see how anyone could exempt the New Testament church from the principle set forth in this passage.

In fact, our Lord's whole point was that the assembly of God's redeemed people is the proper arena in which matters of dispute or discipline should be handled. There is no external court or higher authority on earth to which sin issues may be appealed (1 Cor. 6:2-3).

It is by divine design that discipline should take place in the church. True believers are motivated by a genuine love for one another (1 John 3:14). In such a context, discipline may be administered in love, by loving fellow believers, for the genuine good and edification of the whole body.

THE PURPOSE

Discipline, properly administered, is always motivated by love. Its first purpose is the restoration of the sinning brother: "If he listens to you, you have won your brother" (v. 15). It will also purify the church in that believers will watch their lives to that they'll not have to be confronted.

The goal of church discipline is not to throw people out, shun them, embarrass them, or to be self-righteous, play God, or exercise authority in an abusive or dictatorial manner. The purpose of discipline is to bring people back into a right relationship with God and with the rest of the body. Proper discipline is never administered as retaliation for someone's sin. Restoration, not retribution, is always the goal.

This is obvious from the text of Matthew 18. The Greek word translated "won" in verse 15 is "*kerdaino*," a word often used to speak of financial gain. (The expression is translated "gained thy brother" in the *King James Version*.) Christ thus portrayed the errant brother as a valuable treasure to be won back. That should be the perspective of every Christian who ever confronts a brother or sister about sin.

That is, in fact, the expression of God's own heart with regard to discipline: He sees each soul as a treasure to be recovered. That is the whole context in which Christ spoke these words. The verses immediately preceding these instructions for discipline compare God to a loving shepherd, concerned for each lamb in the flock:

> *"What do you think? If any man has a hundred sheep, and one of them has gone astray, does he not leave the ninety-nine on the mountains and go and search for the one that is straying? If it turns out that he finds it, truly I say to you, he rejoices over it more than over the ninety-nine which have not gone astray. Thus it is not the will of your Father who is in heaven that one of these little ones perish."*
> — vv. 12-14

Every Christian must have that same sense of concern. It's tempting sometimes to take the path of least resistance and avoid confrontation—especially when sin is already drawing a brother or sister away from the fellowship. But that is the very time when we *most* need to get involved. That is the heart of a true shepherd, who will go to any length to recover a missing or wounded sheep and restore him or her to the flock.

Confrontation is not easy, nor should it be. We're not to be busybodies, constantly intruding into others' business. But when we become aware that someone has sinned, we have a duty before God to lovingly confront that person. We cannot protest by saying it is none of our business. Once we become aware of a soul-threatening sin in a fellow believer's life, it is our business to exhort, confront, and labor for purity in the fellowship of the church and victory in the life of the sinning one. These are noble and necessary concerns.

Nonetheless, we must be on guard against abuses and must keep the loving purposes of proper discipline in view at all times. There is a real danger of becoming too fond of chiding one another. Pride can poison the discipline process, just as it pollutes every virtue. That is why Jesus cautioned those who confront to examine themselves before trying to remove the speck from a brother's eye. We must be sure we don't have a log protruding from our own eye (Matt. 7:3-5)!

One person who had seen some discipline cases handled poorly wrote, "If I ever fall into a sin, I will pray that I don't fall into the hands of those censorious, critical, self-righteous judges in the church. I'd rather fall into the hands of the barkeepers, streetwalkers, dope peddlers, because the church people tend to tear each other apart with their gossipy tongues." That is a sad testimony on the reputation of the church.

On the other hand, a person under discipline who refuses to repent is likely to feel abused and mistreated, just as disobedient children sometimes despise the discipline of their parents. It is not at all unusual for an unrepentant person to accuse those who have confronted him of being unloving, unfair, unkind, or otherwise abusive. That is all the more reason for those administering the discipline to take great care to act in love, with careful self-examination and great long-suffering.

THE PERSON

Notice that the discipline process begins at the individual level. "If your brother sins, go and reprove him in private" (v. 15). Discipline is not instituted by a committee. If the offender repents, there is no need to involve others at all. Discipline, if successful, therefore both suppresses the effects of sin and limits the circle of knowledge. Far from broadcasting knowledge of someone's sin unnecessarily, the discipline process confines knowledge of the offense as much as possible. In most cases, if repentance occurs early enough in the process, no one but the offender and the person who confronts ever needs to know about the offense.

The personal, private confrontation prescribed in Matthew 18 also means that church discipline is the responsibility of every believer in the church. It is not something to be delegated to church officials. In fact, if you see a brother in sin, the *wrong* first response is to report his sin to church leaders, or to anyone else. "Go and reprove him in private" (v. 15).

Too many Christians regard discipline as the exclusive domain of church elders. It is not. The purity of the church is every Christian's concern. The responsibility to confront sin that defiles the church lies with the first person to become aware of the sin. Don't defer to someone else. Don't spread the circle of knowledge further than necessary. Above all, don't just say, "Well, I'll pray that my brother will see the light." That may not be enough. You have the light—go and shine it in his eyes!

THE PROVOCATION

What sins are grounds for discipline? Any offense that cannot be safely overlooked without harm to the offender or to the body of Christ (see our discussion in chapter 6).

Matthew 18:15 has been rendered in various English Bible translations with two slightly different senses. Most modern versions read, "If your brother sins, go and reprove him" or something similar. The *King James Version* says, "If thy brother shall trespass *against thee* . . . " (emphasis added). Ancient manuscripts differ on this point. Some include the expression "against thee"; others simply say, "If your brother sins," implying that we should confront one another whether or not we are directly victimized by the sin.

The textual variation turns out to be relatively unimportant, however, when we realize that all disciplinable sins are sins against the entire body of Christ. So whether the other person's sin is *directly* "against thee" or only *indirectly* (because it is a sin that brings a reproach on the whole body), go and show him his fault in private. Suppose you observe a brother in Christ in a morally compromising situation. Should you confront him? By all means. It would be wrong, and ultimately hurtful to the whole body, to reason that since you are not directly victimized by the offense, you have no obligation to confront your brother's sin. That is precisely the sort of situation Paul rebuked the Corinthians for tolerating in their midst (1 Cor. 5).

Some examples of sins committed directly against you include: if someone attacks you physically in anger, steals from you, deceives you, slanders you, or commits a crime of immorality against you. The wrong response in such cases is to retaliate in kind, to return evil for evil, to hold a grudge, or to report the sin to others without having first gone to your brother. Love for him demands that your immediate response be private confrontation.

Indirect offenses against you include any sin that brings a reproach on the church. This includes sins that tend to draw the sinner away from the fellowship of believers—such as habitual worldliness, sloth, negligence of one's spiritual duties, or even doctrinal error. When a brother or sister is drawn away from our fellowship, the loss affects the whole body. So any sin that has the potential of causing such a loss is a sin that should be confronted. Any pattern of disobedience to Christ—or any other sin that brings a reproach on the name of Christ—also is an indirect sin against us, because as Christ's ambassadors we bear His reproach.

Even sins against non-Christians are subject to church discipline, because those sins dishonor Christ in the world's eyes and thus bring a reproach that stains the entire fellowship. So *any* sin you observe is grounds for instituting the discipline—not just those sins by which you are directly victimized. In all such cases, your duty is the same: you must privately confront the offender.

THE PROCESS

But what if the sinning brother refuses to heed your admonition? Then private confrontation is only the first step. Three other steps are very clearly delineated in the passage. Let's examine the whole process, starting with private confrontation.

Step One:
Confront Him with His Sin in Private

"If your brother sins, go and reprove him in private" (v. 15). The verb translated "go" is a present imperative, meaning that this is a command, not a suggestion, not merely an option. If you see your brother in sin, you *must* go.

And go privately first of all. There is no need to involve others at this point. Don't gossip about the offense with others, even under the guise of seeking prayer support. Just go quietly to your brother; tell him his fault between you and him *alone*.

Discipline is difficult with close friends because so much is at stake. Moreover, those who know you best may respond by pointing out some sin of yours. But discipline is also difficult with people we don't know well. We tend to think, *Who am I to intrude into this person's life?* Thus we are intimidated by the thought of confronting friends, and we tend to be indifferent toward people we aren't close to. Either way we must see that what Christ commands here is a solemn duty and is not to be rationalized away for convenience's sake.

What if you are just as guilty as your brother? Did not Jesus suggest that the log in your own eye ought to stop you from dealing with the speck in your brother's? Not at all. "*First* take the log out of your own eye, and *then* you will see clearly enough to take the speck out of your brother's eye" (Matt. 7:5, emphasis added). But if you truly love your brother, you cannot ignore his sin. Having dealt with your own sin, you will then be in a *better* position to confront your brother with a proper spirit of humility. Never is it right to confront a sinning brother with a pious, pontificating attitude, as if to make yourself look good and him look bad. You must go with a loving, humble desire to restore him.

The Greek verb in the phrase "reprove him" (or "show him his fault") is a word that conveys the idea of light exposing something that is hidden. It calls for a clear, precise divulging of the brother's offense. "Reprove him" does not necessarily imply that he is heretofore unaware of his sin. This process is not limited to sins of ignorance. Rather, the phrase means that you should disclose what you know about his sin, so that he will realize his offense is known, thus establishing his accountability for the offense. If he thought his sin was secret, he must realize it has been uncovered. If he thought he could sin without consequence, he must now give an answer.

If the first step of discipline is successful, his answer will be repentance. That will be the end of the process, in which case, "you have won your brother." You will have a bond of intimacy with him that nothing will be able to break.

If he repents, in most cases, nothing more needs to be done. Of course, you will want to encourage him to demonstrate the genuineness of his repentance by doing whatever is necessary to make things right. If any kind of restitution is called for, urge him to follow through. If others have been directly hurt by his sin, he should go to them and seek reconciliation (Matt. 5:23-24). But assuming he demonstrates real repentance, that should end the matter. Uninvolved parties have no need to be told. No further discipline needs to be imposed. You may rejoice in having won your brother. Ideally, this is the final step in the majority of discipline cases.

Step Two:
Take Some Witnesses

Unfortunately, however, that is sometimes *not* the end of the matter. "If he does not listen to you, take one or two more with you, so that by the mouth of two or three witnesses every fact may be confirmed" (v. 16). Sometimes the sinning brother refuses to hear the rebuke. He may deny his guilt; he may deliberately continue in sin; he may try to cover up what he has done. Whatever his response, if it is not repentance—and assuming you are *certain* of his guilt—you must now take one or two other believers with you and confront him again.

The presence of one or two others serves several purposes. First, and most pragmatically, it turns up the pressure. The people you take with you represent the beginning of the whole church's involvement in the matter. The offender is thus put on notice that if he or she continues in sin, the consequences will only grow more severe. Again, however, the proper objective is nothing less than gaining back your brother. Step one is repeated; you must carefully, patiently, lovingly show him his sin again. But this time it is done in the presence of one or two witnesses.

This is another reason for bringing one or two others in step two: they serve as witnesses. The two-witness principle was established in Moses' law (Deut. 19:15) to ascertain guilt beyond reasonable doubt before any verdict could be made—especially in court cases. Therefore, having witnesses in this second step of discipline also suggests that the end of the process will be a form of judgment if the offender does not repent.

The question is sometimes raised whether the "witnesses" must be witnesses to the original offense. Are they brought only to establish the offender's guilt and only when he denies that any offense occurred?

Some do hold that view, but it cannot be the meaning in this context. First of all, if these witnesses were already aware of the offense, they *also* had a duty earlier to go privately and confront the offender, as mandated by verse 15.

Of course, it is also true that if the offender disputes whether the offense actually occurred, there needs to be a second witness or some other objective evidence to establish the offender's guilt. The Old Testament principle cited in verse 16 still applies: every fact must be established by the testimony of at least two or three witnesses. So if a dispute boils down to nothing more than the word of the accused against the word of the accuser, the mere accusation is an insufficient basis for pursuing discipline, and the matter should be dropped.

However, assuming the offender does not dispute the accusation itself and still refuses to repent or forsake the sin, witnesses must be brought in to establish the fact that the offender has been confronted and failed to repent. They are not necessarily witnesses to the original offense, but rather objective parties who will witness the confrontation. They will be able, if necessary, to confirm what was said privately in case the matter needs to be reported to the church (v. 17). They are witnesses to the fact that the discipline process itself has been properly followed. And their presence at this stage is as much a protection for the one being confronted as it is for the one doing the confronting. A person is not to be accused of impenitence before the whole church on the testimony of a single witness. In fact, the two or three others might become witnesses in favor of the accused, if it turns out the accuser is being overly harsh or unfair.

But if the accuser wasn't being too harsh, and if the process moves beyond step two, the fact of the offender's impenitence will need to be established by two or three witnesses.

In many cases the person confronted will respond to this second step with repentance. If so, the matter is settled. Assuming he demonstrates his repentance by forsaking the sin and making things right with any injured parties, this should be the end of the matter. It would be inappropriate at this point to broaden the circle of involvement beyond those who are already witnesses. "My brethren, if any among you strays from the truth, and one turns him back, let him know that he who turns a sinner from the error of his way will save his soul from death, and will cover a multitude of sins" (Jas. 5:19-20). Covering the sin, not exposing it further, is the right response to the sinner's repentance.

Step Three:
Tell the Church

What happens if the offender still refuses to repent? Jesus' instructions are clear: "If he refuses to listen to them, tell it to the church" (v. 17).

This is where many churches balk. It is easy to think of reasons for *not* following this command: It's harsh. People will be offended. It's embarrassing for the person being disciplined. It will tarnish the public image of the church. What if the person being disciplined sues the church? The stark reality of the discipline process might drive unbelievers away. People's sin is best dealt with quietly, out of the limelight.

But in the face of all those arguments stands one powerful reason why the church cannot afford to ignore this important step of discipline: Christ commanded it, and it is therefore required for all who wish to honor Him as Lord.

Bear in mind that the overriding purpose of all discipline is to try to win the offender back. That is the goal of this step as well. The church is to be told about the person's sin not as a matter for gossip, but to enlist the help of the entire congregation in appealing to the sinning one.

The process has the same goal in each step. More people are involved at this point in order to pursue the sinning brother more effectively. In the first step, one individual confronts the sin. If there is no satisfactory response, two or three go, and the appeal is repeated. If there is still no repentance, the whole church is enlisted to appeal to the brother.

Again we see that discipline is the responsibility of the whole church. It is not delegated to an individual. It is not the responsibility of the pastor alone. It is a corporate duty. Once again, this can protect the church from abuses of power, such as that described by the apostle John:

> *I wrote something to the church; but Diotrephes, who loves to be first among them, does not accept what we say. For this reason, if I come, I will call attention to his deeds which he does, unjustly accusing us*

with wicked words; and not satisfied with this, neither does he himself receive the brethren, and he forbids those who desire to do so, and puts them out of the church.

— 3 JOHN 9-10, emphasis added

Diotrephes was evidently abusing his power and influence as a leader in that church in order to turn people away and even excommunicate some singlehandedly. It is never the task of any one man to make such a judgment. Church discipline is a corporate duty, and that is why before anyone is excommunicated, the whole church must be brought into the process. Only *after* everyone in the church has had an opportunity to try to restore the sinning brother is he eventually put out of the church.

After all, the entire church is affected by the offender's sin. If, after all this, the offender repents, it will be the duty of all to reaffirm their love and forgiveness. In 2 Corinthians 2:5-8 Paul gave precisely those instructions:

> *But if any has caused sorrow, he has caused sorrow not to me, but in some degree—in order not to say too much—to all of you. Sufficient for such a one is this punishment which was inflicted by the majority, so that on the contrary you should rather forgive and comfort him, lest somehow such a one be overwhelmed by excessive sorrow. Wherefore I urge you to reaffirm your love for him.*

The whole church ultimately became involved in pursuing this sinning person. Apparently he finally responded with repentance. So Paul in essence said, "Now that he has responded, don't hold him at arm's length and browbeat him. Rather, embrace him and forgive him in love." They had won their brother back.

Dietrich Bonhoeffer was a German theologian who suffered under the Nazi government during World War II. His overall theology we would by no means endorse, but he nonetheless offered some profound insight about why the entire church must be told about an unrepentant brother's sin. Bonhoeffer wrote:

Sin demands to have a man by himself. It withdraws him from the community. The more isolated a person is, the more destructive will be the power of sin over him, and the more deeply he becomes involved in it, the more disastrous is his isolation. Sin wants to remain unknown. It shuns the light. In the darkness of the unexpressed it poisons the whole being of a person. This can happen even in the midst of a pious community. In confession the light of the gospel breaks into the darkness and seclusion of the heart. The sin must be brought into the light. The unexpressed must be openly spoken and acknowledged. All that is secret and hidden is made manifest. It is a hard struggle until the sin is openly admitted, but God breaks gates of brass and bars of iron (Ps. 107:16).

Since the confession of sin is made in the presence of a Christian brother, the last stronghold of self-justification is abandoned. The sinner surrenders; he gives up all his evil. He gives his heart to God, and he finds the forgiveness of all his sin in the fellowship of Jesus Christ and his brother. The expressed, acknowledged sin has lost all its power. It has been revealed and judged as sin. It can no longer tear the fellowship asunder. Now the fellowship bears the sin of the brother. He is no longer alone with his evil for he has cast off his sin in confession and handed it over to God. It has been taken away from him. Now he stands in the fellowship of sinners who live by the grace of God and the cross of Jesus Christ. . . . The sin concealed separated him from the fellowship, made all his apparent fellowship a sham; the sin confessed has helped him define true fellowship with the brethren in Jesus Christ.[1]

But suppose the offender does not repent. How long should the church wait before going to step four? Until it becomes obvious that the offender is simply hardening his heart. No objective time limits are given in Scripture. But I am inclined to think it should be a fairly short time, at most a few weeks, rather than months or years. God Himself demands a response, and a delay only signifies the hardening of the heart (cf. Heb. 4:7).

Step Four:
Regard Him as an Unbeliever

The final step in the discipline process involves excommunication: "If he refuses to listen even to the church, let him be to you as a Gentile and a tax-gatherer" (Matt. 18:17). This does not call for heaping scorn on the person. It is not a command to treat the person badly. It means that the person is to be regarded as an unbeliever. The repeated hardening of his heart calls the reality of his faith into question. From henceforth he should be regarded as an evangelistic prospect rather than a brother in the Lord.

Implicit in this is the revocation of his membership. He is no longer to be deemed a member of the body. Rather, he should be regarded as an unbeliever, and therefore he should not be permitted to participate in the blessings and the benefits of the Christian assembly. In particular, he should not be welcomed as a communicant in the celebration of the Lord's Table. That is precisely what the term *excommunication* means.

But as far as the treatment extended to him by church members is concerned, this is no license for hostility or contempt. In fact, Christ's treatment of heathens and tax collectors is notable chiefly because of how He reached out to them in love. A similar kind of compassionate evangelistic pursuit should characterize our treatment of those who have been excommunicated in this manner, with one significant difference: as long as the "so-called brother" (1 Cor. 5:11) remains unrepentant, believers must not carry on a relationship with that person as if nothing were wrong. In order to send clear signals both to the sinning individual and the watching world, even fellowship in everyday social settings is to be suspended. Paul wrote in 1 Corinthians 5:9-11:

> *I wrote you in my letter not to associate with immoral people; I did not at all mean with the immoral people of this world, or with the covetous and swindlers, or with idolaters, for then you would have to go out of the world. But actually, I wrote to you not to associate*

with any so-called brother if he should be an immoral person, or cov-etous, or an idolater, or a reviler, or a drunkard, or a swindler—not even to eat with such a one.

In 2 Thessalonians 3:6 Paul underscored this distinction between everyday unbelievers and professing Christians who live like unbelievers: "Now we command you, brethren, in the name of our Lord Jesus Christ, that you keep aloof from every brother who leads an unruly life and not according to the tradition which you received from us." Likewise, in Romans 16:17-18 he wrote, "Now I urge you, brethren, keep your eye on those [in the church] who cause dissensions and hindrances contrary to the teaching which you learned, and turn away from them. For such men are slaves not of our Lord Christ but of their own appetites; and by their smooth and flattering speech they deceive the hearts of the unsuspecting." In other words, because of the strong tendency for people to be deceived by someone who *professes* faith in Christ and yet lives a dis-obedient life, the lines must be drawn as clearly as possible. We are supposed to have as little association as possible with such people.

Again, the point is not to be antagonistic or malevolent toward them, but to make clear that willful sin is incompatible with Christian fellowship. Since this person has identified with Christ and is a "so-called brother," it becomes vitally important for the fellow-ship as a whole to demonstrate that this person's deliberate rebellion against Christ is incompatible with a profession of faith in Him.

Even at this point, however, the primary goal with regard to the offender is to win him back. Second Thessalonians 3:15 says, "And yet do not regard him as an enemy, but admonish him as a brother." There is a sense in which you never really let him go; though you put him out of the church and out of your sphere of social fellow-ship, you keep calling him back. If the offender at any time demon-strates genuine repentance, he is to be welcomed back into the fellowship. But until that point, he is to be regarded as an outsider.

Paul, for example, instructed the Corinthian assembly to excommunicate the incestuous man from their midst. He wrote:

> *It is actually reported that there is immorality among you, and immorality of such a kind as does not exist even among the Gentiles, that someone has his father's wife. And you have become arrogant, and have not mourned instead, in order that the one who had done this deed might be removed from your midst.*
>
> — 1 COR. 5:1-2, *emphasis added*

Details of what, if anything, had been done to pursue this man's repentance are not recorded. But his sin was already known to all, and he was continuing impenitently in the grossest kind of immorality. The time for excommunicating him was long past. So Paul exercised his apostolic prerogative and ordered the man excommunicated immediately:

> *For I, on my part, though absent in body but present in spirit, have already judged him who has so committed this, as though I were present. In the name of our Lord Jesus, when you are assembled, and I with you in spirit, with the power of our Lord Jesus, I have decided to deliver such a one to Satan for the destruction of his flesh, so that his spirit may be saved in the day of the Lord Jesus.*
>
> — vv. 3-5

Paul's words are harsh, but they give insight into what excommunication is about. The sinning person is "deliver[ed] . . . to Satan for the destruction of his flesh." In other words, he is given over to the Satan-controlled system of sin and dissipation that he has chosen, where he will reap the full consequences of his sin. The excommunicated person may descend to the very depths of sin before repenting. If he or she is a genuine believer, this should be a further motivation to repent, and the person will be ultimately saved, though by fire (cf. 1 Cor. 3:15). Again, the primary objective is the repentance and restoration of the offender.

A secondary objective at this point, however, is the purity of the larger fellowship. Willful sin is like leaven. If tolerated, it will eventually permeate the entire body. "Do you not know that a little leaven leavens the whole lump of dough? Clean out the old leaven, that you may be a new lump, just as you are in fact unleavened" (1 Cor. 5:6-7). The unrepentant believer must be put out of the assembly.

Notice that Paul characterizes the consequences of the offender's persistent rebellion and subsequent excommunication as "the destruction of his flesh" (v. 5). Sin, especially the deliberate and wanton varieties, often takes a physical toll on the sinner. Sin's natural consequences may include illness, or in extreme cases, even death (1 Cor. 11:30). In the discipline process, the church in essence hands the sinner over to the consequences of his sin.

There's a punitive element in this. In 2 Corinthians 2:6 (quoted above), Paul refers to it as "punishment."

There's also a remedial element, however. In 1 Timothy 1 Paul speaks of "Hymenaeus and Alexander, whom I have handed over to Satan, so that they may be taught not to blaspheme" (v. 20). Suffering the consequences of their own sin would be a learning experience. Paul's hope was no doubt that this would provoke them to repentance.

THE PRESENCE

Jesus went on in Matthew 18 to teach an incredible truth about church discipline: it is one of the instruments by which God Himself mediates His discipline over His people. He is at work in the discipline process. Jesus said:

> *"Truly I say to you, whatever you bind on earth shall have been bound in heaven; and whatever you loose on earth shall have been loosed in heaven. Again I say to you, that if two of you agree on earth about anything that they may ask, it shall be done for them by My Father who is in heaven."*
>
> *– vv. 18-19*

Those verses are often taken out of context and applied to prayer requests of every kind. But they actually apply specifically to the subject of church discipline. "Whatever you bind" and "whatever you loose" refers to the church's verdict in a discipline case. *Binding* and *loosing* were rabbinical terms undoubtedly familiar to the disciples. They referred to the bondage of sin and to liberation from the guilt of it. Jesus was saying that heaven is in agreement with the church's verdict in a properly handled discipline case.

The verb tenses in the previous quotation of Matthew 18:18 are literal renderings. The idea is not that heaven follows the church's lead, but that when discipline is correctly administered, whatever is done on earth has *already* been done in heaven. This is one of the requests in the Lord's Prayer, isn't it? "Your will be done, on earth as it is in heaven" (Matt. 6:10). If God's will is to be done on earth as it is in heaven, the church must practice the proper discipline of sinning members.

This promise is meant as a comfort and encouragement. Too many people think that if the church confronts sin, that is unloving. But the truth is, when a church practices discipline as Christ commanded, that church is simply doing heaven's work on earth.

Verse 19 is also often misunderstood. The Greek word translated "agree" is the same word from which the English word *symphony* is derived. It literally means "to produce a sound together." Whether the verdict involves binding or loosing, when the church is in harmony—and especially the "two or three witnesses" who establish the fact that the sinning individual is unrepentant—the Father is also in agreement. This verse does not mean that anytime you can get two people to agree on something, God has to honor their prayer request. The "two" in verse 19 are two witnesses whose testimony is in agreement. If they are also in agreement with God's will when they impose discipline on a sinning brother, they can be certain that God Himself is working in their midst and on their behalf.

Verse 20 reiterates a similar promise from Christ: "For where two or three have gathered together in My name, there I am in their midst." Not only is the Father acting in accord with us (v. 19), but the Son is participating as well (v. 20).

Although verse 20 is often cited to invoke Christ's presence at prayer meetings, that is a misinterpretation of the intent. God is omnipresent, of course; so He is present whether only one person is praying or fifty. But in this context the "two or three" refers back to the "two or three witnesses" of verse 16. And the verse speaks not merely of Christ's *presence*, but of His *participation* in the discipline process. He joins in the discipline carried out by the church, a fearsome reality for the individual who refuses to repent, but a rich comfort to those who must administer the discipline.

THE PRIORITY

As we have seen throughout the process, the primary goal of all church discipline is to restore the sinning brother or sister. This goal is never abandoned, even after the individual has been excommunicated. And if at any time he repents, he is to be restored and welcomed with great love and compassion. Another passage of Scripture, Galatians 6, outlines three important steps for restoring the brother or sister who has fallen into sin.

Pick Them Up

Galatians 6:1 says, "If a man is caught in any trespass, you who are spiritual, restore such a one in a spirit of gentleness; looking to yourselves, lest you too be tempted." The word translated "trespass" literally means "a side-slip." It refers to a stumble, a blunder, or a fall. The *King James Version* renders it "fault," and some interpreters take it to mean something less than a sin. But it is the very same word translated "transgressions" in Matthew 6:15 ("If you do not forgive men, then your Father will not forgive your transgressions"). The same word is also used in Romans 4:25 ("He who was delivered up because of our transgressions, and was raised because of our justification"). It clearly has reference to sins.

Paul expressly calls for the restoration of the one caught in sin to be handled by "you who are spiritual." That is Paul's term for those who are discerning: "He who is spiritual appraises all things" (1 Cor. 2:15). This is the Spirit-filled believer (Eph. 5:18), in whom the Word dwells richly (Col. 3:16).

The word translated "restore" literally means "repair, mend, or refurbish." It conveys the idea of bringing something damaged back to its former condition. It is the same word used in Matthew 4:21 to speak of James and John mending their nets. It also appears in 1 Corinthians 1:10, where it speaks of reuniting two factions, like the setting of a broken bone. In that verse, the *King James Version* translates the word with the expression "perfectly joined together."

The person who would restore a fallen brother must do so with an attitude of deep humility, "looking to yourselves, lest you too be tempted." That echoes 1 Corinthians 10:12: "Let him who thinks he stands take heed lest he fall." No Christian is invincible. None of us is sin-free; so we are in no position to have a haughty attitude toward those who need restoration. Love for them, and simple humility, demands that we not try to do eye therapy to remove a bit of sawdust from their eye until we have checked to make sure there's no lumber in our own eye.

The role of restorer therefore calls for a mature, discerning, humble believer who is willing to lift up and encourage a brother in need. Don't think, *Well, the job is best left to someone besides me.* This passage is describing the kind of Christian we are *all* supposed to be.

Hold Them Up

There's more. The restorer must also be willing to help shoulder the fallen brother's burden. Verse 2 continues: "Bear one another's burdens, and thus fulfill the law of Christ."

What burden is to be borne? Notice that in this context, Paul's subject is the Christian's *walk*. "Walk by the Spirit" (Gal. 5:16, 25). The picture here is of two travelers. One overtakes the other, who is carrying a load too heavy to bear, which has caused him to stumble ("side-slip," v. 1). So he helps the fallen brother to his feet and shoulders part of the burden.

The word "burdens" represents spiritual weaknesses that can cause a fall. We can help bear such burdens through encouragement, exhortation, and accountability. Something as simple as developing a friendship can have a wonderfully strengthening effect on a weak Christian.

Once a young man came to see me, distraught over his moral failure. He had lived a totally immoral life before becoming a Christian, and he found the memories of his sin were a constant temptation. He had in fact fallen back into immoral relationships on several occasions. He claimed he had tried everything he knew to overcome temptation but was not able to avoid dwelling on evil thoughts, and the evil thoughts sometimes gave way to acts of sin. Trying to help him, I said, "I want you to keep a record of these sins. I'm not interested in the details of your sin, but I do want you to make a record of the incidents. Every time you cultivate ungodly thoughts or commit an immoral act, I want you to record the fact that it occurred. I also want you to note what you were doing at the time that might have sparked the evil thought. And then think it through and record what you *should* have done to flee from the temptation, because Scripture teaches in 1 Corinthians 10:13 that there is always a way of escape." I was hoping to make him review his behavior so he could clearly see patterns of behavior that led him into temptation.

But two weeks later we met again, and when I asked him for his list, he smiled and told me there was no list. "I didn't have anything to record because I didn't fall into those sins. I was so afraid to have to tell you about it that I carefully avoided situations that might cause me to be tempted." It turned out that he knew how to avoid those sins all along. All he needed was some accountability. And that accountability helped lighten his load.

There are many ways to carry someone's load. I often tell people struggling with the bondage of sin to pick up the phone and call me whenever they feel vulnerable to temptation. Praying with someone for victory over a certain sin lifts part of the burden. Sometimes simply having a friend who knows about their struggle can strengthen them and lighten the load.

In every case, however, helping bear the burden entails getting involved in the other person's life. It involves much more than merely saying, "Go in peace, be warmed and be filled" (Jas. 2:16). We have to be mutual burden-bearers.

Build Them Up

Skipping down to verse 6 of Galatians 6, we read, "Let the one who is taught the word share all good things with him who teaches." Paul is still speaking in the context of restoring the sinning brother. At first glance, this verse might seem to have little to do with the restoration process. But here's what Paul is saying: "The one who is taught" refers to the person being restored, and "him who teaches" is the person doing the restoring. The one being taught and the one teaching are supposed to have a ministry of mutual edification with one another.

So this is the process for restoration: *Pick* up your brothers and sisters who have fallen, *hold* them up, and then *build* them up.

I'm convinced that the biblical discipline process, properly observed, would utterly revitalize the church of our generation. Many who have become acclimated to the spirit of our age will no doubt protest that church discipline is not "user-friendly" enough. Years ago when I began to teach on the subject of church discipline in our church, a chorus of voices warned me that if we instituted these principles we would open the doors for a mass exodus from our flock. But the actual results were exactly the opposite. By making clear that we were serious about purity in our fellowship, we not only saw remarkable spiritual growth and maturity among our people, but we also began and continue to experience significant numerical growth as well. People who are committed to Christ are drawn to a fellowship where His word is obeyed.

Church discipline, properly observed, is an ongoing object lesson about how God's own love and forgiveness works. As Hebrews 12:11 suggests, God's discipline may at times seem to serve only negative purposes, but its long-term fruit is always eternal righteousness. Likewise with church discipline. It may sometimes appear harsh and punitive, but its real purpose is ultimately the outworking of forgiveness and mutual encouragement in the visible body of Christ.

⇒⟩⟩

EIGHT

THE BLESSINGS
OF FORGIVENESS

*If I have forgiven anything, I did it for your sakes
in the presence of Christ, in order that no advantage be taken
of us by Satan; for we are not ignorant of his schemes.*

—2 COR. 2:10-11

Unforgivingness is a toxin. It poisons the heart and mind with bitterness, distorting one's whole perspective on life. Anger, resentment, and sorrow begin to overshadow and overwhelm the unforgiving person—a kind of soul-pollution that enflames evil appetites and evil emotions. Such bitterness can even spread from person to person, ultimately defiling many (Heb. 12:15).

Forgiveness is the only antidote. Forgiveness is a healthy, wholesome, virtuous, liberating act. Forgiveness unleashes joy. It brings peace. It washes the slate clean. It sets all the highest virtues of love in motion.

In a sense, forgiveness is Christianity at its highest level.

Second Corinthians 2 contains a vignette on forgiveness that makes a fitting addendum to our study of church discipline and a good concluding summary of the virtues of forgiveness. There the apostle Paul urges the Corinthians to forgive a man who had been under their discipline but had repented of his sin. Paul beseeches them to receive the repentant brother back into their fellowship and to stop punishing him for his offense. In the process, the apostle highlights some of the vast blessings of forgiveness.

Details of the incident that forms the backdrop for Paul's comments are sketchy. We don't know who the individual was whose forgiveness Paul sought. We don't know for certain what he had done. The context seems to suggest that the man's offense involved some sort of personal affront to the apostle. If that is the case, Paul was not merely instructing the Corinthians about forgiveness; he was himself exemplifying Christian forgiveness.

Some commentators surmise that the man referred to in 2 Corinthians 2 is the same person Paul ordered disciplined for incest in 1 Corinthians 5. But what we know about the historical background and timing of the two epistles makes that unlikely. Much had occurred in the interval between 1 and 2 Corinthians. A mutiny had evidently been fomented by someone in the Corinthian assembly. Paul's apostolic credentials had even come into question. That is why a significant portion of 2 Corinthians is devoted to a defense of Paul's apostleship (e.g., 3:1-3; 6:4-10; 10:7-18; 11:5-33; 12:11-13).

It was not surprising that this church gave rise to such a rebellion. Problems at Corinth were rife, despite an auspicious beginning. The apostle Paul himself had founded the church at Corinth (Acts 18) and then spent eighteen months of his life establishing the saints in sound doctrine. But almost as soon as the apostle left Corinth, the church there began to struggle.

The fact that a church existed at all in Corinth was somewhat remarkable. The city was known throughout the Roman Empire for its gross perversion and wickedness. Corinth was filled with brothels. In its pagan temples acts of fornication were thought of as high liturgy, and lasciviousness was regarded as an intense spiritual experience. The young Corinthian church, situated amid so many evil influences, was continually beset with serious problems. The pollution of fleshly paganism began to seep into the church. Word soon came to Paul that abuses and scandals were disrupting the fellowship at Corinth. Some of the brethren had turned the communion service into an occasion for wanton self-indulgence. Worship services at Corinth had become frenzied contests to see who could display the most extraordinary spiritual gifts. Meanwhile, gross sin was being tolerated by people in the fellowship—to such an extreme that even unbelievers in that debauched culture were appalled. Paul's first epistle to the Corinthians addressed those and other serious problems in the church.

Sometime after Paul wrote 1 Corinthians, a rebellion against him broke out in the Corinthian church. Some false teachers (men evidently posing as apostles) came into the church and found a ready audience for their lies and heresies (2 Cor. 11:13-15). Naturally, the false apostles sought to discredit the reigning authority in the Corinthian church—namely, Paul. They made an all-out assault on his character, his life, and his teaching. They did everything they could to disparage him, to impugn his integrity, and to undermine the Corinthians' confidence in his apostolic authority.

Despite the wonderful love Paul had shown the Corinthian church, even though he was the human instrument by whom they had first heard the Gospel, although they owed him their very lives, many in the Corinthian assembly were duped by the lies of the false apostles. They began to question Paul's authority openly. They denigrated his appearance and his speech (2 Cor. 10:10). They questioned his motives and his integrity (1:12). They accused him of vacillating (1:17) and openly voiced doubts about his sincerity (2:17).

To deal with the mutiny, Paul wrote the Corinthians a letter, referred to in 2 Corinthians 7:8. Paul's comments about that letter and the circumstances surrounding it suggest that the epistle to which he refers is not 1 Corinthians, but a different, undoubtedly later epistle—one not preserved as a part of the New Testament canon. (Before 1 Corinthians Paul had also written the Corinthians a letter, mentioned in 1 Corinthians 5:9. The absence of these letters from the canon would indicate that they were never intended to be regarded as Scripture. Had they been God-breathed epistles, they would have been preserved; see 1 Peter 1:25).

In the interim after 1 Corinthians was written, Paul seems to have made a brief visit to Corinth, because twice in 2 Corinthians he speaks of his plans to visit them a "third time" (12:14; 13:1). That visit between 1 and 2 Corinthians was probably a brief fact-finding visit as Paul was en route to somewhere else. The visit evidently did not put a stop to the mutiny. In fact, it may be the case that while in Corinth Paul was assaulted verbally, publicly, and to his face. Paul apparently left Corinth heartsick, heartbroken, and grieved over what he saw and experienced (cf. 2 Cor. 12:20-21). He also gave the Corinthians a stern warning before he left (13:2).

Either during his visit, or (perhaps more likely) in the letter, which was written afterward, Paul instructed the Corinthians to discipline the man referred to in 2 Corinthians 2. This man was obviously a member of the Corinthian church. Perhaps he had also become a ringleader in the rebellion. It may be that his sin involved a personal and public attack on the apostle Paul. All of that would fit well with the context of Paul's remarks.

Whatever the circumstances, sometime after his own visit Paul sent Titus to Corinth to get a firsthand update on the state of things in the church there. Titus went with the express purpose of reporting back to Paul about how the Corinthians had responded to the epistle he had written. One of Paul's concerns was how this man was being dealt with.

So here is the setting for 2 Corinthians: Titus had returned and had given Paul an encouraging report about the Corinthians' repentance (7:6-16). Titus also informed Paul that the Corinthians longed to restore their relationship with him. They were repentant (7:9). They were even mourning over how they had treated Paul (7:7). Best of all, they were indignant about the mutiny that had been fomented in their midst, and they were now zealous to avenge the wrong (7:11).

And the focus of their avenging zeal was evidently this man who had somehow wronged the apostle Paul. They had already pursued him with the discipline process. In fact, the man himself had already repented.

But avenging zeal is not always quenched by the repentance of an offender, and it seems that some in Corinth still wanted to punish this man. They were not satisfied with his repentance. They wanted a measure of vengeance for all the trouble and confusion the man had caused in their fellowship.

One group in particular would have been zealous to avenge any wrongs committed against the apostle Paul. Paul mentioned them in 1 Corinthians 1:12 and 3:4, where he confronted some factious tendencies in the Corinthian fellowship. There he alluded to a group who identified strongly with him—the Paul coalition ("I am of Paul"). It is possible that some of these people who felt such a strong affection for the apostle Paul were the main ones who were still seeking vengeance against this guilty but repentant man.

But not Paul himself. He was more than eager to forgive. Far from siding with those who wanted to inflict more punishment against the offender, he instructed them to forgive and restore the man immediately:

> But if any has caused sorrow, he has caused sorrow not to me, but in some degree—in order not to say too much—to all of you. Sufficient for such a one is this punishment which was inflicted by the majority, so that on the contrary you should rather forgive and comfort him, lest somehow such a one be overwhelmed by excessive sorrow. Wherefore I urge you to reaffirm your love for him. For to this end also I wrote that I might put you to the test, whether you are obedient in all things. But whom you forgive anything, I forgive also; for indeed what I have forgiven, if I have forgiven anything, I did it for your sakes in the presence of Christ, in order that no advantage be taken of us by Satan; for we are not ignorant of his schemes.
>
> — 2 COR. 2:5-11

Paul had the heart of a tender pastor. Though he himself had caused the Corinthians sorrow with his earlier letter of rebuke, causing sorrow was not his goal (vv. 1-4). Motivated only by love for them (v. 4), he had written them through his own tears with no desire to punish them, but only seeking their repentance and the restoration of the broken relationship. He had never used his authority as an apostle to lord it over them but had always sought their joy

(1:24). The sorrow he had aimed to provoke with his letter was sorrow of a godly sort, designed only to secure their repentance in order to liberate them from their sin and unleash the joy again.

That is a good summary of how forgiveness works. It reverses the sorrowful aftermath of an offense and sets right a host of things made wrong by sin.

And in order to make his point, Paul employs this repentant individual as an object lesson for the Corinthians. He instructs them to forgive and restore the man, subjecting him to no further punishment. The apostle's instructions highlight seven blessings of forgiveness.

FORGIVENESS DEFLECTS PRIDE

There is little doubt that Paul himself had instructed the Corinthians to discipline this man until he repented—just as he had instructed them in the case of the incestuous man in 1 Corinthians 5.

But now that the man had repented, it was time to forgive him. And Paul, though probably the target of the man's original offense, took the lead in seeking his forgiveness.

This is a refreshing and godly example. Often the offended party feels justified in withholding forgiveness. Not Paul. He demanded no personal apology. He sought no act of penance. Anyone else might have demanded that the man's case be held open until he could come to Corinth and personally assess the genuineness of the man's contrition. But Paul did not. He was eager to forgive.

This illustrates the absence of pride in Paul's heart. Pride, I am convinced, is the primary reason most people refuse to forgive. They nurse self-pity (which is nothing but a form of pride). Their ego is wounded, and they will not stand for that. Prideful reactions to an offense can run the gamut from those who simply wallow in self-pity to those who retaliate with an even worse offense. All such responses are wrong because they are motivated by pride.

Paul would have none of it. Self-glory, self-protection, ego, pride, vengeance, and retaliation had no place in his heart at all. He did not want pity. He did not encourage those who wanted to take up his offense and see to it that the offender paid in full. Paul did not bask in sympathy offered by others who were angry at the offense against him.

Those are all natural inclinations prompted by sinful pride. When we are offended and someone else expresses outrage at our hurt, our tendency is to lap it up with a selfish delight. Someone says, "You poor thing! Oh, how much you have endured! Oh, how you have suffered! You have made yourself praiseworthy by enduring such excruciating pain!" And we love every word of it.

Paul wanted nothing to do with that. He refused to magnify the offense. "But if any has caused sorrow, he has caused sorrow not to me . . ." (v. 5). In other words, although the man's offense seemed to have involved a personal, perhaps public slight against Paul, the apostle declined to hold it against the man. He waived the personal aspect of the offense completely.

That would defuse anyone who believed that the offender needed additional punishment for Paul's sake. It would take the sword out of their hand. Paul simply minimized his own personal hurt. He refused to take the offense personally. He would not wallow in self-pity. He did not invite commiserating people to join in his despondency. He did not foster bitter resentment. He declined to pursue a personal vendetta. Whatever personal grief and public embarrassment the man's offense might have caused Paul were not important. As far as Paul was concerned, the offense against him was nothing.

And so Paul, by personally forgiving the man, softened the charge against him. The church could deal with the offender with no thought of making him pay for the grief he had caused the apostle. The Corinthian believers did not need to carry out some personal agenda on Paul's behalf. They were not to inflict extra punishment against the offender for Paul's sake. As far as Paul was concerned, no personal score needed to be settled between him and the offender. Paul knew how to be abased and how to abound (Phil.

4:12). He was "well content with weaknesses, with insults, with distresses, with persecutions, with difficulties, for Christ's sake" (2 Cor. 12:10).

Paul did not take this man's offense personally, any more than Jesus took personally the sin of those who nailed him to the cross. Stephen, under the bloody stones, set a similar example (Acts 7:60).

Here is virtue at its noblest. Paul simply rose above the offense and above the offender and took himself out of a victim status.

Modern psychology pushes people in the opposite direction, often teaching them to see themselves as victims and to magnify blame against others. I recently saw a book by one psychologist with a chapter entitled, "You Don't Have to Forgive." That's bad advice. Self-pity is an act of sinful pride. The wounded ego that cannot rise above an offense is the very antithesis of Christlikeness.

Paul was a godly man. He was too humble to seek vengeance when his pride was dented. Personal slights and personal sorrows were not his concern.

He makes a qualifying statement in verse 5: "He has caused sorrow not to me, but in some degree—in order not to say too much—to all of you." Paul was intent on minimizing the man's offense—and not only the offense against him personally. Paul also wanted the Corinthians to downplay their own hurt for the sake of restoring the man. "In some degree" suggests that the sorrow the man had caused the Corinthians was limited in extent. And "in order not to say too much" means "not to exaggerate the point." In other words, "He has caused sorrow to a limited extent, but let's not exaggerate it." It was time to move on, bury the penitent man's offense, and not make it an ongoing crusade in the church.

So Paul utterly dismissed any personal sorrow the man's offense had caused him, and he discouraged the Corinthians from overstating or embellishing the amount of sorrow it had caused *them*. Now that the man had repented, they were not to make more out of the offense than was absolutely necessary. They were particularly forbidden to overdo the significance of the offense against Paul. But they were also cautioned not to overstate the offense against the rest of the fellowship or blow out of proportion the hurt they had suffered. The man had repented. The Corinthians were not to seek vengeance on Paul's behalf. And whatever grief he had caused them should be graciously forgiven too. They were to forgive the man and move on.

Our sinful pride inclines us to respond exactly the opposite way. Pride always wants to demand eye-for-an-eye justice. We want to prolong punishment as long as possible and extract every ounce of suffering in return.

Forgiveness is not like that. It buries the offense as quickly as possible, even at the cost of personal pride. That is the attitude Paul exemplifies in this passage. Paul was a very hard man to offend, simply because he would not take offense. That is a wonderful virtue. It is true godliness and genuine love in action: "[Love] does not take into account a wrong suffered" (1 Cor. 13:5).

Paul had nothing in his heart but love and forgiveness for the offender. He had already forgiven him from the heart. The discipline process needed to be followed until there was repentance. But in his heart Paul harbored no bitterness. And now that the discipline process had borne the desired fruit, Paul was eager to forgive and restore the offender.

True forgiveness sets aside the wounded ego. One of the most beautiful biblical illustrations of this is Joseph. Joseph's own brothers sold him into Egyptian slavery. In Egypt Joseph was falsely accused by Potiphar's wife and then imprisoned for many years. For many people those would have been years of festering resentment and time spent plotting revenge. Not Joseph. When he finally encountered his brothers again, he was in a position to save them from famine. He told his brothers, "Do not be grieved or angry with yourselves, because you sold me here; for God sent me before you to preserve life" (Gen. 45:5).

All Joseph saw was the divine providence that placed him where he was so he could feed his brothers when famine ravaged the land. "For the famine has been in the land these two years, and there are still five years in which there will be neither plowing nor harvesting.

And God sent me before you to preserve for you a remnant in the earth, and to keep you alive by a great deliverance" (vv. 6-7). Where's the ego in that? Where's the "poor me"? Where's the coddled misery? Where's the self-pity? Where's the longing for vengeance?

There isn't any. Forgiveness erases all such evil influences. Forgiveness frees us from the bitter chains of pride and self-pity.

FORGIVENESS SHOWS MERCY

Paul also admonished the Corinthians to show mercy to the repentant offender: "Sufficient for such a one is this punishment which was inflicted by the majority" (2 Cor. 2:6). The discipline the man had already suffered was enough. He had confessed his sin and repented. Paul wanted the Corinthians to back off. Now it was time to show mercy.

The word translated "punishment" in verse 6 is *epitimia*, a Greek word that refers to a legal penalty or a formal censure. It does not refer to personal vengeance or punishment discharged by an individual. Instead it speaks of an official sanction, a corporate reprimand issued "by the majority." It is clear that this speaks of an official, formal act of discipline. The man's offense had been brought before the church, and "the majority" had approved his punishment—which, if the Matthew 18 process was followed, may have gone all the way to formal excommunication.

As we saw in chapter 7, church discipline is not a form of vengeance. It is a biblically mandated formal response from the church with regard to open sin. But the church's action against sinning people in the fellowship is never supposed to be vindictive. Rather, its proper aim is to draw the offender back.

As long as this man remained unrepentant, it was right for the Corinthians to keep away from him. Paul wrote in 2 Thessalonians 3:6, "Now we command you, brethren, in the name of our Lord Jesus Christ, that you keep aloof from every brother who leads an unruly life and not according to the tradition which you received from us." Later he wrote that same church and underscored those instructions: "If anyone does not obey our instruction in this letter, take special note of that man and do not associate with him, so that he will be put to shame. Yet do not regard him as an enemy, but admonish him as a brother" (2 Thess. 3:14-15). He told the church at Rome, "Keep your eye on those who cause dissensions and hindrances contrary to the teaching which you learned, and turn away from them" (Rom. 16:17). Jesus' instructions were similar: "If he refuses to listen to them, tell it to the church; and if he refuses to listen even to the church, let him be to you as a Gentile and a tax-gatherer" (Matt. 18:17). And Paul had already instructed the Corinthian church "not to associate with any so-called brother if he should be an immoral person, or covetous, or an idolater, or a reviler, or a drunkard, or a swindler—not even to eat with such a one" (1 Cor. 5:11).

The Corinthians were simply doing what the rabbis called "binding" (cf. Matt. 16:19; 18:18). The man's sin was bound to him as long as he would not repent, and their discipline was just. As Paul had instructed in the case of the incestuous brother in 1 Corinthians 5:5, they were to "deliver such a one to Satan for the destruction of his flesh." "Remove the wicked man from among yourselves," Paul had told them in that instance (v. 13). The discipline was to be administered publicly, "when you are assembled" (v. 4).

But this man had responded to the church's discipline, and now it was time to show him mercy. The binding had been done, but the loosing was equally important. The binding had been done publicly by the whole body; the loosing should be equally public.

Christians should be more eager to loose than to bind, because forgiveness, not condemnation, epitomizes the heart of our Lord (Luke 9:56, margin; John 3:17). Furthermore, we who live only by the mercy of God should be eager to show mercy to others. When an offender repents, we should restore him in a spirit of gentleness, realizing we too could be in the same situation (Gal. 6:1). We are not to be harsh. We are not to browbeat the repentant brother. We don't put him under a lifetime of penance. We don't make him do something to atone for his sin. We accept his repentance. That should be the end of the issue. That's the whole gist of Ephesians 4:32 and Colossians 3:13, which tell us we should forgive in the same manner Christ forgave us—generously, eagerly, magnanimously, and abundantly. How does God treat a repentant sinner? With total, complete instantaneous forgiveness. He holds forgiveness and love in His heart as He waits for the penitent sinner to come and seek that forgiveness. And then He bestows His mercy with the greatest joy and liberality.

FORGIVENESS RESTORES JOY

Paul, modeling the forgiveness he wanted the Corinthians to show to the offender, was eager to restore the man's joy: "You should rather forgive and comfort him, lest somehow such a one be overwhelmed by excessive sorrow" (2 Cor. 2:7).

Sin destroys joy. David noted this in his great confession of sin in Psalm 51: "Restore to me the joy of Your salvation" (v. 12). Sin always shatters the sinner's joy. But forgiveness restores the joy. Two verses later David wrote, "Deliver me from bloodguiltiness, O God, [the] God of my salvation; then my tongue will joyfully sing of Your righteousness" (v. 14).

So Paul instructs the Corinthians to forgive their brother and end his sorrow. The sorrow of discipline had brought him to repentance; now it was time for joy. The believers in the Corinthian fellowship needed to be more eager to bring the man joy than they were to cause him sorrow.

That is the heart of God. He is always tenderhearted toward repentant sinners. He takes no pleasure in the punishment of the wicked but delights when the wicked repent (Ezek. 18:23, 32; 33:11). "He does not afflict willingly or grieve the sons of men" (Lam. 3:33). God is like the prodigal son's father, who ran to meet his son and embraced and received him "while he was still a long way off" (Luke 15:20).

That is the heart of Christ as well. The prophet Isaiah said of Him, "A bruised reed He will not break, and a dimly burning wick He will not extinguish" (Isa. 42:3; cf. Matt. 12:20). The reed was a shepherd's flute constructed from a soft, hollow, bamboo-like plant. In time the little flutes would become weathered and soft—"bruised." They would lose their fine tone and become difficult to play. The typical shepherd would then simply snap the bruised reed, discard it, and make a new one.

Isaiah said the Messiah would be so tender a shepherd that He would not throw away the little flute that did not play the perfect tune. Instead He would restore the melody and bring back the song.

"Dimly burning wick" refers to a lamp-wick that was old and well-burned or for some other reason smoldered or smoked while it burned, producing an imperfect light and annoying smoke. The common practice was to extinguish the smoking wick and replace it. But the heart of Christ is to use even the smoldering wick, not to throw it away. Instead, He cleanses and trims the wick so that it burns more brightly.

God delights to revive and uplift the heart of the contrite. Elsewhere Isaiah wrote:

> For thus says the high and exalted One Who lives forever, whose name is Holy, "I dwell on a high and holy place, And also with the contrite and lowly of spirit in order to revive the spirit of the lowly and to revive the heart of the contrite. For I will not contend forever, neither will I always be angry; for the spirit would grow faint before Me, and the breath of those whom I have made. Because of the iniquity of his unjust gain I was angry and struck him; I hid My face and was angry, and he went on turning away, in the way of his heart. I have seen his ways, but I will heal him; I will lead him and restore comfort to him and to his mourners, creating the praise of the lips. Peace, peace to him who is far and to him who is near," says the Lord, "and I will heal him."
>
> – ISA. 57:15-19

God desires His people to have fullness of joy. The apostle John wrote, "These things we write, so that our joy may be made complete" (1 John 1:4). Joy is a fruit of the Spirit (Gal. 5:22). And when a Christian under God's discipline repents, God glorifies Himself by restoring that person's joy.

Paul therefore writes to the Corinthians, "so that on the contrary you should rather forgive and comfort him" (2 Cor. 2:7). They were not to hold back their forgiveness; rather they needed to comfort him actively and earnestly, seeking to restore his joy. Hebrews 12:12-13 describes the process: "Strengthen the hands that are weak and the knees that are feeble, and make straight paths for your feet, so that the limb which is lame may not be put out of joint, but rather be healed."

The church cannot set false borders on grace. There are no limits on divine mercy toward penitent people. There are no boundaries on forgiveness. The church must discipline sin in its midst, but we cannot deny a penitent person, no matter how serious his sin may have been.

Someone might protest, "But we want to make sure he will never do it again." We cannot have that assurance. If he sins seventy times seven, we must forgive him that many times.

Refusing to forgive is a sin. And it is a sin that is doubly destructive to Christian joy, because it not only steals the original offender's joy, but it also diminishes the joy of the one who is refusing to forgive. As we have seen repeatedly, failure to forgive brings the unforgiving person under God's discipline. It hinders worship and creates disunity in the fellowship. It is an extremely destructive kind of sin.

Forgiveness reverses all those effects. It restores joy on both sides. It heals the breach caused by sin. It salves the sorrow of both offender and forgiver.

And this should all take place the moment the sinning one repents. As soon as there is repentance, the offender should be restored and strengthened, "lest somehow such a one be overwhelmed by excessive sorrow" (v. 7).

Notice the anonymity of Paul's expression: "such a one." There was no reason to name the man, because he had repented. There was no further need to inform the church of his sin, but only to encourage them to restore him. As soon as the offender acknowledged his own sin and was willing to confess and repent, God wanted him to know joy.

God finds no pleasure in an unending or excessive despair. He seeks our joy, not our sorrow. He does not require sinners to spend a lifetime in pain and despair. A morose obsession with one's own guilt is not a godly virtue. It is actually a kind of self-righteousness. When you see someone who is preoccupied with mourning over sin, refusing to enter into the joy of the Lord, what you're seeing is an artificial spirituality. It is tantamount to refusing God's forgiveness, because forgiveness always brings joy.

FORGIVENESS AFFIRMS LOVE

Paul's instructions for restoring the sinning brother continue: "Wherefore I urge you to reaffirm your love for him" (v. 8). Forgiveness necessarily involves an affirmation of love to the offender. In fact, to withhold forgiveness is to withhold love. Love is the new commandment given to the church by Christ (John 13:34). Love is also called "the royal law" (Jas. 2:8). Therefore, unforgivingness is a very grave sin indeed.

The Greek word translated "reaffirm" in 2 Corinthians 2:8 is significant; it is a technical term that speaks of legally validating a document or a contract. It is the same word used in Galatians 3:15 to speak of the formal ratification of a covenant. Here in 2 Corinthians 2 it undoubtedly refers to a formal, public announcement. As we noted, verse 6 implies that the man had been formally and publicly disciplined. Here Paul suggests that the matter should be concluded with a formal and public reaffirmation of love toward the man. The discipline was announced formally to the whole church; the restoration should likewise be broadcast.

Paul told Timothy that an elder who sins should be rebuked before all, so that others may fear (1 Tim. 5:20). If the purpose of dealing with sin publicly is so that everyone understands how serious sin is, then restoration must also be dealt with publicly so that everyone understands how important forgiveness is. Grace is, if anything, a higher principle than law. Loosing is even better than binding. Since all heaven rejoices when a sinner repents (Luke 15:7), surely the saints on earth should participate in that joy. And so the matter was to be handled publicly.

However, the public affirmation of love should be only a prelude to the display of love that should pour forth from the saints on an individual level toward the restored brother. The Greek word for "love" is *agape*—the love of choice, the love of will, the love of serving with humility. Paul expected something more than a mere formal announcement. The saints were to demonstrate their love to this brother in practical ways.

This is the very character by which a church should be known: "By this all men will know that you are My disciples, if you have love for one another" (John 13:35). How does the world know Christians love one another? What about our love for one another is remarkable, and visible, to a watching world? Is it because we socialize? No. Non-Christians socialize too. It's not our potluck meals or group activities that best display our love toward one another, but our *forgiveness*. Love is best manifested in forgiveness. And the real test of love is how eagerly we forgive when we are offended.

Almost nothing can fracture a church where forgiveness is practiced, because unresolved issues are never left to fester. Offenses are dealt with. They are forgiven. Transgressions are covered. That is why it is so crucial for churches to practice discipline. The discipline process seeks to bring about the forgiveness and reconciliation that keep the unity and love of the church intact.

And when repentance takes place, the affirmation of love to the repentant one should be even more ceremonious than the discipline. Like the father who dressed the prodigal son in the finest clothing, killed the fatted calf, and called his neighbors together for a celebration (Luke 15), we should be lavish with our forgiveness. True forgiveness delights to affirm the sinner's repentance with munificent expressions of love.

FORGIVENESS PROVES OBEDIENCE

We have seen so far that forgiveness is inextricably tied to humility, mercy, joy, and love. Those are all noble virtues—fruit of the Spirit (cf. Galatians 5:22-23). Forgiveness prompts and nurtures all those virtues. But if forgiveness were entirely unrelated to those crucial Christian character qualities, if forgiveness did nothing to cultivate the fruit of the Spirit, it would still be right to forgive.

Why? Because God has commanded that we forgive.

Forgiveness is a simple matter of obedience. That is what Paul means in 2 Corinthians 2:9: "To this end also I wrote that I might put you to the test, whether you are obedient in all things." Their earlier discipline of the offender was one step of obedience. Now they needed to continue showing themselves obedient by restoring their repentant brother.

It is relatively easy to be obedient in some things. Scripture commands us to sing songs of praise to the Lord (Col. 3:16). That is not a difficult thing. The Bible says we're to pray (Luke 18:1). That comes fairly easy, though faithfulness in the task is sometimes a challenge. But of all the commandments Christ gave, it seems one of the hardest things is dealing with sin in the church. That is why many churches avoid discipline altogether. Everything about dealing with sin is difficult. Confronting the sinner privately is hard. Bringing an unrepentant brother's sin before the church is harder still. Pursuing an unrepentant person who has turned his back on the church is one of the most difficult things of all. The further into the process we go, the harder it is to obey.

But the restoration process can also be extremely hard. Picking up the pieces after the offender has repented, restoring him to the fellowship, strengthening him, and affirming love is not easy. Such forgiveness does not come naturally. But it is nonetheless an essential aspect of obedience to the Lord.

The contemporary church has failed in virtually all areas related to dealing with sin. Many churches practice no discipline whatsoever. They do not confront sin. They do not go after the sinner. And ultimately they also forfeit many opportunities to obey in the matter of forgiveness. Their disobedience with regard to disciplining sinners nullifies any opportunity to forgive those who repent.

The converse is also true. Those who do the hard work of confronting and disciplining sin inevitably have more opportunities and a greater willingness to forgive and show love to repentant offenders. Discipline and forgiveness often go hand in hand. And both are equally necessary to maintain the purity and soundness of the church.

Rooting out sin in the church through the discipline process does not necessarily guarantee a pure church. The sin of an offender may be eliminated, but the attitudes and responses of the rest of the flock must also be right (cf. Gal. 6:1). Paul alludes to this in 2 Corinthians 7:12, where he tells the believers, "So although I wrote to you it was not for the sake of the offender, nor for the sake of the one offended." In other words, throughout this episode in Corinth, Paul's chief concern was never merely for the one person who had committed the offense. Nor did he seek this man's discipline in order to vindicate himself (as the offended person). Rather, Paul was mostly concerned with the response of the Corinthian church. He longed to see them demonstrate complete obedience.

The Corinthian church, despite their many shortcomings, were beginning to show signs of the obedience Paul longed to see. The report Titus brought back from Corinth comforted and encouraged him, because they had so far responded exactly as Paul hoped (7:13). All Paul's highest expectations had so far been met, and Titus's own affection for the Corinthians was made to abound (7:14-15). They had obeyed in the matter of the man's discipline. But now they also needed to obey in the matter of his restoration. The same church that had once shown such a wanton neglect of discipline (1 Cor. 5) now was called to prove their obedience in the restoration of a repentant brother. Their discipline had had the desired effect. Now one further test was necessary: they needed to demonstrate forgiveness to the man and thereby prove their obedience in all things.

FORGIVENESS REVITALIZES FELLOWSHIP

Paul further writes, "But whom you forgive anything, I forgive also; for indeed what I have forgiven, if I have forgiven anything, I did it for your sakes in the presence of Christ" (2 Cor. 2:10).

Again we see Paul's humility. He wants to deflect those who might desire to withhold fellowship from the offender for Paul's sake. So Paul is eager to affirm his own personal forgiveness to the offender.

And again he minimizes the offense: "What I have forgiven, if I have forgiven anything, I did it for your sakes"—as if from Paul's perspective the offense was hardly worth noticing in the first place. But he wants to state his forgiveness formally and explicitly for the sake of the Corinthians. No one could say, "We can't receive this man back because of our loyalty to Paul. After all, Paul was the one offended."

Paul, in essence, tells them, "No, it's done. If you have forgiven, I forgive. I want the fellowship restored, for your sakes." He was concerned that unity in the church be reestablished, and complete forgiveness was the only way that would occur. The Corinthians were to hold nothing back for Paul's sake. He wanted the church's fellowship renewed and revitalized. He was eager for the rest of the church to be rejoined with the repentant one. He desired unity in the church. Whatever fracture had been caused by the man's offense must be repaired. Any discord and disharmony must be resolved. Bitterness and vengeance needed to be set aside. The rejuvenation and revitalization of the fellowship took priority over all that. And forgiveness made it all possible.

FORGIVENESS THWARTS SATAN

Finally, Paul urged the Corinthians to forgive, "[so] that no advantage be taken of us by Satan, for we are not ignorant of his schemes" (2 Cor. 2:11).

Satan's whole agenda is undermined by forgiveness. If forgiveness deflects pride, shows mercy, restores joy, affirms mercy, proves obedience, and revitalizes fellowship, imagine how Satan must hate it! Therefore, forgiveness is an essential part of undoing Satan's schemes.

To refuse forgiveness is to fall into Satan's trap. Unforgivingness has all the opposite effects of forgiveness: it hinders humility, mercy, joy, love, obedience, and fellowship—and therefore it is as destructive of individual character as it is of harmony in the church.

First Peter 5:8 says Satan "prowls around like a roaring lion, seeking someone to devour." And one of the ways he devours people is by taking advantage of an unforgiving spirit. Unforgivingness gives him a tremendous advantage.

However, Paul says, "we are not ignorant of his schemes." It is sheer folly to promote Satan's agenda by refusing to forgive. Where unforgivingness reigns, Satan rules. He has his way in a church that refuses to forgive.

But where forgiveness flows freely, Satan's schemes are thwarted.

Forgiveness, then, is the soil in which numerous spiritual fruits and divine blessings are cultivated. Tending and nurturing the soil of forgiveness is one of the surest ways to develop spiritual health and maturity.

On the other hand, as we have seen throughout this book, refusing to forgive is spiritually debilitating. It provokes divine discipline and inflames a host of evils.

Why, then would any Christian ever deliberately withhold forgiveness? We whose very existence depends on the inestimable mercy shown to us in Christ ought to foster a similar mercy in our dealings with one another, and we ought to model forgiveness before a watching world whose greatest need is God's forgiveness.

Think about it like this: Forgiveness is both a blessing and a means to further blessings. Those who refuse to forgive forfeit the multiple blessings of forgiveness. But those who forgive unleash multiple divine blessings, not only on those whom they forgive, but also on themselves. This is the very thing to which we are called.

To sum up, let all be harmonious, sympathetic, brotherly, kind-hearted, and humble in spirit; not returning evil for evil, or insult for insult, but giving a blessing instead; for you were called for the very purpose that you might inherit a blessing.

— 1 PET. 3:8-9

NINE

Answering the Hard Questions About Forgiveness

For You, Lord, are good, and ready to forgive,
and abundant in lovingkindness to all who call upon You.

—Ps. 86:5

I know a young man (we'll call him Jim) who believes he was mistreated by a fellow Christian several years ago. There was a dispute about who was wrong in the incident. Jim brought the matter to the elders of his church for resolution. The elders attempted to investigate the matter but ultimately concluded there was insufficient evidence to determine who was at fault. It was one person's word against the other's, with no other witnesses. The elders finally advised both Jim and the other party to forgive one another and put the dispute behind them.

Jim refused to do that. He had read a popular Christian book on forgiveness, and the book taught that forgiveness can never be granted until the other party repents and seeks forgiveness. Jim now believes he is justified in withholding forgiveness from his brother as long as the other man refuses to admit he was wrong. Jim is determined to see that he gets justice, and he has already spent several years seeking someone who will take up his cause. But almost everyone has given him the same advice: "The issue is petty. It's your word against the other fellow's. This might not be resolved until Christ Himself sorts it out and you lay your differences aside in heaven. Give it up and move on. It is beginning to dominate your life and rob you of opportunities to bear the fruit of the Spirit."

Jim refuses to heed that advice. He believes that God, who hates injustice, would *never* want him to suffer an injury and simply forgive the offender unconditionally. Although numerous Christians have shown him 1 Peter 2:20-23, Jim has somehow managed to explain it away in his own mind. For years he has gone from counselor to counselor, desperately seeking someone who will agree with him and help him pursue justice against this other Christian who Jim says sinned against him. He believes he is obeying the biblical injunction of Colossians 3:13 ("Just as the Lord forgave you, so also should you") because, after all, God does not forgive apart from the repentance of the offender. Thus he has twisted a commandment to forgive into an excuse for withholding forgiveness. (See chapter 6 for a thorough discussion on the question of whether forgiveness is always conditional.)

I don't know whether Jim or the other fellow was at fault in the original dispute. It may well be that both of them were partly wrong. But even if the other fellow was totally at fault, I believe Jim is clearly wrong to hang on to his bitterness and justify his refusal to forgive on the ground that the offender has not repented. This is precisely the kind of situation in which we are supposed to turn the other cheek (Matt. 5:39). Those who keep account of such wrongs, constantly demanding redress of personal affronts, are violating the very spirit of Christ.

As I said at the outset of this book, I am convinced that many, if not most, of the personal problems Christians see counselors for have to do with forgiveness. And there are some difficult questions surrounding this subject of forgiveness.

In this chapter I want to address some of those issues. These are some of the hardest questions about forgiveness that have come my way in thirty years of ministry.

WHAT IS THE DIFFERENCE BETWEEN TRUE REPENTANCE AND A MERE APOLOGY?

Genuine repentance always involves a confession of wrongdoing and a willingness to make things right. An apology often takes the form of an excuse.

The word *apology* comes from the Greek *apologia*, which literally means "a speech in defense of." Apologies are often nothing more than self-defense: "I'm sorry if you took offense, but . . ." Genuine repentance is properly expressed in an admission of wrongdoing and a plea for forgiveness: "It was unthoughtful of me to say that. Will you forgive me?"

Be wary of using merely apologetic language in place of genuine repentance.

TO WHOM SHOULD WE CONFESS OUR SINS?

Confession of guilt must *always* be made to God. Confession is also owed to whomever our sin has injured. The arena of confession should be as large as the audience of the original offense. Public transgressions call for public confession; private sins should be confessed to God alone.

WHAT IF I SIN WITH MY THOUGHTS AGAINST ANOTHER PERSON?

Only actual injuries require confession of a wrong. It would be inappropriate for a man who had a lustful thought to confess that thought to the woman who was the object of his lust. Confession in such cases should be made only to God.

That does not, however, rule out confession in *every* case where the victim is unaware of the offense. If you have quietly slandered someone, that person may be unaware of the offense. Nonetheless, the offense is real. It needs to be made right not only with those who received the original slander, but also with the person who was slandered, even if that person is not yet aware of the offense.

SHOULD I CONFESS MY UNFAITHFULNESS TO MY WIFE, EVEN IF TELLING HER ABOUT IT MAY HURT HER MORE THAN KEEPING IT A SECRET WOULD?

There is no doubt that in some cases confessing a sin may cause as much hurt as the offense itself. Nonetheless, I believe that in all cases the unfaithful party in a marriage relationship broken by adultery should confess the sin to his or her spouse.

Why? For one thing, it takes two people to commit adultery. The other party in the sin already knows about the offense. It compounds your unfaithfulness to share a secret with your cohort in sin but keep your spouse in the dark. The lack of total openness—the need to hide things and keep secrets—will continue to be a barrier to the proper unity of the marriage. Something as serious as a breach in the marital union cannot be repaired if the truth must be kept from your marriage partner. Failure to confess simply compounds lying and cover-ups. That sort of thing will eventually destroy the relationship, whether or not the adultery is repeated.

As difficult as it may be for both you and your spouse, you must deal honestly with a sin like this. If the offended spouse discovers the sin through other means, the hurt that is then caused will be drastically increased. You owe it to him or her to confess.

HOW SHOULD WE HANDLE REPEAT OFFENSES?

Jesus answered this question expressly in Luke 17:3-4: "If your brother sins, rebuke him; and if he repents, forgive him. And if he sins against you seven times a day, and returns to you seven times, saying, 'I repent,' forgive him." Again, our forgiveness is supposed to be lavish, enthusiastic, eager, freely offered, and unconstrained— even for repeat offenders. After all, we are all repeat offenders against God.

BUT WHAT IF THERE IS REASON TO THINK THAT THE OFFENDER'S "REPENTANCE" IS A SHAM?

In normal circumstances, love obliges us to assume the best about those who profess repentance (1 Cor. 13:7). Scripture does suggest, however, that there are certain times when it is legitimate to demand fruits of repentance before assuming that someone's profession of repentance is genuine (Matt. 3:8; Luke 3:8).

One author paints a hypothetical scenario where an offender intentionally punches an innocent person in the nose. After the first offense, the offender asks for, and receives, forgiveness. Moments later, in another unprovoked attack, he punches the same person in the nose a second time. The cycle is repeated a third time, and a fourth, and so on, with the bully professing repentance each time and the victim granting forgiveness each time. That author suggests this is how Jesus' words are to be interpreted: "If he . . . returns to you seven times, *saying*, 'I repent,' forgive him." All the offender needs to do is to say he repents, and the offended person is obliged to forgive.

But that is far too wooden an interpretation of Jesus' words. Our Lord was not suggesting that the disciples should throw discernment out the window when it comes to evaluating a person's repentance. Nothing in the context of Luke 17:3-4 suggests that the offense Jesus had in mind was deliberate or that the repentance was feigned.

In fact, it is important to be wary of feigned repentance in cases like the hypothetical one just described. Such deliberately repeated offenses, especially when accompanied by phony repentance, are evidence of a profoundly evil character and a cynical hatred of the truth. John the Baptist was justified in refusing baptism to the Pharisees until they showed the reality of their profession of repentance (Matt. 3:8).

So there are times when it is sheer folly to accept a mere profession of repentance, especially in the wake of several deliberate repeat offenses.

Nonetheless, even after multiple offenses, the offended person must be prepared to forgive—*eager* to forgive—unless there remains some very compelling reason to doubt the offender's profession of repentance. Even the hardest and most deliberate offender should never be permanently written off; rather, complete forgiveness and reconciliation should remain the offended person's goal.

WHEN IS RESTITUTION APPROPRIATE?

Whenever an actual loss has been caused by a wrong, restitution is certainly appropriate. The granting of forgiveness for the guilt of the offense does not automatically nullify the need to make reparations, especially when the injured party's loss is quantifiable. Whether the loss was caused deliberately (as in a theft) or accidentally (through some form of negligence), restitution should be made.

Under the Old Testament law, most restitution was as nearly as possible matched to the actual loss (Lev. 24:18-21). If your negligence caused you neighbor's ox to die, you had to pay him the value of the ox (Exod. 21:33-34). Deliberate thievery was punished with additional restitution. Someone who stole money had to repay an additional 20 percent (Lev. 6:4-5; Num. 5:6-7). Certain thefts of animals (especially if the stolen animals were killed) required four- and fivefold restitution (Exod. 22:1).

Zaccheus offered fourfold restitution to those he had defrauded, more than the law required (Luke 19:8). That spirit of willingness to make restitution should accompany all true confession of wrongdoing.

Restitution should never be regarded as a meritorious act of penance. The purpose of restitution is simply to restore the value of the damages. Under Moses' law, when restitution was required over and above the actual amount of the loss, the purpose of the restitution was both to punish and to deter.

The one forgiving is free, of course, to forego restitution and to choose to suffer the wrong without demanding repayment. But that is the offended person's option. The offender, if truly repentant, must be willing to right the wrong as much as is possible (cf. Matt. 18:26, 29).

WHAT RESTITUTION CAN BE MADE IF THE OFFENSE WAS A SIN LIKE LYING, SLANDER, DISHONORING ONE'S PARENTS, OR OTHER SINS WHERE NO ACTUAL VALUE CAN BE ATTACHED TO THE DAMAGE?

In some cases tangible restitution is impossible, and yet reparations need to be made. Lies should be confessed and the truth communicated at least as widely as the lie was. Slander needs to be corrected by a sincere effort to restore the offended person's reputation and honor.

Restitution in all such instances begins with a humble confession of the wrongdoing and a willingness to do whatever is reasonable to right the wrong.

IS THE FORGIVER OBLIGATED TO FORGET THE OFFENSE?

"Forgive and forget." The expression has attained the status of a cliché. When we grant forgiveness, does that entail a promise to forget the offense completely?

Yes and no. There is obviously no way to purge the memory of an offense. And the more severe the offense, the more difficult it may be to keep the memory from coming to mind.

I've heard people suggest that God forgets our sins when He forgives. They usually cite Hebrews 8:12 and 10:17: "Their sins and their lawless deeds I will remember no more." Or Isaiah 43:25: "I, even I, am the one who wipes out your transgressions for My own sake, and I will not remember your sins."

But those verses don't say God forgets our sins. They say *He will not remember them*. What's the difference? To forget something is to have no memory of it. Obviously God, who is omniscient, has not lost His memory of our transgressions. Rather, He refuses to call them to mind. He promises not to bring them up.

And that is exactly what is involved in forgiveness. It is a promise not to remind the person of the offense. Jay Adams characterizes this as a threefold promise: "You promise not to remember his sin by bringing it up to him, to others, or to yourself. The sin is buried."[1]

WHAT IF I CANNOT FORGIVE MYSELF?

I realize there are some who teach that a kind of self-forgiveness is necessary. I find this nowhere in Scripture. I've met many people who *claim* to be unable to forgive themselves, but on careful examination this usually turns out to be a kind of sinful pride exacerbated by modern self-esteem philosophy. The person who complains about not being self-forgiving is often simply looking for flattering or consoling words from others as a way of salving the hurt that guilt has caused to their pride.

Jay Adams offers good insight into this question. He writes:

> The problem is not self-forgiveness. Their expressed agony stems from the very fact that, in the worst way, they want to forgive themselves. They want to put it all behind them, they want to bury it once and for all. . . .
>
> The problem is that people who talk this way recognize something more needs to be done. Forgiveness is just the beginning; it clears away the guilt. They also recognize that they are still the same persons who did the wrong—that though they are forgiven, they have not changed. Without being able to articulate it, and using instead the jargon they have heard all around them, they are crying out for the change that will assure them they will never do anything like it again. When, as a counselor, I help them to deal with the problems in their lives that led to the wrong, in such a way that they lead a more biblical lifestyle, I then ask, "Are you still having trouble forgiving yourself?" Invariably, they say no.[2]

WHAT IF THE OFFENSE WAS A GRAVE ONE AND I AM STILL HURTING? SHOULDN'T I WAIT TO FORGIVE UNTIL I CAN BE HONEST ABOUT IT? WOULDN'T IT BE HYPOCRITICAL TO DO OTHERWISE?

Some transgressions, particularly offenses involving marital infidelity, can cause pain so intense that the offended person imagines it is okay to withhold forgiveness in *this* case. They rationalize that Jesus' teaching on forgiveness might be all right for dealing with petty offenses, but a *serious* offense surely justifies a cooling-off period or a time of "emotional healing."

Normally, however, those who take that approach merely allow themselves to seethe, and thus the negative emotions are only fed, and the breach caused by the original offense is made worse by a heart-hardening resentment.

Much of Jesus' teaching on forgiveness was given to teach us *not* to be driven by our passions in such matters. Allowing emotions to take over and control us so that we violate what we know rationally is our duty is the very essence of sensuality. And sensuality is sinful, whether it is the kind of sensuality that leads to sins of lust like adultery, or the kind of sensuality that allows emotions to become a roadblock to forgiveness.

Forgiveness is first of all an act of the will. It is not hypocrisy to will forgiveness when the emotions are screaming for vengeance. Be obedient to the Lord regardless of how you feel. If you refuse to harbor spite or dwell on the offense, evil emotions will be starved. Moreover, the Lord Himself will set your heart right. Right emotions will eventually come if you surrender to Him.

And ultimately a conscious, deliberate, willful choice to forgive is the *only* thing that can free a heart from the bondage of such emotions.

APPENDIX ONE

⋙

HOW ARE WE TO UNDERSTAND THE ATONEMENT?

He had to be made like His brethren in all things, so that He might become a merciful and faithful high priest in things pertaining to God, to make propitiation for the sins of the people.

—HEB. 2:17

There is no way to deal adequately with the subject of God's forgiveness without discussing the doctrine of the Atonement.

It is at the very heart of the Gospel of forgiveness. The Gospel we proclaim is ultimately determined by our view of the Atonement. And no one is truly preaching Christ who is not declaring the true meaning of His death (cf. 1 Cor. 1:23; 2:2; Gal. 3:1). When we take up the subject of the Gospel, we are immediately brought face to face with the doctrine of the Atonement.

We introduced this topic briefly in chapter 1, but because the subject is so crucial, we return to it here for a closer look. As noted in chapter 1, various theories of the Atonement have been set forth historically. And the undeniable reality is that one's view of the Atonement has ramifications for all of one's understanding of the truth revealed by God. A defective view of the Atonement can be utterly disastrous. The annals of church history are filled with examples of people who, having gone astray on this matter, have utterly made shipwreck of the faith.

The doctrine of the Atonement has often been a battleground between Christians and heretics. Many of the primary differences between the true church and the major cults arise directly from the cultists' erroneous views of the Atonement. So these are extremely fundamental issues, and for that very reason they are best *not* left to experts. Rank and file Christians need to have a basic grasp of the doctrine of the Atonement, so they can be on guard against these deadly errors.

The very worst kinds of heresy are often set forth in innocuous-sounding language. Many of these erroneous views of the Atonement contain kernels of truth that sound good, and even biblical. And in recent years virtually all of them have surfaced wearing sheep's clothing. These old, once-discredited errors are now clamoring for acceptance again among evangelicals. Worst of all, a broadening doctrinal tolerance in the evangelical movement has left most believers poorly equipped to identify, much less refute, errors on matters like this.

My aim in this appendix is to outline the major views of the Atonement and explain *why* the erroneous ones are so deadly. If you keep alert for these errors, you will be able to spot some subtle dangers and refute them before they gain a foothold. More important, understanding these issues will strengthen your grasp of the Gospel and make you a better witness for the truth.

CHRIST'S DEATH AS A RANSOM PAID TO SATAN

One of the earliest faulty views of the Atonement was the notion that Christ's death was a payment rendered to Satan. Mark 10:45 says, "The Son of Man [came] . . . to give His life a ransom for many." And 1 Timothy 2:6 teaches that Christ "gave Himself as a ransom for all." According to the view we are now discussing, the "ransom" spoken of in those verses was a fee paid to Satan to purchase the release of sinners from the devil, who supposedly had a claim on their souls. Many of the early Church Fathers seemed to lean toward this notion of the Atonement (often referred to as "the

ransom theory" of the Atonement). This view was more assumed
than argued, however. In the early centuries terms such as *atonement*
and *ransom* were often employed without careful definition.

The early church was consumed with controversies about the
person of Christ. The Gnostic heretics denied the humanity of
Christ, and the Arians attacked His deity. Church apologists in the
first four centuries were kept busy making defenses against such
heresies, and the doctrine of the Atonement simply did not receive
intense scrutiny in those centuries. Consequently, for the most part
the Church Fathers' comments about the ransom of Christ should
not be regarded as studied, conscientious doctrinal statements, but
rather as childlike expressions of an unformed and inadequate doctrine of the Atonement.

A. A. Hodge pointed out that all the elements of a *sound* doctrine
of the Atonement were implicit in the Church Fathers' writings,
though never clearly systematized. Hodge wrote that the Fathers'
more orthodox views on the Atonement, while present, were
nonetheless "often left to a remarkable degree in the background,
and mixed up confusedly with other elements of truth or superstition."[1] Therefore, it is a mistake to read too much significance into
selected Church Fathers' remarks regarding the payment of a ransom to Satan.

The ransom theory in recent years has been revived in a crude
form by various charismatic teachers, especially Kenneth Copeland,
Kenneth Hagin, and others who have been influenced by an early-
twentieth-century charismatic evangelist named E. W. Keynon.[2]
These men teach that Christ purchased ransom for sinners by literally suffering in hell (rather than atoning for sin through His
death on the cross). They surmise that when He died He descended
into hell and suffered there in order to render a payment for sin to
Satan.

But nothing in Scripture implies that Satan has any legitimate
claim on sinners. Satan is not the one who must be propitiated, or
satisfied, before sinners can be redeemed. The biblical word *ransom*
alone simply means "redemption-price." There is no biblical war-

rant to conclude that Satan has any authority to demand such a price for the salvation of sinners. In fact, to think in such terms is to open one's theology to sheer superstition. Satan himself is under God's condemnation (Matt. 25:41); so he is in no position to demand any payment for the souls of sinners.

Furthermore, Scripture clearly teaches that Christ's atonement was a sacrifice *to God*: "Christ . . . loved you, and gave Himself up for us, an offering and a sacrifice to God as a fragrant aroma" (Eph. 5:2). Speaking prophetically of the death of Christ, the prophet Isaiah wrote, "The LORD was pleased to crush Him, putting Him to grief . . . He would render Himself as a guilt offering" (53:10). The guilt offering was an offering given to God, and as this verse suggests, the purpose of Christ's dying was to satisfy the claims of *God's justice*, not to compensate the devil.

CHRIST'S DEATH AS AN EXAMPLE OF RIGHTEOUSNESS

Another faulty view of the Atonement is the notion that Christ's death serves primarily as a moral example. This opinion (sometimes called "the moral influence theory" of the Atonement) has surfaced throughout church history in various incarnations. It was propounded by Peter Abelard in the early twelfth century, in reaction to Anselm's views (see below). Abelard denied that God's justice demanded any payment for sin and asserted that the redeeming value of Christ's death consisted mostly in the example He left for sinners to follow.

A nearly identical theory was set forth during the Reformation by a heretical group known as the Socinians. The forerunners of modern liberalism, the Socinians insisted that God's predominant attribute is His love, which virtually cancels out His wrath. They therefore believed that God is inclined to pardon sinners without demanding any payment.

The Socinians argued that sins can be forgiven, or they can be atoned for, but not both. If sins are forgiven, no payment is necessary. Whatever is paid for is not really forgiven. We know from

Scripture that God forgives generously, gladly (Neh. 9:17; Isa. 55:7; Mic. 7:18). Therefore, said the Socinians, the death of Christ could not have been any kind of *payment* for sins. Rather, Christ's death served as an example of obedience and love to believers, pointing the way to life.

Multitudes have evidently found that subtle argument persuasive—to the utter detriment of the church. The tragic legacy of this view of the Atonement can be seen in the effects of liberal theology on all the mainline denominations.

Furthermore, the argument itself is patently unbiblical. Remember, the gist of the Socinian argument is this: divine forgiveness is so lavish that it renders a payment for sin unnecessary; sins are freely remitted without any payment to satisfy divine justice. In particular, the idea that a blood sacrifice is required to buy forgiveness is regarded as barbaric by most who hold this view of the Atonement.

But what does Scripture say? "Without shedding of blood there is no forgiveness" (Heb. 9:22). Scripture teaches that divine forgiveness is rooted and grounded in a blood atonement. Far from making a payment for sins unnecessary, divine love was expressed in God's willingness to pay for sins with His Son's blood.

Furthermore, once you embrace the notion that Christ's death is nothing but an example, you have boxed yourself into the purest kind of works-salvation. It becomes the sinner's responsibility to rescue and reform himself.

If Christ's redemptive work is only an example to us, it accomplishes nothing objective on our behalf. Redemption from sin becomes a subjective matter of each sinner's following His example. Again, the inevitable result is some sort of works-salvation.

CHRIST'S DEATH AS A DEMONSTRATION OF GOD'S JUSTICE

Another erroneous view of the Atonement is the one we mentioned briefly in chapter 1—"the governmental theory." This is a compromise position between the orthodox view (below) and the moral influence theory of the Socinians and modern liberals. The governmental theory takes the position that Christ's death was a *demonstration* of God's wrath against sin, but not an actual payment on behalf of sinners. According to this view the cross displays both God's wrath against sin (seen in the severity of Christ's sufferings) and God's love (seen in Christ's willingness to endure those sufferings). However, according to this view, the sufferings were not a vicarious payment for anyone's sins. Christ's death was merely a public display of what God's wrath against sin would look like—not a real substitution that actually paid sinners' debt. So rather than satisfying divine justice on our behalf, Christ's death serves to move sinners to repentance by revealing both the goodness and the severity of God. Like the Socinians, advocates of the governmental theory believe God forgives sin without a payment, simply setting aside sin's penalty on behalf of those who repent.

The governmental theory approaches the Atonement from a legal standpoint. God's law and His moral government have been challenged by sin. Christ's death reveals to sinners the severity of God's law against sin. Thus the dignity and standard of the law are thereby maintained, so God can be just in forgiving, even though He simply waives sin's penalty.

In this view, Christ did not actually pay the price of sin on anyone's behalf. Like the Socinian view, this theory suggests that the Atonement accomplished nothing objective on the sinner's behalf; it was merely a symbolic gesture. Redemption therefore is primarily a subjective issue hinging completely on the sinner's response. The governmental theory necessarily leads to an extreme form of Arminianism (a doctrine that emphasizes human responsibility at the expense of divine sovereignty) or even Pelagianism (a denial that man's fallen condition renders him unable to save himself).

The earliest advocate of the governmental theory was Hugh Grotius, a Dutch theologian in the early seventeenth century. Grotius's theory was embraced by several New England theologians in the seventeenth and eighteenth centuries, including Charles Finney. The governmental theory is once again enjoying a revival through the influence of groups like Youth With A Mission (YWAM) and several popular Christian authors and youth speakers.

Its tendency, however, is deadly. The governmental theory alters the Gospel so that rather than being a message about what God has done for sinners, the emphasis is on what the sinner must do. Carried to its logical end it often involves a denial of the crucial doctrine of justification by faith. Like the Socinian theory of the Atonement, the governmental theory leaves the sinner ultimately responsible to reform and redeem himself.

George Otis, a modern advocate of the governmental theory, describes the moral dilemma his view aims to solve:

> God loves man, He loves him so much, He wants this intimate fellowship with him. But He also recognizes that sin is a horrible, powerful thing and He doesn't want it to start spreading out of control in the universe. And to allow man, to help man to understand how He viewed sin and how terrible sin really was, He attached a sanction to it and that sanction was death.
>
> So what is God going to do? Is He going to, in effect, condone sin? And say "Okay, I know I said, 'The soul that sinneth it shall surely die'—but in this case, the soul that sinneth it shall live, because I really like you and I really don't want you to die"?
>
> But then what's going to happen when the next person sins? God really likes him too. And the same with the next one and pretty soon nobody's going to die for their sin. But the other alternative, of course, is that everybody dies. And that's not too hot an alternative either. So this is God's government problem. How can God, as the righteous moral governor of the universe, whose responsibility it is to uphold the law of the universe and to uphold righteousness and to protect society. How is He going to get out of this dilemma? This is God's governmental problem.[3]

According to Otis, God met the "dilemma" by making a dramatic display of divine justice in the death of Christ. Otis quotes Romans

3:24: "God *displayed* [Christ] publicly as a propitiation in His blood through faith. *This was to demonstrate His righteousness*, because in the forbearance of God He passed over the sins previously committed" (emphasis added).

Passing over the crucial concept of propitiation (which necessarily speaks of satisfying God's wrath), Otis homes in on the word *demonstrate* and insists that Christ's dying was *only a demonstration* of divine justice, not an actual payment for sin. He says:

> Christ did not pay the debt or literally suffer the penalty of the law for His people. He prepared the way for our debt to be remitted. Or in plain language, dispensing with all metaphor, He made it consistent and proper and honorable for sin to be forgiven according to the prescribed terms of the Gospel.
> The truth is Christ paid no man's debt.[4]

Echoing the historic view of both the Socinians and the governmental theorists, Otis also claims that the forgiveness of sins requires no payment:

> On a personal basis God could say the second after a sin is committed, "hey, I forgive you." He doesn't hold any grudges or bitterness. He doesn't need to be paid back before He can forgive. There are no strings attached to His love. But He's got to be careful in His role, not as our father, but in His role as righteous, moral governor of the universe, that He's not careless in extending forgiveness so that it encourages others to sin. He can't do that.[5]

So according to the governmental theory, the Atonement was necessary only to salvage God's reputation, not as an actual substitution on sinners' behalf.

Charles Finney embraced this view of the Atonement because he began with the assumption that neither sin nor righteousness could be imputed from one person's account to another. Finney insisted that the idea of imputation, transferring guilt from the sin-

ner to Christ, was inherently unjust.[6] Therefore he also ruled out
the transfer of Christ's righteousness to the sinner (despite Rom.
4:5; Phil. 3:9). This led him to deny several vital evangelical doctrines, such as justification by faith and the doctrine of original sin.

Regarding justification by faith, Finney denied that God justifies
the ungodly (cf. Rom. 4:5). Instead, he taught that in order to be justified, sinners must actually *become* perfectly righteous. He wrote:

> There can be no justification in a legal or forensic sense, but
> upon the ground of universal, perfect, and uninterrupted
> obedience to law. This is of course denied by those who hold
> that gospel justification, or the justification of penitent sin-
> ners, is of the nature of a forensic or judicial justification.
> They hold to the legal maxim, that what a man does by
> another he does by himself, and therefore the law regards
> Christ's obedience as ours, on the ground that he obeyed for
> us. To this I reply: . . . His obedience could no more than jus-
> tify Himself. It can never be imputed to us. . . . It was natu-
> rally impossible, then, for Him to obey on our behalf.[7]

On what ground did Finney believe Christians were to be justified? Only their own obedience to the law could possibly justify
them. Finney's whole argument was that a sinner cannot be justified
by the imputation of another's righteousness. Therefore, he was left
with one option: he had to embrace a theology of self-justification.
It was, any way you look at it, a doctrine of salvation by works. In
other words, it was a different gospel, and not true Christianity.

The legacy of Finney's own theological journey shows in micro-
cosm where the governmental theory of the Atonement inevitably
leads. Finney saw clearly the consequences of his doctrine of the
Atonement. He plainly stated that not only justification, but also
regeneration, must be the sinner's own work, not God's. He wrote:

> [Sinners] are under the necessity of first changing their hearts,
> or their choice of an end, before they can put forth any voli-
> tions to secure any other than a selfish end. And this is plainly

the everywhere assumed philosophy of the Bible. That uni-
formly represents the unregenerate as totally depraved [a
purely voluntary condition, not a constitutional depravity,
according to Finney], and calls upon them to repent, to make
themselves a new heart.[8]

All of these errant views grew out of Finney's commitment to the
governmental model of the Atonement. They are the inevitable
result of a consistent application of that view.

The governmental view is often found alongside a strong
emphasis on revivalism. I mentioned in chapter 1 that a major Web
site advocating this theology is called "Revival Theology
Resources."

But the revivalism you'll find linked with the governmental
theory of the Atonement inevitably has a strongly man-centered
emphasis. They insist that revival is the result of human choices and
human actions, not a sovereign work of God. In fact, the whole
emphasis of this theology is not on what God does on our behalf,
but on what we must do to better ourselves.

That is the inevitable result of a theology that portrays the
Atonement as anything other than an objective work God does on
behalf of those whom He redeems. Deny that the Atonement
means Christ paid for sin on sinners' behalf, and you must
inevitably define salvation in terms of what the *sinner* must do.

This also forces a redefinition of the significance of the Cross.
Rather than emphasizing what Christ accomplished there, governmental theorists must define the Cross in terms of how it can
change the human heart. Rather than seeing the atoning work of
Christ as an objective, finished work, this theory defines the
Atonement as a subjective potential. George Otis, whose messages
on the Atonement are quoted above, provides a classic example of
this. He says: "The power of the cross does not lie in some vague,
abstract, ethereal cosmic transaction. The power of the cross, the
power of the blood of Christ, lies in its ability to literally, literally,
literally, literally subdue the human heart."[9]

By characterizing substitutionary atonement as "some vague, abstract, ethereal cosmic transaction," Otis denigrates the idea of an objective, finished work. He is left only with the subjective elements of salvation. This is the inevitable result of the governmental theory of the Atonement. And as we see in the legacies of Charles Finney and numerous other advocates of this view, the results are ultimately fatal to the true Gospel.

THE TRUTH: CHRIST'S DEATH AS A PENAL SUBSTITUTION

Here is the true doctrine of the Atonement as taught in Scripture: Christ's death was a substitution for sinners. God imputed the guilt of their transgressions to Christ and then punished Him for it. Christ's righteousness is also imputed to those who believe. This we established in chapter 1, but allow me to review some biblical texts that underscore these truths:

• *Isaiah 53:5-6*: "He was pierced through for our transgressions, He was crushed for our iniquities; the chastening for our well-being fell upon Him, and by His scourging we are healed. All of us like sheep have gone astray, each of us has turned to his own way; but the LORD has caused the iniquity of us all to fall on Him."
• *2 Corinthians 5:21*: "He made Him who knew no sin to be sin on our behalf, so that we might become the righteousness of God in Him."
• *Galatians 3:13*: "Christ redeemed us from the curse of the Law, having become a curse for us."
• *1 Peter 2:24*: "He Himself bore our sins in His body on the cross, that we might die to sin and live to righteousness."
• *1 Peter 3:18*: "Christ also died for sins once for all, the just for the unjust."
• *1 John 2:2*: "He Himself is the propitiation for our sins."

The Atonement was a full payment of the price of sins, to satisfy both the wrath and the righteousness of God, so that He could forgive sins without compromising His own holy standard.

As noted above, A. A. Hodge argues that all the elements of this view have been an essential part of Christian doctrine from the beginning. "With few exceptions," Hodge wrote, "the whole church from the beginning has held the doctrine of Redemption in the sense of a literal propitiation of God by means of the expiation of sin."[10] Hodge also pointed out that the clearer the church's conception of the Atonement has been, the more true vitality and strength the church has enjoyed. The decline of understanding of the doctrine of the Atonement has always been accompanied by a corresponding decline in the spiritual health of the visible church.

As we noted, however, in the early centuries, sound views on the Atonement were mixed with much confusion and were often all but obscured by superstition generated by the ransom theory.

A fuller understanding of the Atonement finally began to come clearly into focus with the work of Anselm of Canterbury (1033-1109). Anselm was the first great theologian to focus his energies on trying to understand the Atonement as a doctrine. The ground he laid in defining the Atonement ultimately became the foundation on which the Protestant Reformation was built.

Subsequent church history reveals that when the penal-substitution aspects of the Atonement have been emphasized and understood, the church has prospered. When these doctrines have been challenged or obscured, the church has fallen into serious decline.

WHAT IS THE UNFORGIVABLE SIN?

*"Any sin and blasphemy shall be forgiven people,
but blasphemy against the Spirit shall not be forgiven. And whoever
shall speak a word against the Son of Man, it shall be forgiven
him; but whoever shall speak against the Holy Spirit,
it shall not be forgiven him, either in this age,
or in the age to come."*

–MATT. 12:31-32

We have seen repeatedly that God is by nature forgiving. The theme of forgiveness runs through Scripture from beginning to end. Even as Moses descended from Sinai with the tablets of the law, God emphasized His willingness to forgive: "Then the LORD passed by in front of him and proclaimed, 'The LORD, the LORD God, compassionate and gracious, slow to anger, and abounding in lovingkindness and truth; who keeps lovingkindness for thousands, who forgives iniquity, transgression and sin" (Exod. 34:6-7). One could say that both law and Gospel are designed to teach us about forgiveness—the law by underscoring our need of forgiveness, and the Gospel by actually offering forgiveness to sinners who have seen that need.

Forgiveness therefore is an integral part of what defines the moral character of God. God is an eager forgiver. Anyone who turns to Him in genuine repentance—even the worst of sinners—will find mercy granted abundantly, lavishly, generously.

But there is a sinful tendency in most unbelievers to doubt whether God will truly forgive *their* sins. I often encounter people who seem positive that certain sins they commit are unforgivable. Is that true? Is there any sin that God won't forgive? Does the severity and the amount of sin put one beyond forgiveness?

I'm sure you would agree that the worst conceivable sin would be to kill Jesus Christ. I can't imagine any sin being more wicked than that. Of course, that's exactly what men did to the Son of God. Yet while our Lord was hanging on the cross and about to die, He prayed for His executioners: "Father, forgive them; for they do not know what they are doing" (Luke 23:34). If killing God's Son is forgivable, certainly the *degree* of sin will not forfeit forgiveness.

What about the *amount* of sin? When anyone—whether he is a seventy-year-old profligate who has lived a life steeped in immorality or a seven-year-old child whose worst sin was being naughty—turns to God in confession and repentance, God will forgive him.

Finally, is there any *kind* of sin that God won't forgive? A survey of Scripture will show that God forgives idolatry, murder, gluttony, fornication, adultery, cheating, lying, homosexuality, blasphemy, drunkenness, extortion, and every other kind of sin imaginable, including self-righteousness. He even forgives those who reject Christ. If He didn't, then no one could ever be saved. Everyone, to one degree or another, rejected Christ before they were saved.

Yet there was one group of people who rejected Christ and discovered that there is indeed one sin God will not forgive. The Pharisees hounded Jesus throughout His ministry, rejecting both His works and His words. The epitome of their rejection resulted in these scathing words of our Lord: "Any sin and blasphemy shall be forgiven people, but blasphemy against the Spirit shall not be forgiven. And whoever shall speak a word against the Son of Man, it shall be forgiven him; but whoever shall speak against the Holy Spirit, it shall not be forgiven him, either in this age, or in the age to come" (Matt. 12:31-32). What is blasphemy against the Spirit, and what led the Pharisees to sin in such a way? Let's back up in

Matthew to establish the context and discover the nature of the unpardonable sin.

HOW A HEALING LED TO REJECTION

During Jesus' ministry in Galilee, on one occasion "there was brought to Him a demon-possessed man who was blind and dumb, and He healed him, so that the dumb man spoke and saw" (v. 22). Christ's ministry was filled with many such events. Both the people and religious leaders already had been exposed to scores of instantaneous, total, permanent, and verifiable healings performed by the Lord (vv. 9-15; cf. 4:23-25; 8:2-4; 9:1-8). The source of His supernatural powers was no longer open to scrutiny, either by the multitudes or the religious leaders.

Yet most of the people were ambivalent about Jesus' identity and the source of His power. The scribes and Pharisees, however, were far beyond ambivalence. They were no longer skeptical and resentful of Jesus; they considered Him a threat to their power and had become adamantly hostile.

It appears that Jesus performed this particular healing to force the Pharisees to make their animosity public. This man, who was demon-possessed, blind, and unable to speak (possibly associated with deafness), suddenly and miraculously began to speak and see. And he did so to such a degree that "all the multitudes were amazed, and began to say, 'This man cannot be the Son of David, can he?'" (v. 23).

Apparently, this particular miracle proved to be unusually overwhelming, since "the multitudes were amazed." The Greek verb indicates that the people were totally astounded, filled with amazement and wonder. Such a response reveals that Jesus purposely intensified the supernatural character of this miracle.

The reaction of the people revealed that they recognized this miracle as a possible messianic sign: "This man cannot be the Son of David, can he?" "Son of David" was one of the many scriptural titles for the Messiah (2 Sam. 7:12-16; Ps. 89:3; Isa. 9:6-7). That the people were seriously considering the possibility that Jesus was the Messiah put the Pharisees under intense pressure to disprove such a notion.

THE EPITOME OF REJECTION

In their rush to counter the reaction of the multitudes, the Pharisees unwittingly walked into the trap Jesus had set for them: "When the Pharisees heard it, they said, 'This man casts out demons only by Beelzebul the ruler of the demons" (v. 24). The Pharisees in effect were claiming that Jesus wasn't the Messiah, but was rather the very antithesis of the Son of David—the servant of "Beelzebul the ruler of demons." "Beelzebul" was the pagan deity considered to be the prince of demons, Satan himself.

The Pharisees had put themselves in quite a quandary. Jesus' power was obviously supernatural, and it could only come from one of two possible sources: God or Satan. Since the Pharisees had already refused to recognize that Jesus was from God, they were forced to claim that He was an agent of Satan.

While the Pharisees were attempting to attract the crowd to their position, Jesus was keenly aware of what they were doing. He then proceeded to confront their accusation on all its illogical points.

The Absurdity of the Accusation

First, Jesus attacked the logical absurdity of their charge: "Any kingdom divided against itself is laid waste; and any city or house divided against itself shall not stand. And if Satan casts out Satan, he is divided against himself; how then shall his kingdom stand?" (vv. 25-26). It is logical that any kingdom, city, or house that is divided against itself would destroy itself. The same would thus be true of the spirit world. Satan is far too shrewd to order his minions to fight against each other and destroy his plans to work in the lives of people.

It is true, however, that evil is destructive by nature, and often evil agents are self-destructive (Mark 5:13). Demonic forces may occasionally fight with each other. But satanic forces would never wage outright war against one another. It was absurd to accuse Jesus of casting out demons by the power of Satan.

The Prejudice of the Accusation

Jesus next proceeded to reveal the corrupt, wicked bias of the Pharisees' hearts: "And if I by Beelzebul cast out demons, by whom do your sons cast them out? Consequently they shall be your judges" (v. 27). "Sons" was often used as an epithet for disciples or followers (see 2 Kings 2:3). The Pharisees revealed their prejudice by approving of the exorcisms performed by their followers. Such activity they would never claim as ungodly, and certainly not satanic. Yet when Jesus cast out demons *and* every kind of disease, they attributed His works to Satan.

The basic reason people reject Christ is not lack of evidence but personal bias. Those who are steeped in evil works avoid at all costs exposure to the righteousness of Christ. The Pharisees represent all children of darkness, who cannot and will not tolerate His light (John 3:19). They look instead for ways to justify their own wickedness and to destroy anyone who dares to expose them.

Since the Pharisees supported the exorcisms of their followers, Jesus was justified in suggesting that those followers judge the logic of the Pharisees' accusation of Christ. Who was the source of the sons' exorcisms? If it was Satan, they would condemn themselves and any of the religious leaders who supported them. If it was God, that would refute the Pharisees' accusation of Jesus.

The Rebelliousness of the Accusation

The third and basic reason behind the Pharisees' accusation was their rebellion against God, which Jesus exposed in this manner: "But if I cast out demons by the Spirit of God, then the kingdom of God has come upon you. Or how can anyone enter the strong man's house and carry off his property, unless he first binds the strong man? And then he will plunder his house. He who is not with Me is against Me; and he who does not gather with Me scatters" (vv. 28-30).

The only remaining possibility was that Jesus performed His miracles by the power of God, and thus He had to be the Messiah. Any Jew familiar with the Scriptures knew that all the miracles Jesus performed were prophesied as accompanying the Messiah (Isa. 29:18; 35:5-6). Since the Messiah was to be Israel's eternal King, the logical extension was that the kingdom of God (represented as the sphere of Christ's rule in any place or age) had arrived as well.

The proof of Jesus' claim was in all the miracles He did. He used the picture of a thief breaking into a strong man's house. A thief could not begin to carry out any loot unless he tied up the strong man first. Likewise, Jesus could not cast out Satan's demons unless He already had bound him. And only God could enter the house of Satan, successfully bind him, and carry off his property. Only God could have such power and authority.

Jesus then established the Pharisees' relationship to Him: if they were not for Him, they were against Him. Those are the only two possible relationships; there can be no neutral ground. The Pharisees' accusation revealed their rebellion and their status as enemies of God.

EXAMINING THE UNPARDONABLE SIN

How far men can proceed in sin and lose the opportunity to be saved is the basis for what Jesus then said to the Pharisees: "Therefore I say to you, any sin and blasphemy shall be forgiven men, but blasphemy against the Spirit shall not be forgiven. And whoever shall speak a word against the Son of Man, it shall be forgiven him; but whoever shall speak against the Holy Spirit, it shall not be forgiven him; either in this age, or in the age to come" (vv. 31-32).

Blasphemy is a form of sin, but here Jesus treats the two separately, emphasizing blasphemy as the most extreme form of sin. Jesus uses "sin" to describe all ungodly thoughts and actions, and he uses "blasphemy" to represent any conscious condemnation and rejection of God. Those who blaspheme God are guilty of defiantly defaming or mocking Him (cf. Mark 2:7). The Old Testament penalty for it was death by stoning (Lev. 24:16).

Yet Jesus even says that God will forgive blasphemy when it is confessed and repented of. The apostle Paul experienced such forgiveness: "I was formerly a blasphemer and a persecutor and a violent aggressor. And yet I was shown mercy, because I acted ignorantly in unbelief; and the grace of our Lord was more than abundant, with the faith and love which are found in Christ Jesus" (1 Tim. 1:13-14). Peter blasphemed Christ (Mark 14:71), but the Lord forgave and restored him. Any believer can blaspheme, since any thought or word that defames the Lord's name is blasphemy.

Even blasphemy against Jesus will be forgiven: "Whoever shall speak a word against the Son of Man, it shall be forgiven him" (Matt. 12:32). "Son of Man" refers to the Lord's humanity, and thus to His life on earth in His incarnation. If people misjudge Jesus and sin against Him with less than full exposure to the evidence of His deity, forgiveness is still possible if they believe once they have received full knowledge. Paul's conversion certainly attests to that; prior to his salvation he "acted ignorantly in unbelief" (1 Tim. 1:13).

There is one form of blasphemy, however, that God will not forgive, and that is "blasphemy against the Spirit" (Matt. 12:31-32). This is a deliberate rejection of Christ in full light of the Holy Spirit's testimony. These men had spurned the Spirit-wrought conviction that Christ's claims were all true and rejected Him for politcal reasons (John 11:47-48). When people have been exposed to the evidence that proves the source of all the Lord's words and works, and still reject Jesus as the Messiah, they are beyond forgiveness and are settled in their unbelief. It is inconceivable for those of us who know and love the Lord to understand how anyone who is given such full revelation could reject and condemn Him.

Those who refuse to believe in Christ lose the opportunity ever to "be forgiven . . . either in this age, or in the age to come" (Matt. 12:32). "This age" refers to all human history, and "the age to come" speaks of eternity. Forgiveness is forever unavailable for those who blaspheme the Holy Spirit.

The people in view in this passage heard Jesus teach and preach God's truth, yet refused to believe. They saw the divine power of the Holy Spirit working in and through Him, healing every kind of disease, casting out every kind of demon, and forgiving every kind of sin; yet they accused Him of deceit, falsehood, and demonism, attributing His power to Satan. God can do nothing for those who reject Christ as God in that manner and in the face of such overwhelming evidence. Commentator William Hendriksen says of such people:

> Their sin is unpardonable because they are unwilling to tread the path that leads to pardon. For a thief, an adulterer, and a murderer there is hope. The message of the gospel may cause him to cry out, "O God be merciful to me, the sinner." But when a man has become hardened, so that he has made up his mind not to pay attention to the . . . Spirit . . . he has placed himself on the road that leads to perdition.[1]

During Jesus' earthly ministry, the Pharisees and all others who blasphemed the Spirit cut themselves off from God's mercy. God had offered them His mercy in Christ, yet they rejected and ridiculed Him as satanic. The writer of Hebrews offers a stern warning to all who follow in the footsteps of the Pharisees and reject Christ in spite of exposure to the truth and the biblical record of His supernatural works:

> *How shall we escape if we neglect so great a salvation? After it was at the first spoken through the Lord, it was confirmed to us by those who heard [the apostles], God also bearing witness with them, both by signs and wonders and by various miracles and by gifts of the Holy Spirit according to His own will. . . . For in the case of those who have once been enlightened and have tasted the heavenly gift and have been made partakers of the Holy Spirit, and have tasted the good word of God and the powers of the age to come, and then have*

fallen away, it is impossible to renew them again to repentance, since
they again crucify to themselves the Son of God, and put Him to
open shame.

−HEB. 2:3-4; 6:4-6

During World War II action in the North Atlantic, an American naval force was engaged in battle on a particularly dark night. In the midst of the battle, one of the aircraft carriers was exposed to attack from the enemy, so a blackout was ordered. Yet six planes were heading back to the carrier from a mission and could not land without runway lights. Their request for the ship to turn on the lights just long enough so they could land was denied because to do so would jeopardize the lives of thousands of men. When the planes ran out of fuel, the pilots were forced to ditch in the freezing water, and all the crew of those six planes died.

God also reaches a point when He turns out the lights, and the opportunity for salvation is then gone forever. The one who rejects the full light of salvation will have no more light. He has lost forever his opportunity for forgiveness.

Two Classic Sermons on Forgiveness

Therefore let it be known to you, brethren,
that through Him forgiveness of sins is proclaimed to you, and through
Him everyone who believes is freed from all things, from which
you could not be freed through the Law of Moses.

—ACTS 13:38-39

C.H. Spurgeon
Forgiveness Made Easy

Forgiving one another, even as
God for Christ's sake hath forgiven you.[1]

—EPH. 4:32

The heathen moralists, when they wished to teach virtue, could not point to the example of their gods, for, according to their mythologists, the gods were a compound of every imaginable and, I had almost said, unimaginable vice. Many of the classic deities surpassed the worst of men in their crimes: they were as much greater in iniquity as they were supposed to be superior in power. It is an ill day for a people when their gods are worse than themselves. The blessed purity of our holy faith is conspicuous, not only in its precepts, but in the character of the God whom it reveals. There is no excellency that we can propose but we can see it brightly shining in the Lord our God; there is no line of conduct in which a believer should excel but we can point to Christ Jesus our Lord and Master as the pattern of it. In the highest places of the Christian faith you have the highest virtue, and unto God our Father and the Lord Jesus be the highest praise.

We can urge you to the tenderest spirit of forgiveness by pointing to God who for Christ's sake has forgiven you. What nobler motive can you require for forgiving one another? With such high examples, brethren, what manner of people ought we to be? We have sometimes heard of men who were better than their religion, but that is quite impossible with us; we can never, in spirit or in act, rise to the sublime elevation of our divine religion. We should constantly be rising above ourselves, and above the most gracious of our fellow Christians, and yet above us we shall still behold our God and Saviour. We may go from strength to strength in thoughts of goodness and duties of piety, but Jesus is higher still, and evermore we must be looking up to Him as we climb the sacred hill of grace.

At this time we wish to speak a little concerning the duties of love and forgiveness; and here we note, at once, that the apostle sets before us the example of God Himself. Upon that bright example we shall spend most of our time, but I hope not quite so much as to forget the practical part, which is so much needed in these days by certain unforgiving spirits who nevertheless assume the Christian name. The theme of God's forgiving love is so fascinating that we may linger awhile, and a long while too, upon that bright example of forgiveness that God has set before us; but from it all I hope we shall be gathering grace by which to forgive others even to seventy times seven.

We shall take the text word by word, and so we shall obtain the clearest divisions.

I. The first word to think about is *"for Christ's sake."* We use these words very often; but probably we have never thought of their meaning. Let us touch thereon with thoughtfulness, praying the good Spirit to instruct us. "*For Christ's sake*"; all the good things that God has bestowed upon us have come to us "for Christ's sake," but especially the forgiveness of our sins has come "for Christ's sake." This is the plain assertion of the text. What does it mean? It means, surely, first, *for the sake of the great atonement that Christ has offered.* The great God can, as a just Lawgiver and King, readily pass by our offenses because of the expiation for sin that Christ has offered. If sin were merely a personal affront toward God, we have abundant evidence that He would be ready enough to pass it by without exacting vengeance; but it is a great deal more than that. Those who view it as a mere personal affront against God are but very shallow thinkers. Sin is an attack upon the moral government of God; it undermines the foundations of society, and were it permitted to have its way it would reduce everything to anarchy and even destroy the governing power and the Ruler himself.

God has a great realm to govern, not merely of men that dwell on the face of the earth, but beneath his sway there are angels and principalities and powers, and we do not know how many worlds of intelligent beings. It would certainly be a monstrous thing to suppose that God has made yonder myriads of worlds that we see sparkling in the sky at night without having placed some living creatures in them; it is far more reasonable to suppose that this earth is an altogether insignificant speck in the divine dominion, a mere province in the boundless empire of the King of kings. Now, this world having rebelled against God high-handedly, as it has done, unless there were a satisfaction demanded for its rebellion, it would be a tolerated assault upon the dominion of the great Judge of all, and a lowering of His royal influence over all His domain. If sin in man's case were left unpunished, it would soon be known through myriads of worlds, and in fact by ten thousand times ten thousand races of creatures, that they might sin with impunity; if one race had done so, why not all the rest? This would be a proclamation of universal license to rebel. It would probably be the worst calamity that could happen—that any sin should go unpunished by the supreme Judge.

Sometimes in a state, unless the lawgiver executes the law

against the murderer, life will be in peril, and everything will become insecure, and therefore it becomes a mercy to write the death-warrant. So is it with God in reference to this world of sinners. It is His very love as well as His holiness and His justice that, if I may use such a term, compels Him to severity of judgment; and so sin cannot and must not be blotted out until atonement has been presented. There must first of all be a sacrifice for sin, which, mark you, the great Father, to show His love, Himself supplies, for it is His own Son who is given to die, and so the Father Himself supplies the ransom through His Son, that Son being also one with Himself by bonds of essential unity, mysterious but most intense. If God demands the penalty in justice, He Himself supplies it in love. 'Tis a wondrous mystery, this mystery of the way of salvation by an atoning sacrifice; but this much is clear, that now God for Christ's sake has forgiven us, because satisfaction has been made to the injured honor of the divine government, and justice is satisfied.

I want you to consider for a moment how readily God may now blot out sin since Christ has died. The blotting out of sin seems hard until we see the cross, and then it appears easy enough. I have looked at sin until it seemed to blind me with its horror, and I said within myself, "This damned spot can never be washed out; no fuller's soap can change its hue; sooner might the Ethiopian change his skin or the leopard his spots. O sin, thou deep, eternal evil, what can remove thee?" And then I have seen the Son of God dying on the cross, and read the anguish of His soul, and heard the cries that showed the torment of His spirit when God His Father had forsaken Him, and it has seemed to me as if the blotting out of sin were the easiest thing under heaven. When I have seen Jesus die, I have not been able to understand how any sin could be difficult to remove. Let a man stand on Calvary and look on Him whom he has pierced, and believe and accept the atonement made, and it becomes the simplest thing possible that his debt should be discharged now that it is paid, that his freedom should be given now that the ransom is found, and that he should be no longer under condemnation since the guilt that condemned him has been carried away by his great Substitute and Lord. It is then because of what Jesus Christ has suffered in our stead that God for Christ's sake has forgiven us.

The second rendering of the text would be this, that God has forgiven us *because of the representative character of Christ*. It should never be forgotten that we originally fell by a representative. Adam stood for us, and he was our federal head. We did not fall personally at the first, but in our representative. Had he kept the conditions of the covenant, we would have stood through him; but inasmuch as he fell, we fell in him. I pray you cavil not at the arrangement, because there lay the hope of our race. The angels probably fell individually, one by one, and hence they fell irretrievably; there was no restoring them. But as we fell in one Adam, there remained the possibility of our rising in another Adam; and therefore in the fullness of time God sent forth His Son, Jesus Christ, born of a woman, made under the law, to become the second Adam. He undertook to remove our burdens and to fulfil the conditions of our restoration. According to God's covenant He had to appear in our nature, and that nature in the fullness of time He assumed. He had to bear the penalty; that He has done in His personal suffering and death. He had to obey the law; that He has done to the utmost.

And now Christ Jesus, having borne the penalty and fulfilled the law, is Himself justified before God and stands before God as the representative of all who are in Him. God for Christ's sake has accepted us in Him, has forgiven us in Him, and looks upon us with infinite and changeless love in Him. This is how all our blessings come to us—in and through Christ Jesus; and if we are indeed in Him, the Lord not only forgives us our sin, but He bestows upon us the boundless riches of His grace in Him. In fact, He treats us as He would treat His Son; He deals with us as He would deal with Jesus. Oh, how pleasant to think that when the just God looks upon us, it is through the reconciling medium—He views us through the Mediator. We sometimes sing a hymn that says:

> *Him and then the sinner see,*
> *Look through Jesus' wounds on me.*

And this is just what the Lord does. He counts us just for the sake of our Saviour's atonement and because of His representative character.

Now go a little further. When we read "for Christ's sake" it surely means *for the deep love that the Father bears Him*. My brethren, can you guess a little of the love that the Father has toward the Only-begotten? We cannot pry into the wondrous mystery of the eternal filial relationship of the Son of God lest we be blinded by an excess of light; but this we know, that they are one God—Father, Son, and Holy Spirit; and the union that exists between them is intense beyond conception. "The Father loves the Son" was always true, and it is true now; but how deeply, how intensely He loves the Son no mind can conceive. Now, brethren, the Lord will do great things for the sake of a son whom He loves as He loves Jesus, for in addition to the fact of His eternally loving Him, as being one with Him by nature and essence, there is now the superadded cause of love arising out of what the Lord Jesus has done as the servant of the Father. Remember that our Lord Jesus has been obedient to His Father's will—obedient to death, even to the death of the cross; wherefore God has highly exalted Him and has given Him a name that is above every name. One of the sweetest thoughts, to my mind, that I sometimes feed on when I am alone is this—that *God the Father will do anything for Christ*. Here is another piece of a honeycomb—*when I can plead Christ's name, I am sure to be heard*. "For Christ's sake" is a plea that always touches the heart of the great God. Show that your receiving such and such a blessing will glorify Christ, and the Father cannot withhold it, for it is His delight to honor Jesus.

We speak after the manner of men, of course, and on such a theme as this we must be careful; but still we can only speak as men, being only men. It is the joy of the Father to express His love to His Son. Throughout all ages They have had fellowship one with another; They have always been one in all their designs; They have never differed upon any points and cannot differ. And you notice that when our Lord says, "Father, glorify thy Son," He is so knit with the Father that He adds, "that thy Son also may glorify thee." Their mutual love is inconceivably great, and therefore, brethren, God will do anything for Jesus. God will forgive us for Christ's sake; yea, He has done so in the case of thousands around me. And thou, great sinner, if you will go to God at this moment and say, "Lord, I cannot ask You to forgive me for my own sake, but do it out of love for Your dear Son," He will do it, for He will do anything for the sake of Jesus. If you are at this time conscious of sin so as to despair of yourself, it is well that you should be so, for self-despair is only common sense, since there is nothing in yourself upon which you can rely. But do catch at this hope—it is not a straw, it is a good, substantial life-buoy—ask forgiveness for the sake of Jesus, for God will do anything for Jesus, and He will do anything for you for His dear Son's sake.

So we read our text once more in the light of a truth that grows out of the love of God; namely, that *God does forgive sin for the sake of glorifying Christ*. Christ took the shame so that He might magnify His Father, and now His Father delights to magnify Him by blotting out men's sin. If you can prove that any gift to you would reflect glory upon Christ, you may depend upon the fact you will have it. If there is anything under heaven that would make Christ more illustrious, the Father would not spare it for a moment. If you see that for you to have your sin forgiven would raise the fame of the Saviour, go and plead that argument with God, and you shall surely prevail. Will it not make Christ glad if He saves such a sinner as you are? Then go with this argument in your mouth: "Father, glorify Your Son by exalting Him as a glorious Saviour in saving me." I find this often a great lever to move a heavy load, to say unto God, "Lord, You know the straits I am in. You knowest how undeserving I am. You know what a poor, undone creature I am before You. But if Your dear Son shall help and save me, the very angels will stand and wonder at His mighty grace, and so *it will bring glory to Him*, and therefore I entreat You, be gracious unto me."

You are certain to prevail if you can plead that it will glorify Christ, and surely you would not wish to have a thing that would not glorify Him. Your prayer shall always be answered if your heart is in such a state that you are willing to have or not to have, according as it will honor your Lord. If it will not glorify Christ, be more than content to do without the choicest earthly good; but be doubly grateful when the boon that is granted tends to bring honor to the ever dear and worshipful name of Jesus. "For Christ's sake." It is a precious word; dwell upon it, and lay up this sentence in the archives of your memory—the Father will do anything for the sake of Jesus Christ, His Son.

II. Now, secondly, we pass on to observe what it is that we are told in the text has been done for us, and to us, for Christ's sake. "God for Christ's sake *hath forgiven you*."

First notice, that He has done this *certainly*. The apostle does not say he hopes so, but he says, "God . . . for Christ's sake *hath* forgiven you." Are you in the number of the forgiven, my dear hearer? Have you believed in the Lord Jesus Christ? Then, as surely as you have believed, God for Christ's sake *has* forgiven you. Have you put your trust in the atoning sacrifice? Then God for Christ's sake *has* forgiven you. You have not begun to be a Christian, I hope, with the idea that one day, at some future period, you may obtain forgiveness. No. "God . . . for Christ's sake *hath* forgiven you." Pardon is not a prize to be run for, but a blessing received at the first step of the race. If you have believed in Jesus, your sin is all gone; all your sin has been erased from the records of the past, never to be accounted against you again ever. The moment a sinner looks to Christ, the burden of his sin rolls off his shoulders, never to return. If Christ has washed you (and He has if you have believed in Him), then you are clean every whit, and before the Lord you stand delivered from every trace of guilt.

Pardon is not a matter of hope, but a matter of fact. Expectation looks for many a blessing, but pardon is a realized favor that faith holds in her hand even now. If Christ took your load, your load cannot remain on your own back; if Christ paid your debts, then they do not stand in God's books against you. How can they? It stands to reason that if your Substitute has taken your sin and put it away, your sin lies no more on you. God for Christ's sake has forgiven you. Get hold of that grand truth, and hold it, though all the devils in hell roar at you. Grasp it as with a hand of steel: "God for Christ's sake has forgiven me." May each one of us be able to say that. We will not feel the divine sweetness and force of the text unless we can make a personal matter of it by the Holy Ghost.

Then notice that God has forgiven us *continuously*. He not only forgave all our sins at the first, but He continues daily to forgive, for the act of forgiveness is a continuous one. I have sometimes heard it said that we were so forgiven when we first believed that there is no need to ask for further forgiveness; to which I reply: We were so completely forgiven when we first believed that we ought continually to ask for the perpetuity of that one far-reaching act, that the Lord may continue to exert toward us that fullness of forgiving grace that absolved us perfectly at the first, that we may continue to walk before Him with a sense of that complete forgiveness, clear and unquestioned. I know I was forgiven when first I believed in Christ; and I am equally sure of it now. The one absolution continues to ring in my ears like joy bells that never cease. Pardon once given continues to be given. When through doubt and anxiety I was not sure of my pardon, it was still true, for he that believes on Him is not condemned, even though he may write bitter things against himself. Beloved friend, catch hold of that, and do not let it go. Divine pardon is a continuous act.

And this forgiveness on God's part was *most free*. We did nothing to obtain it by merit, and we brought nothing wherewith to purchase it. He forgave us for Christ's sake, not for aught that we had done. True, we did repent, and we did believe, but He gave us repentance and faith, so that He did not forgive us for the sake of them, but purely because of His own dear love, because He delights in mercy and is never more like Himself than when He forgives transgression, iniquity, and sin.

Remember, also, that He forgave us *fully*. It was not here and there a sin that He blotted out, but the whole horrible list and catalog of our offenses He destroyed at once. The substitution of our Lord has finished that matter even to perfection.

> *Because the sinless Saviour died,*
> *My sinful soul is counted free;*
> *For God, the Just, is satisfied*
> *To look on Him and pardon me.*

All our transgressions are swept away at once, carried off as by a flood, and so completely removed from us that no guilty trace of them remains. They are all gone! O believers, think of this, for *all* is no little thing: sins against a holy God, sins against His loving Son, sins against the Gospel as well as against the law, sins against man as well as against God, sins of the body as well as sins of the mind, sins as numerous as the sands on the seashore and as great as the sea itself—all, *all* are removed from us as far as the east is from the west. All this evil was rolled into one great mass and laid upon Jesus; and having borne it all, He has made an end of it forever. When the Lord forgave us, He forgave us the whole debt. He did not take the bill and say, "I strike out this item and that," but the pen went through it all: *PAID*. It was a receipt in full for all demands, Jesus took the handwriting that was against us and nailed it to His cross, to show before the entire universe that its power to condemn us had ceased forever. We have in Him a full forgiveness.

And let it be remembered that this forgiveness that God has given us for Christ's sake is an *eternal* forgiveness. He will never bring up our past offenses and a second time impute them. He will not find us on an evil day and say, "I have had great patience with you, but now I will deal with you according to your sins." Far otherwise; he who believes in Jesus has everlasting life and will never come into condemnation. Irreversible is the pardon of heaven. "The gifts and calling of God are without repentance." He never repents what he has given, or forgiven. 'Tis done, 'tis done forever: Jehovah absolves, and the sentence stands fast forever. "There is therefore now no condemnation to them which are in Christ Jesus." "Who shall lay any thing to the charge of God's elect? It is God that justifieth. Who is he that condemneth?" Blessed be God for His eternal pardon!

And since I could not find a word to finish with but this one, I will use it: he has *divinely* pardoned us. There is a truth, reality, and emphasis in this, for though a man should forgive all you have done against him, if you have treated him very badly, it is more than you could expect that he should quite *forget* it. But the Lord says, "Their sins and iniquities will I remember no more forever." If a man has played you false, although you have forgiven him, you are not likely to trust him again. An old proverb says, "Never ride a broken-kneed horse," and it is not a bad proverb either. But see how the Lord deals with His people. When Peter was set on his legs again he was a broken-kneed horse, and yet see how gloriously the Lord rode that charger on the day of Pentecost. Did he not go forth conquering and to conquer? The Lord lets bygones be bygones so completely that He trusts pardoned souls with his secrets, for "the secret of the Lord is with them that fear him"; and He entrusts some of us with his choicest treasures, for Paul said, "He hath put me in trust with the gospel, though I was a blasphemer." He commits to our keeping that priceless casket that encloses the best hope of men, namely, the Gospel of Jesus. "We have this treasure in earthen vessels."

This shows how perfect is our forgiveness—nay, I must put it, how *divine* is the forgiveness that we have received. Let us rejoice in that grand promise that comes to us by the mouth of Jeremiah of old: "In those days, and in that time, saith the Lord, the iniquity of Israel shall be sought for, and there shall be none; and the sins of Judah, and they shall not be found: for I will pardon them whom I reserve." Here is annihilation—the only annihilation I know of— the absolute annihilation of sin through the pardon that the Lord gives to His people. Let us sing it as though it were a choice hymn: "The iniquity of Israel shall be sought for, and there shall be none."

III. Now, if you have drunk into the spirit of our subject you will be strengthened to hear what I have to say to you upon a point of practice: "*Forgiving one another*, even as God for Christ's sake hath forgiven you."

"Forgiving one another, even as God for Christ's sake hath forgiven you." Now observe how the apostle puts it. Does he say "forgiving another"? No, that is not the text. It is "forgiving *one another*."

One another! Ah, then that means that if you have to forgive today, it is very likely that you will yourself need to be forgiven tomorrow, for it reads, "forgiving *one another*." It is turn and turnabout, a mutual operation, a cooperative service. In fact, it is a joint-stock business of mutual forgiveness, and members of Christian churches should take large shares in this concern. "Forgiving one another." You forgive me, and I forgive you, and we forgive them, and they forgive us, and so a circle of unlimited forbearance and love goes around the world. There is something wrong about me that needs to be forgiven by my brother, but there is also something wrong about my brother that needs to be forgiven by me, and this is what the apostle means—that all of us are to be mutually exercising the sacred art and mystery of forgiving one another.

If we always did this, we would not endure those who have a special faculty for spying out faults. There are some who, whatever church they are in, always bring an ill report of it. I have heard this sort of thing from many—"There is no love among Christians at all." I will tell you the character of the gentleman who makes that observation; he is both unloving and unlovely, and so he is off the track of the pilgrims of love. Another cries, "There is no sincerity in the world now." That man is a hypocrite; you can be quite sure of that. Judge a bird by its song, and a man by his utterance. The censorious measure our corn, but they use their own bushels. You can know very well what a man is by what he says about others. Judging other men by their own judgment of their fellows—that is a gauge of character that very seldom will deceive you. Their speech betrays their heart. "Show me your tongue, sir! Now I know whether you are sick or well." He who speaks with an ill tongue about his neighbor has an ill heart; rest assured of that. Let us engage in our Christian career with the full assurance that we will have a great deal to forgive in other people, but there will be a great deal more to be forgiven in ourselves. Let us count on having to exercise gentleness, and needing its exercise from others. "Forgiving one another, even as God for Christ's sake hath forgiven you."

Note again: when we forgive, it is a poor and humble business compared with God's forgiving us, because we are only forgiving one another—that is, forgiving fellow servants—whereas when God forgives us, the Judge of all the earth is forgiving, not his fellows, but his rebel subjects, guilty of treason against His Majesty. For God to forgive is something great; for us to forgive, though some think it great, should be regarded as a very small matter.

Then reflect upon the matter to be forgiven. Our Lord in His parable tells us that the fellow servant owed a few pence, but the servant himself was debtor to his master for many talents. What we owe to God is infinite, but what our fellow creature owes to us is a very small sum. What did he do who has so much offended you? "He said a very shameful thing about me." That was very bad of him, no doubt. "Then he played me a very nasty trick and acted very ungraciously; in fact, he behaved scandalously, and if you hear the story you will be quite indignant." Well, I am indignant. He is a bad fellow, there is no doubt about it; and so are you. So were you certainly when you first came to God; bad as he was to you, you have been much worse to the Lord. I will warrant that his blacks toward you are whites compared with your blacks in the presence of God. "Oh, but you would not believe how basely he acted." No, and I dare say I should hardly believe it if I heard how base you have been to the Lord. At any rate, it should make our eyes fill with tears to think how we have grieved our God and vexed His Spirit. Some of us have had so much manifest forgiveness, so much outward sin forgiven, that for us to forgive ought to be as natural as to open our hands. After such forgiveness as the Lord has bestowed on some of us, we should be wicked servants indeed if we were to take our brother by the throat and say, "Pay me what thou owest." We should deserve to be given over to the tormentors by our angry Master if we did not count it joy to pass by a brother's fault.

If anyone here who is a Christian finds it difficult to forgive, I am going to give him three words that will help him wonderfully. I would put them into the good man's mouth. I gave them to you just now and prayed you to get the sweetness of them. Here they are again: "For Christ's sake." Cannot you forgive an offender on that ground? Ah, the girl has acted very shamefully, and you, her father, have said some strong things, but I beg you to forgive her for Christ's sake. Cannot you do it with that motive? It is true that your son has behaved very wrongly, and nothing hurts a father's heart more than the wicked conduct of a son. You did in a fit of anger say a very stern thing and deny him your house forever. I entreat you to eat your words up for Christ's sake. Sometimes when I have been pleading a case like that, the person I have been persuading has kindly said, "I will do it for you, sir." I have said, "I will thank you if you will do it at all, but I would rather you would have said you would do it for my Master, for what a blessed Master He has been to you! Do it for His sake."

I may be speaking very directly to some of you. I hope I am. If there be any of you who have gotten into a bad state of heart and have said you never will forgive a rebellious son, do not say so again until you have looked at the matter for Christ's sake. Not for the boy's sake, not for your neighbor's sake who has offended you, not for any other reason do I urge you to mercy, but for Christ's sake. Come, you two brothers who have fallen out, love each other for Christ's sake. Come, you two sisters; come, you two friends who have been alienated—get together and end all your ill feeling, for Christ's sake. You must not keep a drop of malice in your soul, for Christ's sake. Oh how this charming word melts us, and as it melts it seems to leave no trace of anger behind it. For Christ's sake our love suffers long and never fails.

I do not know how to put this next word I am going to say. It is a paradox. You must forgive or you cannot be saved; at the same time, you must not do it from compulsion—you must do it freely. There is a way of carrying this into practice, though I cannot explain it in words. You must forgive not because you are forced to, but because you heartily do it. Remember, it is of no use for you to put your money into that offering box as you go out unless you remember first to forgive your brother. God will not accept the gifts, prayers, or praises of an unrelenting heart. Though you leave all your substance to His cause, He will not accept a penny of it if you die in an unforgiving temper. There is no grace where there is no willingness to overlook faults. John said, "He that loveth not his brother whom he hath seen, how can he love God whom he hath not seen?" The very prayer that teaches you to ask for mercy bids you say, "Forgive us our debts, as we forgive our debtors." Unless you have forgiven others, you read your own death-warrant when you repeat the Lord's Prayer.

Finally, I want to say to you all, brethren, that as brothers and sisters in Christ Jesus, if we are to forgive one another, there must also be some other things that we ought to do. And the first is, do not let us provoke each other to offend. If I know that a man does not like a certain thing, I will not thrust it in his way. Do not say, "Well, if he is short-tempered, I cannot help it; he should not be so ready to take offense. I cannot be always paying deference to his absurd sensitiveness." No, but, brother, your friend is very ready to take offense, and you know that he is; have respect, then, to his infirmity of temper, such as you would have if he were afflicted in body. If you have rheumatism or gout, your friends do not go stamping across the room and saying, "He ought not to mind that; he ought not to feel it." Kindhearted people step across the floor with a light step, for fear they should hurt the poor suffering limb. If a man has a diseased mind and is very irritable, treat him gently, pity his infirmity, and do not irritate him.

A friend wrote me a short while ago a letter of serious complaint against a brother who had been very angry with him and had spoken very sharply while irritated. I felt bound to hear the other side of the story, and I was obliged to say, "Now, you two brothers are both wrong. You, my brother, lost your temper. But you, my other brother, irritated him, so that I do not wonder he did lose his temper. And when you saw he had lost his temper, why did you not go away or do something to quiet him? No, but you remained to increase the wrath, and then wrote to expose him." I blame the wood for burning, but what shall I say of the bellows? It was wrong to blaze, but was it right to fan the flame? Very often when a man is angry, he may not be the only one to blame. Therefore, brothers and sisters, if we are to forgive each other, do not let us provoke each other to the point of offense.

In the next place, do not see offenses where they do not exist. Oftentimes a man has been offended at another for no reason at all. One person has said of another as he passed him in the street, "He will not even nod to me. He is too proud to acknowledge me because I am a poor man." Now, that beloved friend who was thus blamed could not see much further than his hand, for he was short-sighted. Another has been censured for not hearing, though he was deaf, and another for not shaking hands when his arm was crippled. Do not imagine offenses where they are not intended.

Next, do not take offenses where they *are* intended. It is a splendid thing if you will not be offended. Nothing makes a man feel so small as when you accept what he intended for an insult as if it were a compliment and thank him for it. Can you master yourself to that point? Remember, when you have conquered yourself, you have conquered the world. You have overcome everybody when you have so fully overcome your own spirit that you remain content with that which naturally would excite your wrath.

Then, if you must be offended, dear brother, do not exaggerate an offense. Some good women, and *men* also, when they come as tale-bearers, make a great many flourishes and additions. They go a long way around, and they bring innumerable beliefs and suggestions and hints and hearsays into the business, until a fly's egg becomes as huge as ever was laid by an ostrich. I begin coolly to strip off the feathers and the paint, and I say, "Now, I do not see what that point had to do with it, or what that remark has in it. All I can see when I come to look at the bare fact is so-and-so, and that was not much, was it ?" "Oh, but there was more intended." Do not believe that, dear brother, dear sister. If there must be something wrong, let it be as little as you can. If you have a telescope, look through the large hole and minify instead of magnifying, or better still, do not look at it at all.

A blind eye is often the best eye a man can have, and a deaf ear is better by far than one that hears too much. "Also take no heed," says Solomon, "unto all words that are spoken, lest thou hear thy servant curse thee." Something you have done may irritate a servant, and he may make remarks that are unbecoming and impertinent. Don't hear what he is muttering. Keep out of hearing; he will be sorry tomorrow, and if he thinks you did not hear him, he will continue in your service and be faithful to you. What would *you* do if *your* master held you accountable for every word and if he scrutinized every sentence that you uttered? How would you live at all if he reckoned sharply with you? No, dear friends, as you are to forgive one another, do not take offense; and when offense is given, do not exaggerate it, and if you can, do not even observe it.

Then again, do not publish offenses. There has been something very offensive said. What now? Do not repeat it. Do not go first to one, and then to another and say, "Now this is quite private, and mind you keep it a secret—So-and-so has spoken shamefully." Better that you should let your heart break than go up and down with a firebrand in this fashion. If a brother has done wrong, why should you do wrong also? And you will be doing wrong if you publish his fault. Remember how the curse came upon Noah's son for exposing his father. How much better it is for us all when there is anything wrong to go backward and cover it, without even looking at it ourselves, if we can help it. Cover it up! Charity covers a multitude of sins. Not only one, two, three sins will charity cover, but she carries a cloak that covers a whole host of faults.

Above all, my brethren, and with this I close, never in any way, directly or indirectly, avenge yourselves. For any fault that is ever done to you, the Master says unto you, "Resist not evil." In all things bend, bow, yield, submit. "If you tread on a worm, it will turn on you," some say. Is a worm your example? Christ will be mine. It is a shocking thing when a Christian man forgets his Lord and finds an excuse for himself among the poor creatures under his feet. But if it must be so, what does a worm do when it turns? When you have trodden on a worm, does it bite? Does the worm hurt anyone? Ah, no. It has turned, but it has turned in its agony and writhed before you, that is all. You may do that, if you must. Brother, the most splendid vengeance you can ever have is to do good to them who do you evil, and to speak well of them who speak ill of you. They will be ashamed to look at you; they will never hurt you again if they see that you cannot be provoked except to greater love and larger kindness.

This ought to be the mark of Christians. Not "I will bring the law against you," or "I will avenge myself," but "I will bear and forbear even to the end." "Vengeance is mine; I will repay, saith the Lord." Do not take into your hand that which God says belongs to Him. Rather, as He for Christ's sake has forgiven you, so also forgive all those who do you wrong. "How long am I to do that?" says one. "I would not mind doing it three or four times." There was one of old who would go the length of six or seven, but Jesus Christ said, "Seventy times seven." That is a very considerable number. You may count whether you have yet reached that amount, and if you have, you will now be glad to begin again, still forgiving, even as God for Christ's sake has forgiven you.

May God help us to be patient to the end. Christ Jesus must be the object of our imitation. This is the kind of doctrine that Christ Himself preached, and therefore, since He preached continually this love to our neighbor, and also forgiveness of our enemies, we ought both to preach and to practice it. Go and believe in Him, and be imitators of Him, remembering that He forgave His murderers upon the cross on which He accomplished our redemption. May His Spirit rest upon you evermore. Amen.

ALEXANDER MacLAREN
THE FORGIVING SON OF MAN

*But that ye may know that the Son of Man hath power
on earth to forgive sins, (then saith he to the sick of the palsy,)
Arise, take up thy bed, and go unto thine house.*

—MATT. 9:6

The great example of our Lord's teaching, which we call the Sermon on the Mount, is followed in this and the preceding chapter by a similar collection of His works. These are arranged by the evangelist with some care in three groups, each consisting of three miracles, and separated from each other by other matter. The miracle to which our text refers is the last member of the second triad, of which the others are the stilling of the tempest and the casting out of demons from the two men in the country of the Gergesenes (Gadarenes).

One can discern a certain likeness in these three incidents. In all of them our Lord appears as the Peace-bringer. But the spheres in which He works are different in each. The calm that was breathed over the stormy lake was peace, but of a lower kind than that which filled the souls of the demoniacs when the power that agitated them and made discord within had been cast out. Even that peace was lower in kind than that which brought repose by assurance of pardon to the poor paralytic. Forgiveness is a loftier blessing than even the casting out of demons. The manifestation of power and love rises steadily to a climax.

The text subordinates the mere miracle to the authoritative assurance of pardon and thus teaches us that the most important part of the incident is not the healing of disease, but the accompanying forgiveness of sins. Here we have noteworthy instruction given by our Lord Himself as to the relation between His miracles and that perpetual work of His, which He is doing through the ages and today, and will do for us if we will let Him. It towers high above the miracle, and the miracle is honored by being its attestation. We deal, then, with this narrative as suggesting great principles over and above the miraculous fact.

MAN'S DEEPEST NEED IS FORGIVENESS

How strangely irrelevant and wide of the mark seems Christ's response to the eager zeal of the bearers and the pleading silence of the sufferer! "Son," or as the original might more accurately and tenderly be rendered, "Child," "be of good cheer; thy sins be forgiven thee." That sounded far away from their want. It was far away from their wish; but it was the direct answer to the man's true need. Possibly in this case the disease was the result of early profligacy—

A sin of flesh avenged in kind.

Probably, too, the paralytic felt, whatever his four kindly neighbors may have done, that what he needed most was pardon, for Christ casts not His pearls before eyes that cannot see their luster, nor offers His gift of pardon to hearts unwounded by the consciousness of sin. The long hours of compelled inactivity may have been not unvisited by remorseful memories, and the conscience may have stirred in proportion as the limbs stiffened. Be that as it may, it is to be observed that our Lord points to the miracle as a proof of His power to pardon, given not to the palsied man, but to the cavillers standing by, as if the former needed no proof, but had grasped the assurance while it was yet unverified. Thus both Christ's declaration and the swift acceptance of it seem to imply that in that motionless form stretched on its pallet an inward tempest of penitence and longing raged, which could only be stilled by something far deeper than any bodily healing.

At all events, the plain lesson from Christ's treatment of the case is that our deepest need is pardon. Is not our relation to God the most important and deep-reaching relation that we sustain? If that be right, will not everything else come right? As long as that is wrong, will not everything be wrong? And is it not true that whatever may be our surface diversities, we all have this in common, that we are sinners? King and clown, philosopher and fool, cultured and ignorant are alike in this, that "all have sinned, and come short of the glory of God." Royal robes and linen jackets cover the same human heart, which in all is gone astray, and which in all writhes more or less consciously under the same unrest, the consequence and token of separation from God.

Hence is seen the wisdom of Christ and the adaptation of His Gospel to all men, in that it does not trifle with symptoms, but goes direct to the deep-lying and often latent disease. It is wasted time and energy to dally with surface and consequential evils. The only way of making the fruit good is to make the tree good, and then it will bring forth according to its kind. Cooling draughts are alleviations for the sick, but the cure must be something more potent. The source of all sorrow is sin, for even to the most superficial observation, the greater part of every man's misery comes either from his own wrongdoing or from that of others; and for the rest of it, the judgment of faith that accepts the declaration of God regards it as needed because of sin, in order to discipline and purify.

The first thing to do in order to stanch men's wounds and redress their misery is to make them pure, and the first thing to do in order to make them pure is to assure them of God's forgiveness for their past impurity. So the sarcasms that are often launched at religious men for "taking tracts to people when they want bread" and the like are excessively shallow and simply indicate that the critic has but superficially diagnosed the disease and is therefore woefully wrong about the needed medicine. God forbid that we should say a word that even seemed to depreciate the value of other forms of philanthropic effort, or to be lacking in sympathy and admiration for the enthusiasm that fills and guides many self-sacrificing and earnest workers amid the squalor and vice of our complex and half-barbarous "civilization." It is the plain duty of

Christian people heartily to rejoice in and to help all such work and to recognize it as good and blessed, being as it is a direct consequence of the Christian view of the solidarity of humanity and of the stewardship of possession.

But we must go a great deal deeper than aesthetic or intellectual or political or economic reforms can reach before we touch the real reason why men are miserable. The black fountainhead must be stanched, or it is useless trying to drain the bog and make its quaking morass solid, fertile soil. We shall effectually and certainly cure the misery only when we begin where the misery begins, where Christ began, and deal first with sin. The true "saviour of society" is he who can go to his paralyzed and wretched brother and, as a minister declaring God's heart, say to him, "Be of good cheer; thy sins be forgiven thee." Then the palsy will go out of the shrunken limbs, and a new energy will come into them, and the sufferer will rise, take up his bed, and walk.

FORGIVENESS IS EXCLUSIVELY A DIVINE ACT

We read that there were sitting by, with jealous and therefore blind eyes, a company of learned men, religious formalists of the highest order, gathered, as one of the other evangelists tells us, out of every corner of the land, as a kind of ecclesiastical inquisition or board of judges to report on this young Galilean teacher, whom His disciples unauthorizedly called Rabbi. They were as unmoved by the dewy pity in Christ's gaze as by the newborn hope beginning to swim up into the paralytic's dim eyes. But they had a keen scent for heresy, and so they fastened with sure instinct on the one questionable point: "Why doth this man speak blasphemies? who can forgive sins but God only?" (Mark 2:7). Formalists, whose religion is mainly a bundle of red tape tied around men's limbs to keep them from getting at things that they would like, are blind as bats to the radiant beauty of lofty goodness and insensible as rocks to the wants of sad humanity.

But still these scribes and doctors were perfectly right in the principle that they conceived Jesus to be violating. Forgiveness is an exclusively divine act. Of course that is so. Sin is the perversion of our relation to God. The word *sin* is meaningless unless the deed be thought of in reference to God. The same act may be regarded as being sin or crime or vice. As sin, it has to do with God; as crime, it has to do with public law and with other men; as vice, it has to do with a standard of morality and may affect myself alone. The representatives of national law can pardon crime. The impersonal tribunal of morals is silent as to the forgiveness of vice. God alone has to do with vice or crime considered as sin, and He alone against whom only we have sinned can pardon our transgression.

God only can forgive sins, because the essential in forgiveness is not the remission of external penalty, but the unrestrained flow of love from the offended heart of Him who has been sinned against. When you fathers and mothers forgive your children, does the pardon consist simply in sparing the rod? Does it not much rather consist in this, that your love is neither deflected nor embittered anymore by reason of your child's wrongdoing, but pours on the little rebel, just as before the fault? So God's forgiveness is at bottom, "Child, there is nothing in My heart to you but pure and perfect love." Our sins fill the sky with mists, through which the sun itself cannot but appear a red ball of lurid fire. But it shines on the upper side of the mists all the same and all the time, and thins them away and scatters them utterly, and shines forth in its own brightness on the rejoicing heart. Pardon is God's love, unchecked and unembittered, granted to the wrongdoer. That is a divine act exclusively. The carping doctors were quite right: "who can forgive sins but God only?"

Such forgiveness may coexist with the retention of some penalties for the forgiven sin. "Thou wast a God that forgavest them, and Thou tookest vengeance on their inventions." When sins are crimes, they are generally punished. The penalties of sins considered as vices or breaches of the standard of morality are always left, for the evil thing done has entered into the complex whole of the doer's past, and its "natural issues" are not averted, though their character is modified when they are borne in consciousness of God's forgiveness. Then they become merciful chastisement, and therefore tokens of the Father's love. The true penalty of evil, considered as sin, is wholly abolished for the man whom God forgives, for that penalty is separation from God, which is the only real death, and he who is pardoned and knows that he is, knows also that he is joined to God by the pouring on him, though unworthy, of that infinitely placable and patient love. Pardon is love rising above the dark dam that we have piled up between us and God and flooding our hearts with its glad waters.

We might add here, though it be somewhat apart from our direct purpose, that the forgiveness of sin is a possibility, in spite of modern declarations that it is not. When we venture to ask, with the humility that becomes a mere believer in Christianity when addressing our modern wise men, why forgiveness is impossible, we are referred to the iron links of necessary connection between a man's present and his past, and are assured that in such a universe as we live in, neither God nor man can prevent the seed sown from springing, and the sower from reaping what he has sown. But we may take heart to answer that we, too, believe that "whatsoever a man soweth, that shall he also reap" and then may ask what that has to do with the scriptural doctrine of forgiveness, which leaves that solemn law quite untampered with insofar as the iron links that the objectors contemplate are concerned, and proclaims this as the very heart of God's pardon, that the sinful man, who forsakes his sin and trusts in Christ's sacrifice, will be treated as if his sin were nonexistent, insofar as it could interfere with the flow of the full tide of God's love.

But we need a definite conveyance of this divine forgiveness to ourselves. If we have ever been down into the cellars of our own hearts and seen the ugly things that creep and sting there, a vague trust in a vague mercy from a half-hidden God will not be enough for us. The mere peradventure that God is merciful is too shadowy to grasp and too flimsy for a troubled conscience to lean on. Nothing short of the King's own pardon, sealed with His own seal, is valid; and unless we can come into actual contact with God and hear, somehow, with infallible certitude from His own lips His assurance of forgiveness, we shall not have enough for our soul's needs.

CHRIST CLAIMS AND EXERCISES THIS DIVINE PREROGATIVE OF FORGIVENESS

The fact that Jesus answered the muttered thought of these critics might have convinced them that He exercised other divine prerogatives and read men's hearts with a clearer eye than ours. *He* must be rightly addressed as "Lord" of whom it can be said, "There is not a word in my tongue, but, lo, O LORD, thou knowest it altogether." If He possess the divine faculty of reading hearts, He is entitled to exercise the divine power of forgiving what He discerns there.

But mark His answer to the objectors. He admits their premises completely. They said, "No man can forgive sins, but God only." Now, if Jesus were only a man like the rest of us, standing in the same relation to God as other saints, prophets, and teachers, and having nothing more to do with God's forgiveness than simply to say to a troubled heart, as any of us might do, "Brother, cheer up; I tell you that God forgives you and all who seek His pardon," if His words to the paralytic were, in His intention, only ministerial and declaratory, then He was bound, by all the obligations of a religious teacher, to turn to the objectors and tell them that they had misapprehended His meaning. Why did He not say to them in effect, "I speak blasphemies? No, I do not mean that. I know that God alone forgives, and I am only telling our poor brother here, as you might also do, that He does. The blasphemy exists only in your misunderstanding of My meaning"?

But Christ's answer was not in the least like this, though every sane and devout teacher of religion would certainly have answered so. In effect He says, "You are quite right. No man can forgive sins, but God only. I forgive sins. Then who do you think that I, the Son of man, am? I claim to forgive sins. It is easy to make such a claim, easier than to claim power to raise this sick man from his bed, because you can see whether his rising follows the word, whereas the other claim cannot be visibly substantiated. Both sentences are equally easy to say, both things equally impossible for a man to do; but the doing of the one is visible, and the other is not. I will do the visible impossibility, and then you can judge whether I have the right, as I allege, to do the invisible one."

Clearly there is in this answer of Jesus a distinct claim to forgive sins as God does. The objection that He meets and the manner of meeting it alike forbid us to take the power to "forgive sins" in this context in any but the highest divine sense. Now, this claim seems to bring us face to face with a very distinct alternative, which I venture to urge on your consideration. To offer the choice of being impaled on one or other horn of a dilemma is not the best way of convincing hesitating minds of the truth; but still it is fair, and to some it may be cogent, to say that a very weighty "either/or" is here forced on us. Either the Pharisees were right, and Jesus Christ, the meek, the humble, the religious sage, the pattern of all self-abnegation, the sweet reasonableness of whose teaching eighteen centuries have not exhausted nor obeyed, was an audacious blasphemer, or He was God manifest in the flesh. The whole incident compels us, in all honest interpretation, to take His words to the sick man as the Pharisees took them, as being the claim to exercise an exclusively divine prerogative. He assumed power to blot out a man's transgressions and vindicated the assumption, not on the ground that He was declaring or bringing the divine forgiveness, but on the ground that He could do what no mere man could.

If Jesus Christ said and did anything like what this narrative ascribes to Him—and if we know anything at all about Him, we know that He did so—there is no hypothesis concerning Him that can save His character for the reverence of mankind, but that which sees in Him the Word made flesh, the world's Judge, from whom the world may receive, and from whom alone it can *certainly* receive, divine forgiveness.

JESUS CHRIST BRINGS VISIBLE WITNESSES
OF HIS INVISIBLE POWER TO FORGIVE SINS

Of course, the miracle of healing the paralytic was evidence in very complete and special form, inasmuch as it and the forgiveness that it was wrought to attest were equally divine acts, beyond the reach of man's power. We may note, too, that our Lord here teaches us the relative importance of these two, subordinating the miraculous healing to the higher work of giving pardon. But we may permissibly extend the principle and point to the subsidiary external effects of Christianity in the material and visible sphere of things as attestations of its inward power, which only he who feels his burden of sin falling from his shoulders at the cross knows as a matter of experience. The manifest effects of the Christian faith on individuals, and of the less complete Christian faith that is diffused through society, do stand as strong proofs of the reality of Christ's claim to exercise the power to forgive. The visible results of every earnest effort to carry the Gospel to men, and the effects produced in the lives of the recipients, do create an immense presumption in favor of the reality of the power that the Gospel proclaims that Jesus exercises. We may admit the extravagance, the coarseness, the narrowness, that too often deforms such efforts and dwarfs the spiritual stature of their converts. But when the bitterest criticism has blown away as froth, is there not left in the cup a great deal that looks and tastes very like the new wine of the kingdom? Passions tamed, hopes hallowed, new and noble direction given to aspirations, self subdued, the charities of life springing like flowers where there were briers and thorns or waste barrenness, homes made Bethels, houses of God, that were pandemoniums—these and the like are the witnesses that Jesus Christ advanced no rash claims, nor raised hopes which He could not fulfill, when He said, "Thy sins be forgiven thee."

Whenever Christ's forgiving power enters a heart, life is beautified, purified, and ennobled, and secondary material benefits follows in its train. We have a right to claim the difference between so-called Christian and non-Christian lands as attestations of the reality of Christ's saving work. It is a valid answer to much of the doubt of today. If you wish to see His credentials, look around. His own answer to John's messengers still remains applicable: "Go and tell John the things that ye see and hear." There are miracles, palpable and visible, still wrought by Jesus Christ, more convincing than were those to which the forerunner was directed when his faith faltered. It is still true that "His name, through faith in His name, makes men whole," and that in the presence of unbelievers, who may test the cure. The dead are still raised, deaf ears are opened, dormant faculties are quickened, and, in a thousand channels, the quick spirit of life flows from Jesus, and "everything lives whithersoever that river cometh." Let any system of belief or of no-belief do the like if it can. This rod has budded. Let the modern successors of Jannes and Jambres do the same with their enchantments.

These thoughts yield two very plain lessons. One is addressed to professing followers of Jesus Christ. You say that you have received in the depths of your spirit the touch of His forgiving hand, blotting out your sins. Nobody can tell whether you have or not except by observing your life. Does it look as if your profession were true? The world takes its notions of Christianity a great deal more from you, its professors, than it does from preachers or apologists. You are the books of evidences that most men read. See to it that your lives worthily represent the redeeming power of your Lord, and that men, looking at your beautiful, holy, and gentle life, may be constrained to say, "There must be something in that religion that makes him such a man."

The other lesson is for us all. Since we are all alike in that forgiveness is our deepest need, let us seek to have that prime and fundamental necessity supplied first of all; and since Jesus Christ assures us that He exercises the divine prerogative of forgiveness and gives us materials for verifying His claim by the visible results of His power, let us all go to Him for the pardon that we need most among all our needs, and which He and only He can give us. Do not waste your time trying to purify the stream of your lives miles down from its source; let Him heal it and make the bitter waters sweet at the Fountainhead. Do not fancy, friend, that your palsy or your fever, your paralysis of will toward good, or the diseased ardor with which you follow evil and the consequent restless misery, can be healed anywhere besides. Go to Christ, the forgiving Christ, and let Him lay His hand upon you. Listen to the blessed words from His own sweet and infallible lips, words that will work like a charm upon all your nature: "Son, be of good cheer; thy sins be forgiven thee." "Daughter, thy faith hath made thee whole; depart in peace." Then shall the eyes of the blind be opened, then shall the lame man leap as a hart, and the tongue of the dumb sing. Then limitations, sorrows, and the diseases of the spirit shall pass away, and forgiveness will bear fruit in joy and power, in holiness, health, and peace.

NOTES

Chapter 3:
If We Confess Our Sins . . .

1. Bob George, *Growing in Grace* (Eugene, OR: Harvest House, 1990), 67.
2. Bob George, *Classic Christianity* (Eugene, OR: Harvest House, 1989), 193-194.
3. Ibid., 195.
4. Ibid., 193.
5. Ibid., 194 (emphasis in original).
6. For a thorough discussion on the security of salvation, see John MacArthur, *Saved Without a Doubt* (Wheaton, IL: Victor, 1992).
7. Matthew Henry, *Matthew Henry's Commentary on the Bible*, 4 vols. (Old Tappan, NJ: Revell, n.d.), 4:page unknown.

Chapter 5:
Forgiving One Another

1. See Appendix 3 for a further discussion of this passage.

Chapter 6:
Just As God Has Forgiven You

1. Jay Adams, *From Forgiven to Forgiving* (Amityville, NY: Calvary, 1994), 34.
2. Ibid.
3. Jay Adams cites this verse but argues that it calls only for the preparation of the heart for forgiveness. He suggests that the command "forgive" in this verse merely means that the one praying should be "ready to forgive" (ibid., p. 30). But Adams believes actual forgiveness does not occur until the offender asks for forgiveness. The person who has "forgiven" in this manner therefore cannot regard the forgiveness as complete until he confronts the offender, obtains that person's repentance, and formally grants forgiveness.
4. Matthew Henry, *Matthew Henry's Commentary* (Old Tappan, NJ: Revell, n.d.), page unknown.

Chapter 7:
If Your Brother Sins

1. Dietrich Bonhoeffer, *Life Together* (New York: Harper & Row, 1954), 112-113.

Chapter 8:
Answering the Hard Questions About Forgiveness

1. Jay Adams, *From Forgiven to Forgiving* (Amityville, NY: Calvary, 1994), 25.
2. Ibid., 64.

Appendix 1:
How Are We to Understand the Atonement?

1. A. A. Hodge, *The Atonement* (Memphis: Footstool, n.d.), 267.

2. See John MacArthur, *Charismatic Chaos* (Grand Rapids, MI: Zondervan, 1994), 278ff.

3. George Otis, Jr., "The Atonement" (transcribed from a message delivered at a series of YWAM meetings in Tacoma, Washington, autumn 1981). Transcripts of these messages are available on the World Wide Web at: http://www.concentric.net/~for1/otisa.htm.

4. Ibid.

5. Ibid.

6. Finney spends a considerable amount of time in his *Autobiography* arguing against "that theological fiction of imputation" (Old Tappan, NJ: Revell, 1908), 56ff.

7. Ibid., 362.

8. Charles Finney, *Systematic Theology* (Minneapolis: Bethany House, 1994), 249.

9. Otis, ibid.

10. Hodge, 269.

Appendix 2:
What Is the Unforgivable Sin?

1. William Hendricksen, *The Exposition of the Gospel According to Matthew* (Grand Rapids, Mich.: Baker, 1973), 529.

Appendix 3:
Two Classic Sermons on Forgiveness

1. All Scripture references in these classic sermons are from the *King James Version*.

Scripture Index

General Index